To my beautiful, resilient mother.

Viet Kieu

murdoch books
Sydney | London

Viet

Recipes remembered from Vietnam

Kieu

Thi Le with Jia-Yen Lee

Photography by Mark Chew
Styling by Kirsten Jenkins

Juke Joint

The opportunity to write this book presented itself via my restaurant, Anchovy, which had always been a medium through which I refined my thoughts and approach to Vietnamese cuisine. By extension, this book, *Viet Kieu*, has allowed me to use the tools of my trade as a chef-restaurateur to explore dimensions of both my Vietnamese ancestry and identity that the rigidity of a restaurant did not always allow.

In using this book, I hope it comes through clearly that the foundations of Vietnamese food are informed by its history, geography and ethnic tribes, which date all the way back to the 10th century BCE. As cooks, however, we should remember that the essence of Vietnamese cuisine is informed by locally available quality produce, and the cook's ability to adapt. It is my hope that the recipes outline the essential elements, so that you have the freedom to use ingredients in your local market to bring the dishes to life.

There are aspects of Vietnamese cuisine that are easy to execute and others that require patience and perseverance. The cross section of recipes within reflects this depth – recipes for easy weeknight dinners, some to attempt when a weekend of cooking beckons, and recipes that exist perhaps most for posterity.

To that end, this book was written in conversation with my partner in life and work Jia-Yen Lee, and it has been our intention to tell the stories of these dishes and their relationship to Vietnamese cuisine in a way that reflects the generations and adaptations that have come before.

Thi Bich Phuong Le

Contents

An introduction

J.Y.

Passports are often romantically posed as keys to the world, the missing link that helps the wanderlust traveller discover themselves. We forget that passports simply document the mechanics of who we are. Thi's passport contains traces of her identity at a surface level: Thi Bich Phuong, an Australian of Vietnamese ancestry who was born in a refugee camp in Malaysia in 1985. A round-the-world backpacking trip, a popular undertaking among Australian youth, brought Thi back to Malaysia for the first time in 2007. There was much confusion at the Malaysian immigration counter about this person whose prints were everywhere but Malaysia, despite the fact that she was born there. It felt like Thi was an international baby with no real roots or place to call home, and with an artificial sense of belonging wherever she found herself. Truthfully, it still does.

Like many migrants or refugees of her generation, Thi has always had questions about how she fits into her environment. She has regularly contended with the competing dualities of her cultural identity and her social experiences. This conflict cultivated Thi's loathing for labels. Growing up in Sydney's western suburbs, she was too 'oriental' to fit in with her Anglo-Saxon school mates. Drive 40 minutes south-east to Cabramatta, Sydney's Vietnamese enclave, and she was too far removed from the accepted Aussie-Vietnamese flavour. She shared the same skin tone, the same hair colour and a phonetically familiar name. However, her social currency among her Cabramatta peers diminished with her fashion choices (ripped shorts, faded T-shirt and flip-flops – very beach Australiana, very Western Sydney) and her grasp of Vietnamese (rudimentary at best). Thi struggled to find her place: too Asian to be a 'Westie'; too 'ocker' by way of the local Cabramatta yardstick.

Thi had a parallel experience when she travelled back to Vietnam in her earlier years. In her mum's hometown of Cà Mau, the southern-most province of Vietnam, she was seen as a curiosity, an outlier, a product of Western culture. Here was a person, a viet kieu, who looked Vietnamese but did not dress like one. Those ripped shorts defied expectations of how a viet kieu visiting the motherland in the early 2000s would dress – they did not signal wealth or wellbeing garnered from a life overseas. In a gesture motivated by either pity or concern, Thi's aunty in Cà Mau tried to buy her new clothes, resulting in an awkward faux pas for Thi. This just served to further reinforce the stigma of an identity stereotype that has confined Thi throughout her life.

Society's insistence on labels would continue to aggravate Thi through her teenage and early adult years, only this time the stakes felt higher as a young person grappling with identity politics: heterosexual V homosexual. Which flavour of a lesbian was she? Lipstick, butch, dyke, baby dyke? Thi did not consider the labels useful and found that they bore no relevance on a night out in town. It was a point of frustration for her – that she continued to find herself shackled by labels among peers who sought to be inclusive.

There is another label that had quietly defined Thi in her younger years and the depression she cycled in and out of. It explained the livid anger brewing inside her as she matured into a young adult; it commanded her abuse of tobacco, alcohol and hard drugs. The adults thought it apt to stick the label of 'miscreant western suburbs youth' on her and call it a day. The label that would have been more helpful was 'child sex abuse survivor'.

It has taken Thi a long time to work through the trauma of being a survivor, and longer still to work through her family's attitude and lack of care for the actions that one of its members inflicted on her. The effects of this trauma would go on to exert their influence throughout various points of Thi's life – her volatile relationships with her partners; her reaction to triggers that a layperson would consider unremarkable; the physical and emotional outbursts that have manifested from the stresses of running a small business.

Years later, this fixation on labels would come back to define Thi's professional career, as the notion of 'modern Asian' cuisine was taking off alongside the ambiguous zone of 'modern Australian'. The latter was often defined by a loose use of accessible native Australian ingredients in modern compositions – a bit of protein, a creamy component, a vividly coloured oil – served on ceramic plates hand-thrown by the chef.

Food media tried, and struggled, to pigeonhole Thi and her cooking, especially in the early days of our restaurant. The breadth of Anchovy's menu stretched from the Vietnamese flavours of Thi's ancestral kitchen, to the Turkish-Arabic-Filipino nuances of her Western Sydney childhood, through to the European and miscellaneous Southeast Asian influences from her experience in professional kitchens and her penchant for travel respectively. Some unkindly shuffled Thi's cooking into the pan-Asian-cum-fusion-cum-Asian-confusion genre.

I often described the restaurant's cuisine to customers by simply saying: *Imagine a Vietnamese person growing up in Australia*. Those with lived experience got it. Those without often nodded, but we were never sure if they truly understood.

In the simplest terms, viet kieu (or việt kiều in Vietnamese) is a term used to refer to people of Vietnamese ancestry living outside of Vietnam. Historically, the term has been used pointedly to describe those who left the country, with particular reference to the migration that followed the capture of Saigon by North Vietnamese forces in 1975. Its modern-day connotations are more complex – including the prejudiced ongoing notion in Vietnam of 'us' and 'them', or, in Australian parlance, the 'Southies' and the 'Northies'; or being a pawn in the minefield of extended-family customs and pop quizzes.

Being a viet kieu is a label that Thi has come to embrace. As an adult on return trips to Vietnam, Thi is no longer viewed as a curiosity who can wield a pair of chopsticks. Instead, she has been able to use the label as an icebreaker, as people ask: *Why are you here, where do you live, where were you born?* Thi's answer to the latter is inevitably met with a knowing nod: *Pulau Bidong* – one of the camps for vượt biên, the Vietnamese term for those who crossed the border or escaped. In her naturalised home of Australia, Thi recognises that she is neither native nor adopted but simply acculturated.

'The dishes in this book reflect the essence of Vietnamese cuisine: produce, locality, adaptability and freshness. Take them, adapt them, then own them and the way you want to make them.'

It took a while to distil exactly what would make up this book. Would it be a book of typical – we are loath to use the word 'traditional' in this context – Vietnamese food that people might know or expect? Would it be an ambitious book of contemporary dishes based on our restaurant? Would it lean into Thi's experience as a chef across largely European-style restaurants? Would it look at the building blocks of flavour that make up Vietnam's long and layered culinary history? After much contemplation, it turned out that these were not the right questions for us to be asking.

The story of Thi's food comes in the stories of her life. Vietnamese in name, born in a Malaysian refugee camp, and raised in suburban Australia, Thi experienced deep trauma but found acceptance in the queer community, and an escape in cooking. Thi's stained history meant that while growing up she carried a deeper than usual loathing for food associated with her Vietnamese heritage, and yet she came around to celebrating it. This book, while being a cookbook at its core, would need to tell those personal stories. In this way, the book became *Viet Kieu*.

Thi's memories of her past are muddied and fragmented, in many instances repressed. Her self-expression and self-discovery have been articulated as recipes, the tool of her trade. When we started to tell this story, it felt easier to tell it in two voices: Thi's own voice, which you will see in the recipes themselves and in some of the stories, and in other places my voice, as Thi's partner in life and work. The stories you encounter among the recipes are not chronological. Some of them deal with heavy topics. We have tried to avoid the typical Vietnamese approach of saving face and talking around a problem; these social conventions denied Thi justice in her younger years. Other stories give you a glimpse of the sparkling personality and the talent, beyond the pain.

The dishes in this book reflect the essence of Vietnamese cuisine: produce, locality, adaptability and freshness. Use the recipes as a guide, not the be all and end all. Take them, adapt them, then own them and the way you want to make them. Some of the recipes in this book are for standalone dishes that require time and cooperation from you to yield success. Others are forgiving and also thrive when paired with proteins and star ingredients of your choice.

This is a book that extends on Thi's ongoing journey: to catalogue and learn about Vietnamese dishes and cooking techniques, combined with a reverence for produce and locality, even if it yields uncommon substitutions; to explore the forces that have shaped her life and perspective; and to capture the complexities of what being a viet kieu means to her and her food. It is a resource that showcases virtues of the Vietnamese character – pluck, adaptability, and an unending appetite for freshness and flavour. Consider this book a looking glass into the essence of Vietnamese cuisine and the life of a viet kieu in the twenty-first century, wherever you are in the world.

PRAWN NOODLES
GARLIC
AROY-D
COCONUT MILK

A Vietnamese pantry

Thi

A disgruntled customer once asked me why our bánh mì shop only sold Vietnamese filter coffee and not espresso-based coffee. I said it was because Vietnam was colonised by the French and not the Italians. The Vietnamese pantry is very much a product of its past and geography – of its ethnic groups and their connection with the land, of historical trade and invasions, of its early Chinese influence then later French and American ties, of regional variations informed by climate and topography.

The items listed here are hardly exhaustive – it may even sway further from a central Vietnamese palate as my own experiences lean towards southern and northern Vietnamese cuisine. If you are unable to find an ingredient at your local supermarket, Southeast Asian and East Asian grocers are likely to yield success. I have on occasion chanced upon ingredients in Indian, Malaysian and Thai grocers in Melbourne.

Sauces + liquids

Fish sauce The lifeblood of the Vietnamese. Fish sauce has its own nuances, as olive oil does. The brand I use as an all-rounder is Three Crabs – it is great for seasoning, but has sufficient lightness to stand alone as a dipping sauce.

Oyster sauce I use Megachef Premium Oyster Sauce for its gluten-free nature. Take note of the percentage of oyster extract used across the different brands on the market, opting for brands that use a higher percentage of oyster extract.

Mushroom sauce I use Megachef Premium Mushroom Sauce, which is thick and glossy with the consistency of oyster sauce; it is not mushroom soy.

Soy sauce I use a few different brands of soy sauce, depending on application. Dark and light soy have been introduced into my repertoire by way of Chinese cookery traditions.

All-purpose soy sauce Adds a layer of savouriness to dishes, and does not colour in the same way that dark soy does. My preferred all-purpose soy is Megachef Gluten-Free Soy Sauce, which, as it turns out, is quite high in sodium content.

Dark soy sauce Imparts a rounded, aromatic component, a touch of sweetness and a dense, dark colour. My preferred brand is Pearl River Bridge Superior Dark.

Light soy sauce Perceptibly saltier compared to dark soy but actually contains a lower sodium content. My preferred brand for cooking is Pearl River Bridge Golden Label Superior Light. I would use light soy to flavour food but not to dip, as I find the sodium content interferes with, for example, raw fish. In these situations, I would lean towards Japanese shoyu, which has an even lower sodium content.

Maggi Original Seasoning A soy alternative and an omnipresence in so many bánh mì shops. It yields a different flavour dimension from soy sauce as it is wheat-based.

Viet caramel (nước hàng, nước màu or karamel masakan in Malay) A caramel for savoury applications (see page 218) to add colour and depth, rather than sweetness. The north makes it with sugar and water, whereas the south leans on coconut water. In the Anchovy kitchen, we call it 'caramel with a K', referring to the Malay term on our bottle.

Hoisin (tương đen) A versatile sauce of Chinese roots that does not contain seafood, despite the promise in its name, which literally translates to 'seafood sauce' in Cantonese. Used for dipping, marinades and as an accompaniment to noodle dishes such as phở in southern Vietnam.

Sa tế A spiced condiment defined by the use of lemongrass, not to be confused with the Malay satay sauce. There are several brands on the market and even more variations online. The version I make packs a spicier punch; see page 41.

Cooking wine A generic term for wine destined for cooking rather than for drinking, via the addition of salt. The properties that cooking wine brings include layering (adding and enhancing) flavour and dispelling smells. Common varieties in Asian grocers are rice wines of Chinese descent, including mijiu and its aromatic sub-variety shaoxing wine. There is a recipe for rượu nếp or glutinous rice wine on page 254.

> **Shaoxing wine** The cooking wine I lean on the most; it is made with glutinous rice, and wheat bran is often used in the fermentation process. In the absence of shaoxing wine, a light-bodied fino sherry makes a reasonable substitute (similarly dry, saline, nutty and aromatic).

White vinegar Used for pickling and for acid balance. I find white vinegar to be more abrasive than its cousin, rice vinegar. Commonly derived from grain or chemically made with acetic acid.

Rice vinegar A milder relative of white vinegar that is derived by fermenting rice. I prefer using rice vinegar for its more delicate qualities.

Nước chấm Translates to 'dipping water.' There are a variety of nước chấm, though the most widely recognised is nước mắm chấm, the fish-sauce based dipping sauce tuned to the southern Vietnamese palate. There are several types of nước chấm covered in this book; see pages 34–36.

Mắm tôm bắc Fermented shrimp paste of northern Vietnamese tradition. It is purple in colour and is runnier compared to kapi (of a Thai tradition, lightly dried but still in paste form) or belacan (of a Malay tradition, commonly dried into blocks).

Stocks Any culinary powerhouse will recommend a good stock in lieu of water. A few notes on preparing stocks in the oriental tradition. Clarity is king, and achieved through careful stock management, including cleaning the bones and not cutting your ingredients too small, discarding and replacing the stock water immediately after the bones and water first comes to the boil, and diligently skimming impurities from the surface. Simmer your stock, and never let it come to the boil again after the first boil. Layer flavours using natural ingredients, such as dried seafood for salt and dried fruits or berries for sweetness. Finally, never rush your stock. A lot of dishes in this book call for stock, based on the recipe on page 43. I make a big batch and freeze it into 1 litre (4 cup) containers.

> **Master stock** From the Chinese culinary traditions and, despite its name, is commonly used as a poaching liquid or a marinade rather than as a true stock. Its preparation and management rails against several principles of European cookery: use it repeatedly, across a variety of proteins; store to reuse, boil to refresh. It can be used perpetually with careful management; flavour and depth are layered over time.

Young coconut juice A staple in southern Vietnamese cuisine and historically used as a sweetener in braised or steamed dishes. Coconut water in Tetra Paks make a suitable alternative; look for a variety with a higher percentage of young coconut juice, as opposed to mature coconut juice.

Coconut milk Appears more regularly than coconut cream in the Vietnamese kitchen's savoury repertoire. If I had it my way, I would milk my own coconuts; failing which, my go-to brands are Kara in savoury dishes and Aroy-D in sweets, as Aroy-D is looser. Remember that the quality of coconuts used will inform the end product as much as the quantity of extract used – the packaging will never tell you anything about the coconut quality, but your tastebuds will.

Coconut cream Appears more regularly than coconut milk in the Vietnamese kitchen's sweets repertoire. It is derived from coconut milk that has been allowed to settle, and has a higher percentage of fat. Do remember to shake your package well to help re-emulsify its contents if you are sourcing your coconut cream from a retail shelf.

Fats + oils

Pork lard A delicious addition to any kitchen. Mum always had a plate next to the stove where a hunk of pork back fat would sit. It would be swiped across hot surfaces as required to leave the goldilocks quantity of lubrication.

Olive oil I do use olive oil in my cooking, which perhaps betrays my early experience in an Italian kitchen. Regardless, olive oil adds another dimension of complexity to Vietnamese sauces while remaining complementary. My go-to olive oil for dressings has always been the first harvest olive oil from Rose Creek Estate, a small, local family business – vibrant and fresh, with a delicate fruitiness, a distinct herbaceous quality, and a really clean finish.

Spring onion oil (mỡ hành) See page 44 to make your own spring onion (scallion) oil. Substitute a component of oil for butter for a more unctuous version.

Garlic oil A condiment or flavour enhancer. Minced garlic that is heated up in hot oil and used to finish a variety of dishes, often going straight off the flame and into a roiling pot of hot broth.

Annatto oil Widely used in Vietnamese cuisine to enhance a dish's appearance. See page 45 for annatto (or achiote) oil method.

Sesame oil You are more likely to find sesame seeds than sesame oil in Vietnamese cuisine. There are two varieties – pressed from white sesame seeds and from black sesame seeds. It is often the latter that is referenced when sesame oil is called for.

Butter Mayonnaise and butter are both known as bơ within the Vietnamese lexicon, though the former is more accurately spelt out in full as sốt bơ trứng (egg butter sauce). It is also the same reason that mayonnaise is confused for butter in many bánh mì shops.

Spices + flavours

Pepper (black, white and red) Pepper is grown in Vietnam and the Vietnamese are liberal in its use. Always toast and crack as required. Black pepper has a stronger and more pronounced flavour compared to white pepper, which I find to be milder and more floral. Red peppercorns (as opposed to red capsicums/bell peppers) are fruitier than their associates and infinitely harder to come by; I associate them with Phú Quốc in Vietnam.

Mắc khén A mountain pepper indigenous to northern Vietnam. Related to Szechuan peppercorns, with similar numbing properties, but milder. It lends a distinct citrus note to dishes or spice mixes.

Star anise On a recent trip to Hanoi, we came across star anise so fresh that it was bright vermillion in colour, with a felt-like surface. The intensity made me reflect on the lifeless pack of star anise that sat in my pantry. Look for whole star anise.

Cassia The mountains of northern and central Vietnam hold the honour of being home to Saigon cinnamon; it is a variety of cassia that contains a high concentration of essential oils.

Clove In *The Flavour Thesaurus*, Niki Segnit describes cloves as 'sweet rusty nails', which has stuck with me since the day I read it. Used in phở broths.

Cardamom pods (green and black) Two very different spices. Green cardamom poses a sweeter and fresher note while black cardamom smells like it looks – smoky, bitter and earthy. Black cardamom is used in phở and other dishes.

Turmeric As a powder and a root. Used to impart both colour and flavour.

Madras curry powder In the Vietnamese repertoire from the Tamils by way of the French. An essential ingredient in Vietnamese curry.

Sesame seeds Make appearances in portable foods, such as bánh tiêu and bánh căn, as well as in rice paper bánh tráng mè.

Granulated white sugar Southern Vietnamese cuisine has a substantially sweeter palate compared to its central and northern counterparts. White sugar is a recent introduction to the cuisine, with palm sugar (jaggery) and coconut juice historically being the dominant sweetening agent.

Palm sugar There are several varieties of palm-based sweeteners on the market, each with their own subtleties. The palm sugar that I use in this book refers to Thai palm sugar from the palmyra palm, which is lighter in colour and flavour than gula melaka, coconut palm sugar from Malaysia, which I also rely on in different applications. In some circles, palm sugar is classed as a type of jaggery, which is used as an umbrella term for unrefined sugars. Please note that jaggery also commonly refers to cane sugar, which is much sweeter than palm sugar.

Mushroom seasoning I am not a proponent of bouillon powder, with its aggressive onion and garlic powder qualities, artificial flavours and startling sodium content. But this vegetarian bouillon powder alternative is as functional as instant coffee granules – a quick way to add a distinct flavour to a dish without the accompanying moisture content.

Ferments + pickles

Pickled vegetables A staple in Vietnamese cuisine, with the most commonly sighted being daikon (white radish) and carrot across bánh mì outlets globally. They also make appearances in various nước chấm (pages 34–36), as accompaniments to meals (like cà pháo, page 229) as well as standalone ingredients (such as mustard greens, page 64).

Fermented rice It is perhaps unsurprising that rice grains find themselves fermented or used as an agent of fermentation in a cuisine and culture where rice plays such an integral role. Rice is fermented to make the southern cơm mẻ (page 243), or as rượu (page 254), and used as an agent of fermentation in nem chua (page 188).

Fermented seafood Always a favoured part of my arsenal for the depth and range of flavour they introduce to various dishes. They range from the mild and less intrusive mắm tép (page 32) through to the adventurous ba khía (page 50) to the downright obnoxious chẻo mắm tôm (page 37). I do also lean on blocks of belacan – shrimp paste of the Malay tradition.

Fermented bean curd (chao) Fermenting and brining lend salt and depth to this radioactive cube of flavour, used both as a marinade and a condiment to dip. White fermented bean curd (often simply known without its colour descriptor) is the most common variant used in this book, regardless of protein choice. There are many ready-to-eat versions on the market, and a recipe on page 68. You can also find versions with added chilli; do not confuse with the red version of the Chinese cookery tradition, which contains added red yeast rice, and which I have not yet come across in Vietnamese cookery.

Dried + salted

Dried fruits An elegant way to impart sweetness to a dish without the crystalline quality of processed white sugar.

Dried longans Slightly chewy and sometimes smoky on the nose, possibly a result of the drying process. Edible once rehydrated, and make the perfect hiking snack.

Dried red dates (jujubes) Typically sold whole, edible in their dried form, and used to impart sweetness in broths or sauces. Not to be confused with medjool dates.

Dried mandarin peel Used to add an additional dimension to braises, soups and even congee. Orange or tangerine peels make for a great substitute.

Dried seafood Dried fish is an integral component of southern Vietnamese cuisine (see page 57). Preserved fish is often used as a flavouring agent in soups or stocks. Dried prawns or shrimp and their skins are fantastic flavour enhancers for stocks and stir-fries and used in place of sodium alternatives; see page 54.

Salted eggs As the name suggests, salted, typically achieved using a brine. Salted eggs can be used to supplement the sodium and flavour in dishes, and to bring an alternative textural dimension. A worthwhile undertaking if you have access to happy duck or hen eggs.

Chả Refers broadly to a range of seasoned and processed meats, the most recognisable being chả lụa, meatloaves that make up the classic cold cut bánh mì. Regional variations include chả cá (fish cakes) from the south and chả huế from the Huế region.

Flours + starches

Rice flour Called for in a number of bánh recipes, in part due to the historical resourcefulness of inhabitants around the rice-growing regions. For a higher rate of success in these recipes, do find yourself wet-milled rice flour (particularly the Erawan brand) as opposed to dry-milled rice flour. The hydration content will be the difference between chasing the high of success and tipping the failure into your bin. I have never found success using rice starch in place of rice flour; it works well as a thickener but is only soluble in hot water.

Glutinous rice flour Glutinous or sticky rice has a lower amylose content and is naturally more sticky or tacky. Not interchangeable with rice flour where the intended application is to attain texture.

Cornflour (cornstarch) Used as a thickener in slurries, for binding, for dusting, and to form a protective barrier for proteins when using the Chinese velveting technique (see page 186). Cassava or tapioca starch is also used as a thickener.

Wheaten starch Wheat flour that has been processed to remove the protein (gluten) from the starch. The caveat is that only wheaten starch that is labelled gluten free is truly gluten free. Hardly makes an appearance in Vietnamese cuisine but commonly used in Cantonese cookery to achieve a translucent aesthetic; I have added it to the noodle recipe on page 78 on my mother-in-law's advice.

Mung bean starch Yet another thickener that shares wheaten starch's natural ability to achieve a clear aesthetic (think bean thread noodles). Its water-absorption capabilities are relatively low, which means its use in sweets like bánh lọt (page 266) yields a crunchier end product.

Rice + noodles

Jasmine rice Known interchangeably as steamed rice and long-grain rice, it is the dominant variety of rice grown in Vietnam and the point of origin for most rice-based bánh dishes in this book.

Glutinous (sticky) rice Stickier and tackier than jasmine rice, which affects the style in which this particular variety of rice is eaten. I would not drown it in sauce or soup, but I do use it in making congee as I find it produces a better texture. I also use glutinous rice to brew rice wine as the higher starch content yields more fermentable sugars to sustain the brewing process.

Rice noodles Just like pasta, there are lots of rice noodles available on the market.

Mai fun (Cantonese) Round and the smallest in diameter. Typically used in the islands of Southeast Asia and also known as bee hoon.

Bánh hỏi Pressed rice vermicelli noodles, similar in fineness to mai fun. Rather than being laid out flat as they are extruded, the noodles are pressed together to form a mesh.

Lai fun (Cantonese) Round and thicker yet in diameter, the noodle that traverses Southeast Asia, finding a home in the islands in laksa and further up the peninsula in bún bò huế.

Bánh canh Rounder and thicker than lai fun, and extra chewy from the addition of tapioca starch. Many recipes often call for udon noodles as a substitute, but wheat-based udon noodles often lack several qualities yielded by bánh canh, including the chewiness, the starchiness (which helps thicken a soup base) and the gluten-free factor.

Bánh lọt (drop noodle, silver needle) Typically in the Vietnamese sweets territory and a lovely fluorescent green in colour. They do exist in a savoury form and free from colour closer to the Cambodian border, where these noodles are known as lort cha. Bánh lọt are typically pushed through a press; silver needle noodles are similar, but hand-rolled to achieve the needly points they're named after.

Bánh phở Flat and typically around 5 millimetres (¼ inch) in width, typically found on the peninsula, in viet cooking and cult dishes like pad Thai.

Hor fun (kway teow, Cantonese) Flat and much wider, going as thick as 3 centimetres (1¼ inches), found across Southeast Asia.

Phở chiên Square puffed noodles. Native to Hanoi and cut from layers of rice noodle sheets before being twice fried (see page 186).

Bánh ướt Flat sheets from which bánh phở, hor fun and phở chiên are cut.

Rice paper Most commonly associated with rice paper rolls and cuốn, but there are various types of rice paper for various dishes. Bánh tráng or bánh đa are used for the aforementioned rice paper rolls. The compositions of both rice and tapioca starches vary; the latter is used to increase the tensile strength of the rice paper to help prevent tearing.

Herbs + aromatics

Ginger A rhizome with a multitude of applications. Young ginger has a milder taste and is more tender compared to old ginger, which is infinitely spicier (and more expensive to buy). Best and easiest to peel with a spoon. Buy larger knobs rather than small broken pieces.

Galangal Used more widely in northern Vietnamese cuisine and also dishes towards Cambodia. It is a relative of, and thus shares similar properties to, ginger. Always best to use younger because it is less dry and woody.

Lemongrass My dream is to move my restaurant to the northern end of Australia, where the weather is hotter and lemongrass is in abundance– the aroma of freshly plucked lemongrass surpasses anything that is store bought. Use the bulbous end of the lemongrass rather than just the leafier stalky parts. It is easiest to cut lemongrass at an angle, and easier still to smash the stem with the back of your cleaver before attempting to cut it.

Tamarind Most commonly found in their industrialised form, as powders, concentrates, pastes or blocks. A sweet-sour fruit, tamarind's many forms add to its versatility. Most of the tamarind references in this book lean on tamarind blocks, to which water is added to obtain either a pulp or water.

Garlic Invest in good-quality local garlic for a richer flavour – it's worth it. Avoid pre-minced options; always peel, chop and smash fresh garlic just before cooking. This simple technique makes a big difference in your dishes.

Chilli I make reference to several types of chilli in this book, both in fresh and dried forms.

Red bullet Unsurprisingly bullet-shaped, and somewhat moderate in intensity. My preferred all-purpose fresh chilli. Dried bullet chillies are great for imparting colour (if used liberally) and a little heat for some sauces – soak before using.

Green scud Slender, the length of one's pinky, and potent in heat. I find the heat of scud chillies to be more linear and pointed compared to bullet chillies. Green scuds have a more herbaceous note and are a great addition to something richer and creamier, like a fish pie. The heat levels of dried scud chillies are more robust as the drying intensifies the heat and flavour; I blitz these up as the cheat's shortcut to chilli powder. The use of the word 'scuds' is particular to Australia – the word is a David Thompson invention.

Red bird's eye Similar to green scuds, red bird's eyes or Thai chillies are also slender and pinky length. They yield a touch more fruitiness than scuds.

Spring onions (scallions, green shallots or green onions) An allium of several different names. I adore the earthier flavour of spring onions grown in dirt as opposed to those grown in water. The caveat is that the dirt found in the bulbous folds of the spring onions is often missed, resulting in a sandy mouthful.

Shallots French shallots are often more accessible. However, my preference is always to source Asian red shallots for their superior quality – they are firmer and less mushy, with a stronger, sharper and sweeter flavour.

Fried shallots When prepared properly, they add a mildly caramelised sweetness and a textural dimension to a dish. Store-bought shallots are acceptable in a pinch, but make an afternoon of it and fry yourself some shallots (page 71).

Garlic chives Not to be confused with French chives, garlic chives are, as the name suggests, more garlicky. Their anatomy is flatter and more grass-like, and may or may not come with a bulb at the tip. A good alternative if making spring onion oil. Refrigerate wrapped in damp paper towels.

Garden mint The most pedestrian of mint varieties, which retains its ability to take a dish to a whole other level, but I do seek out young spearmint when possible.

Fish mint A heart-shaped leaf that is quite savoury in flavour, some say fishy. Grows well in the shade and has the propensity to take over your garden.

Vietnamese mint Also known as laksa leaf in some circles, and more likely to be found in southern than northern Vietnamese cuisine.

Shiso A leaf of a vibrant dark purple and just as vibrant a flavour. I like introducing shiso into my herb plates for a pop of colour.

Rice paddy herb A herb that grows at the edges of ponds and rice paddy fields. It yields a distinct citrusy and cumin flavour. Makes up the backbone flavour of some dishes like canh chua (page 86).

Sawtooth coriander (culantro) A relative of coriander (cilantro) with an elongated shape and saw-toothed leaves. If mortgage repayments were not an issue, this would be my go-to. It offers an intense, peppery flavour perfect for enhancing dishes.

Chinese celery Not to be confused with Western celery, Chinese celery looks like parsley, with its thin stalks and triangular-toothed leaves, but tastes like a more intense version of celery. In its absence, the more tender part of celery leaf can be used as a substitute.

Curry leaf Fragrant leaves that add a unique aroma to curries and stews. Best used fresh to maximise flavour; I recommend growing your own at home.

Makrut lime leaf Distinctive leaves with a strong citrus aroma. They add brightness and complexity to Southeast Asian dishes.

Nasturtium Edible flowers and leaves with a peppery kick and vibrant colour. Great for salads and wrapping small bites – and a perfect suburban foraging endeavour!

Betel leaf Widely used in Southeast Asian dishes, often for wrapping. Their aromatic, slightly bitter flavour adds depth. Give the leaves a kiss of heat to unleash their fragrance.

Sesame leaf Deliciously nutty and aromatic, these are often used in Korean dishes. Versatile for wraps, salads, and garnishes, I use them as an alternative when betel leaf is not available.

Lettuce and larger leaves Opt for large, crisp leaves for wrapping. During winter, Japanese mustard greens, castelfranco radicchio or sorrel all make great alternatives.

Banana leaf Fresh banana leaf has a delectable fragrance with a grassy sweetness. The frozen or steamed and vacuum-packed leaves work as substitutes. I find that a little heat, such as passing the leaf over the stovetop, helps with its pliability.

Pandan An aromatic green leaf. Used for imparting flavour via infusing and, to a lesser extent, for colour. Pandan has a sweet, almost vanilla-like perfume that is slightly grassy. Using fresh pandan for colouring can be disheartening as it yields an olive-green hue; pandan extract gives a more vibrant aesthetic.

Young mango or guava leaf If you come across these rare leaves, consider buying a lottery ticket! If you are lucky, you can find them in Vietnamese markets when in season. Opt for the younger, tender shoots, as they are tangy and add a fresh, citrusy flavour to dishes – great for wrapping.

Dried lily buds Lily flowers are typically dried and used in soups or stews. They are chewy with an earthy flavour. They are easiest to handle when knotted, which also imparts an aesthetic quality.

Shiitake mushrooms Used more commonly in northern Vietnamese cuisine, possibly due to its proximity to China.

Wood ear mushrooms A type of fungus that has the texture of cartilage. It is brown and typically sold dry, either in whole pieces or sliced thin. Fresh wood ear mushrooms have an ethereal lightness and should be sought out particularly where they are the star of the dish, or even one of the supporting actors. The dried version will suffice when the recipe calls for it to be mixed with many other ingredients (for the nem rán recipe on page 218).

Equipment essentials
Meat tenderiser/stabber
Mortar and pestle
Food processor
Blender
Sharp knife
Cleaver
Wok
Barbecue/hibachi
Stockpot
Morning glory stem shredder
Spice infuser

The Vietnamese mum's garden
Garden mint
Fish mint
Vietnamese mint
Shiso
Lemongrass
Rice paddy herb
Sawtooth coriander (culantro)
Tomatoes
Lettuce
Spring onion (scallion)
Curry leaf
Makrut lime
Nasturtium
Malabar spinach

HANOI 27.5
NUOC MAM
GINGER
VINEGAR

Staples, sauces + condiments

FEED ME!

This chapter is the bedrock of my cooking. The balance of flavours in dressings is particularly important. I think it is such an essential skill as a cook to be able to differentiate and understand ingredients as they become more sour, spicy and bitter, and how sugars develop through fruit or how they alter and mellow through the processing of caramelisation. One of my pet hates is rancid acid. It rears its hideous head in poorly executed Southeast Asian dressings and, unfortunately, the odd cocktail – puckery acid without the brightness.

Mắm tép nước sốt giấm

Shrimp vinaigrette

Makes about 250 ml (1 cup)

25 g (1 oz)	galangal, peeled
25 g (1 oz)	ginger, peeled
15 g (½ oz)	garlic cloves, peeled
200 g (7 oz)	nước chấm base (page 34)
100 g (3½ oz)	mắm tép (cincalok)
75 ml (2½ fl oz)	arbequina olive oil, or other fruity, delicately flavoured oil
½ teaspoon	smoked chilli powder
½	lime, juiced

There are a few varieties of fermented (mắm) prawn and shrimp sauces in the Vietnamese pantry: tép, ruốc and tôm. The table below outlines the key differences.

Like its cousins, mắm tép can be pungent and is thus often diluted with ingredients such as lime and sugar. I have used the principles of a vinaigrette to lighten the mắm tép in this base recipe, which has allowed me to pair it with ingredients like pipis (see page 122) to complement each ingredient's saline quality.

For this recipe, I have used the Malay variety of shrimp sauce called cincalok, which is readily available in Asian grocers.

1 Using a mortar and pestle, pound the galangal, ginger and garlic until smooth. Add the nước chấm base and mix well.
2 Mix the mắm tép, olive oil and toasted chilli powder through.
3 Add the lime juice and taste. The dressing should have strong galangal and ginger flavours on the front palate; the saltiness from the mắm tép should be apparent, but so too should the acid from the lime, with the olive oil rounding out the palate, so adjust the flavours as needed.
4 Keep in the fridge for up to 1 week.

	Mắm tép	Mắm tôm	Mắm ruốc
Ingredients	Small prawns or krill	Larger prawns	Prawns and other crustaceans
Origin	Regional differences	Northern	Central
Consistency	Visibly bitsy	Smooth and wet	Smooth and wet
Colour	Shades of pink and orange	Purple	Pinkish grey

Nước chấm

Nước chấm base

Makes about 750 ml (3 cups)

250 ml (1 cup)	rice vinegar
250 ml (1 cup)	fish sauce
250 ml (1 cup)	water
250 g (9 oz)	sugar

The starting point for a lot of the other nước chấm that follow. Make a sizeable batch and keep it in your fridge, adding aromatics for the other variations when the time calls for it. Nước chấm ớt (see note) is a versatile variation.

1. Mix all the ingredients together in a saucepan and bring to the boil, skimming off any scum that rises to the surface.
2. Remove from the heat and leave to cool.
3. Pour into a sterilised jar and seal. Your nước chấm base will keep for up to 4 months in the fridge, to use as required.

Note

To make nước chấm ớt, pound two or three garlic cloves and two chillies (any type, and more for an extra spicy kick) in a mortar and pestle. Add 1 cup (250 ml) of nước chấm base. Season with fresh citrus juice (lemons or limes) as desired.

Nước chấm Hanoi

Hanoi-style

Makes about 800 ml (28 fl oz)

120 ml (4 fl oz)	white vinegar
100 ml (3½ fl oz)	fish sauce
500 ml (2 cups)	water
100 g (3½ oz)	granulated white sugar
75 g (2½ oz)	garlic cloves, minced
1	red bullet chilli, minced
20 g (¾ oz)	cracked black pepper
	vegetable pickle (page 62), to garnish

I prefer this dipping sauce over the southern-style nước chấm, which I find to be sweeter and, on occasion, too viscous. I love the use of black pepper in this variation; my preference is to have a lot of it.

1. Combine the vinegar, fish sauce, water, sugar, garlic, chilli and pepper in a saucepan and heat until the sugar has dissolved. Bring to the boil, then skim off any scum that rises to the surface.
2. Serve the dipping sauce garnished with well-drained vegetable pickle, taking care not to use the pickling brine.

Note

You can make a larger batch of the dressing, without the garlic or vegetable pickle, and keep it in a sterilised jar in the fridge for up to 3 months. You can also simply mix all the dressing ingredients together without boiling, but the dressing will have a substantially shorter life span.

Nước chấm mắm tôm

Shrimp dressing

Makes about 200 ml (7 fl oz)

30 g (1 oz)	garlic cloves, peeled
20 g (¾ oz)	red bird's eye chillies (or more if you like it hotter)
70 g (2½ oz)	mắm tôm bắc (fermented shrimp paste)
1 tablespoon	sugar
30 ml (1 fl oz)	hot water
30 ml (1 fl oz)	neutral-flavoured oil
30 ml (1 fl oz)	lime juice or calamansi juice

The key ingredient in this is mắm tôm bắc, a fermented shrimp paste also known as the mắm tôm of the north or mắm tôm Hanoi. It's available from Asian grocers.

1. Using a mortar and pestle, pound the garlic and chillies to a smooth paste.
2. Add the mắm tôm bắc, sugar and water and stir to loosen the mixture.
3. Warm the oil in a small saucepan until just smoking, then pour it over the spice mixture.
4. The dressing is best used straight away, with each diner adding their desired amount of lime or calamansi juice. (Lime juice adds a more savoury acid, while calamansi adds a brighter aspect.) If you would like the dipping sauce to be more tart, add more lime juice – or add less lime juice if you would prefer it to be more salty.

Nước chấm tương hột

Fermented soy bean sauce

Makes about 450 ml (16 fl oz)

30 ml (1 fl oz)	peanut or vegetable oil
50 g (1¾ oz)	red Asian shallots, minced
50 g (1¾ oz)	garlic cloves, minced
50 g (1¾ oz)	peanut butter (no added salt or sugar), or other nut paste
40 g (1½ oz)	salted soy beans (tương hột)
200 ml (7 fl oz)	water
2 tablespoons	soy sauce
1 tablespoon	sesame oil
1 tablespoon	brown sugar
1 tablespoon	tapioca starch
1 teaspoon	Chinese five spice

To serve

fried shallots (page 71
vegetable pickle (page 62),
crushed nuts

Rich and nutty, this sauce is a nice counterpoint to the fish-sauce based nước chấm that most people are familiar with. This sauce originates from the south and uses salted soy beans. Best eaten with rice paper rolls and white cut pork (page 196).

1. Warm the peanut oil in a small saucepan over medium heat. Add the shallot and garlic and fry for 1–2 minutes, until fragrant.
2. Add the remaining ingredients, stirring thoroughly, then bring to the boil. Remove from the heat and leave to cool completely.
3. Portion into individual bowls, allowing 150 ml (5 fl oz) per person, and garnishing each with fried shallots, pickles and crushed nuts.
4. Without the garnishes, the nước chấm will keep in a sealed jar in the fridge for up to 1 week.

Nước mắm gừng

Ginger sauce

Makes about 150 g (5½ oz)

50 g (1¾ oz)	old ginger, peeled and roughly chopped
2	garlic cloves, peeled
1	red bullet chilli, stem removed
100 g (3½ oz)	nước chấm base (page 34)
3 teaspoons	lime juice (or to taste)

Spiced with the warming heat of ginger, this has to be one of my all-time favourite dipping sauces in the Vietnamese repertoire. It works best with game meats, poultry and even fish. It is a rare nước mắm to find in restaurants; when you do, they have often skimped out on the ginger or have made it far too sweet.

1. Place the ginger, garlic and chilli in a small blender and pulse until finely chopped, or pound to a smooth paste using a mortar and pestle.
2. Stir the nước chấm base and lime juice through, adding more lime juice to your liking.
3. The dipping sauce is best used straight away, but will keep for 3–4 days in the fridge.

Note

I like to I char my aromatics (onions, shallots, garlic, chillies and the like, as in the shrimp sauce opposite) to intensify their flavour and add a roasted dimension. I usually leave the skin on, to protect them, and skewer smaller ingredients, such as chillies, to keep them together. Start on medium–high heat on your stove or, better still, a barbecue (which means clean-up will be less tedious, and you will be less likely to set off your fire alarm). If using a gas hob, place wire mesh or a rack over the hob so your aromatics don't fall through. Once charred on one side, turn the aromatics over and roast the other side. It will feel like you are cremating them, but do char them further than you think you need to. Once cooled, the skins should slip away easily, if needed.

Chẩm chéo

Green chilli + mắc khén relish

A spice mix from the Tái ethnic tribe of northern Vietnam; mắc khén from the region is the defining spice. The mix can be either wet or dry depending on the chilli used (fresh or dried). There are several profiles of chẩm chéo; this is but one of the many versions. It is best eaten with grilled meats, although I also find great joy eating this alongside tinned sardines and crackers.

Makes 100 g (3½ oz)

3	green scud chillies, roughly chopped
1	red bird's eye chilli, roughly chopped
1 teaspoon	sea salt
1 tablespoon	mắc khén or mountain peppercorns
3	garlic cloves, peeled
30 g (1 oz)	young tender lemongrass
30 g (1 oz)	coriander (cilantro) leaves, roughly chopped
30 g (1 oz)	calamansi juice or lime juice

1. In a mortar and pestle, pound the chillies with the salt, mắc khén and garlic until smooth.
2. Add the lemongrass and pound, then incorporate the coriander.
3. Add the calamansi juice, to taste. It should be peppery, a little spicy, citrusy and seasoned.
4. Store in an airtight container in the fridge for up to 2 days.

Chèo mắm tôm

Shrimp sauce

An outrageously spicy and addictive chéo. Its flavour is aggressive – punchy, pungent and searingly spicy. Best paired with something simple and mild, like raw or steamed vegetables, or with a dish of a similar kick such as acacia omelette (page 228).

Makes about 400 g (14 oz)

3	red Asian shallots, skin on
2	garlic cloves, skin on
30	green scud chillies
pinch of	sea salt
4 tablespoons	Thai shrimp paste (kapi)
1 tablespoon	raw sugar
150 ml (5 fl oz)	lime juice
30 g (1 oz)	pea eggplants, kept whole
75 g (2½ oz)	shredded green mango flesh

1. Char the shallots, garlic and chillies on a hot chargrill pan or barbecue until blackened and tender in the centre; this can take 15–30 minutes, depending on the size of the shallots (see note opposite). Remove from the heat and leave until cool enough to handle.
2. Squeeze the shallots and garlic cloves out of their skins. Roughly chop the charred aromatics, then transfer to a mortar. Add the salt and pound with a pestle until you have a generally smooth paste with a few small chunks.
3. Add the shrimp paste and sugar and pound until incorporated, then stir the lime juice through. If the flavour is too spicy, you can add a little more sugar to balance the heat.
4. Add the pea eggplants and mango and lightly pound to crush the vegetables. Check the consistency; if the mixture is too thick, add water to your liking, being careful not to dilute the sauce too much.
5. Your sauce is ready to eat straight away, but will keep in an airtight container in the fridge for up to a week.

Nước me
Tamarind base

Makes about 600 g (1 lb 5 oz)

100 g (3½ oz)	palm sugar (jaggery)
100 ml (3½ fl oz)	fish sauce
100 ml (3½ fl oz)	tamarind water (from below)

Tamarind water (see notes)

200 g (7 oz)	tamarind block
600 ml (21 fl oz)	boiling water

As the name suggests, a base recipe that forms the foundation of other sauces in this book. It keeps well in the fridge in a clean container, so do not stress about the larger yield. Use it with pipis or clams (see page 102) or even grilled fish.

Tamarind water

1 Break the tamarind block in a bowl and pour the boiling water over. Leave to soak overnight so the tamarind dissolves.

2 The next day, transfer the mixture into a blender. Blend, then strain, keeping the water. Discard the pulp.

Tamarind base

3 Cut the palm sugar into small pieces using a sharp knife and place in a saucepan.

4 Add the fish sauce and 100 ml (3½ fl oz) of the tamarind water and bring to the boil over medium heat, stirring occasionally. Remove from the heat.

5 Skim off any scum that has risen to the surface and leave to cool. The mixture should be loose and velvety. If it is too thick, add more water and bring back to the boil.

6 The tamarind base will keep for up to 3 months, stored in a clean, airtight container in the fridge.

Notes

– The basic ratio of ingredients in the tamarind water is one part tamarind to three parts water, so you can scale the recipe up or down to use in other dishes. Alternatively, you can buy tamarind water at your local Asian grocer.

– To make nước chấm me, pound two or three garlic cloves and two chillies (any type, and more for an extra spicy kick) in a mortar and pestle. Add a cup of tamarind base, and adjust the sweetness with fresh lime juice.

wok: lemongrass sa tế (page 41)
small saucepan: nước chấm base (page 34)
fry pan: fermented soy bean sauce (page 34)
ramekin: all the ingredients for pineapple mắm nêm (page 40)
takeaway container: pineapple mắm nêm (page 40)

Mắm nêm khóm

Pineapple mắm nêm

An anchovy sauce tempered with pineapple. The base of mắm nêm, like many of its cousins featured in this book, displays the hallmarks of a fermented seafood product – it is an acquired taste, tastes better than it smells, and is something I would avoid getting on my clothes for a night out in town.

Makes 4–6 serves

2 tablespoons	grapeseed or vegetable oil
¼ stem	lemongrass, thinly sliced
2–3	garlic cloves, minced
2	red bird's eye chillies, finely minced
2½ tablespoons	caster (superfine) sugar
150 g (5½ oz)	very ripe pineapple, either fresh or tinned, drained and blitzed
30 g (1 oz)	mắm nêm ăn lien (see note)

Dressing

120 ml (4 fl oz)	grapeseed or vegetable oil
65 ml (2¼ fl oz)	rice vinegar
35 ml (1¼ fl oz)	fish sauce
3 teaspoons	sesame oil
pinch of	smoked chilli powder

1. Warm the oil in a frying pan over medium heat and fry the lemongrass, garlic and chilli for about 3 minutes, until fragrant. Add the sugar and stir until dissolved.
2. Stir in the pineapple and mắm nêm and bring to the boil, then remove from the heat and set aside to cool.
3. Whisk all the dressing ingredients together, then stir the dressing through the pineapple mixture. Adjust the flavourings to your taste, by adding more rice vinegar if required.
4. Any left-overs will keep in an airtight container in the fridge for up to 2 months.

Note

Mắm nêm ăn liền is unfiltered fish sauce that has been cooked out, ready to eat –you can find it in Vietnamese grocers. Some versions already have garlic and chillies added, so adjust the recipe accordingly.

Muối tiêu chanh

Salt, pepper + citrus

The holy trinity. As Vietnamese a condiment as nước mắm, and as indispensable as tomato sauce in a sporting arena. This combination works with citrus of any description including lemons, calamansi and kumquats. You can also add chilli, either powdered or sliced into thin rounds.

Makes 1–2 serves

2 teaspoons	sea salt
2 teaspoons	peppercorns (black, white or red)
½	lime (or other citrus), cut into wedges

1. Toast the salt and pepper in a dry frying pan over medium heat for 1 minute.
2. Transfer to a mortar and pestle or spice grinder and pound or blitz. The fineness of the pepper is entirely optional – I like mine with varying levels of cracked pepper, while my mum likes her pepper resembling a fine powder.
3. Squeeze the lime (or other citrus) juice over the salt and pepper mixture to your liking, and use as a dip.
4. The mixture will keep indefinitely in an airtight container in the pantry to use as required.

Sa tế
Lemongrass sa tế

Makes about 800 g (1 lb 12 oz)

160 g (5½ oz)	lemongrass
200 g (7 oz)	red Asian shallots
50 g (1¾ oz)	garlic cloves, peeled
40 g (1½ oz)	red bird's eye chillies, stems removed
300 ml (10½ fl oz)	vegetable oil
60 ml (¼ cup)	fish sauce
⅓ teaspoon	sea salt
1 tablespoon	raw sugar
50 g (1¾ oz)	toasted white sesame seeds (optional)

Not to be confused with satay sauce (spelt 'sate' in Indonesia), which is also a spiced sauce but typically containing peanuts and found most commonly in the cuisine of Southeast Asia's Malays. A defining feature of Vietnamese sa tế is the use of lemongrass. It is often employed to stir-fry or to boost a soup (such as in bún bò huế), rather than just as dip, as is common with its Malay cousin. Mum used to top this sauce over pan-fried flounder.

1. Remove the tough outer layers of the lemongrass until you reach the tender, pale inner stem. Trim the root end and the top of the stem, discarding the dry, fibrous parts, then roughly chop and set aside.
2. Repeat this same process with the shallots.
3. In a small food processor, roughly pulse the lemongrass, shallots and chillies separately. Do not over-blend the ingredients, as it will make your frying harder.
4. Heat the oil in a wok over high heat until it just starts to smoke.
5. Add the minced lemongrass, garlic and chilli and stir-fry for about 1 minute, then reduce the heat to medium and fry until aromatic and lightly coloured.
6. Take the pan off the heat and stir in the fish sauce, salt and sugar. Check the seasoning. It should be slightly sweet, spicy and salty.
7. If using sesame seeds, stir them in now.
8. Set aside to cool, then transfer to a clean airtight container. The sauce will keep in the fridge for up to 5 weeks.

Nước sốt củ riềng và hạt
Galangal + nut dressing

Makes about 300 ml (10½ fl oz)

50 g (1¾ oz)	galangal, peeled and roughly chopped
2	garlic cloves, peeled
1	red bird's eye chilli, roughly chopped
180 g (6 oz)	nước chấm base (page 34)
70 g (2½ oz)	roasted peanuts or cashews, crushed
1 tablespoon	lime juice (or to taste)

Inspired by the northern parts of Vietnam and Laos, this is a versatile sauce for fried snacks and fish dishes.

1. Using a mortar and pestle, pound the galangal into a coarse paste. Add the garlic and chilli and pound until smooth.
2. Stir the nước chấm base through, then the nuts and lime juice. The dressing should be sweet and sour, with a slight nuttiness, and should also be quite loose, with heat or spice from the galangal rather than the chilli.
3. The dressing is best used straight away, but will keep in an airtight container in the fridge for up to 3 days.

Sốt chanh ớt xanh
Green chilli + lime dressing

Makes about 250 ml (1 cup)

35 g (1¼ oz)	coriander (cilantro) roots, washed well
25 g (1 oz)	garlic cloves, peeled
10 g (¼ oz)	green scud chillies
75 ml (2½ fl oz)	lime juice, strained
55 g (¼ cup)	caster (superfine) sugar
55 ml (1¾ fl oz)	fish sauce

I have always enjoyed the versatility of this dressing. It is my go-to for grilled seafood, saline sweetness being a perfect foil for the vibrance of chilli and lime. Equally, I have used it to dress freekeh salads that I have packed J.Y. for lunch. There is length in the spice, which is tempered by the sweetness and chased by a savoury acid component.

This dressing is one that really hones the palate and gives you the vocabulary to understand and express the flavour of ingredients. Do not be scared of the chilli and resist the temptation to use coriander stalk or leaf in place of the root. If you end up with a doughnut-shaped sauce, which is to say a sauce with no mid-palate, add more chillies and coriander root. It does keep for a few days after making; just hold the lime and add before serving.

1. Blend all the ingredients in either a mortar and pestle or a mini food processor. (I prefer the texture of the sauce made using a mortar and pestle, but feel free to take whichever route suits you.)
2. Check the seasoning and adjust to your liking. This dressing is best used soon after making.

Nước sốt gừng ngọt
Sweet ginger dressing

Makes about 400 ml (14 fl oz)

90 ml (3 fl oz)	arbequina olive oil or grapeseed oil
80 ml (⅓ cup)	lime juice, strained
50 ml (1¾ fl oz)	fish sauce
40 g (1½ oz)	ginger, peeled, then finely grated or Microplaned
30 ml (1 fl oz)	sweet ginger vinegar (see opposite)
30 ml (1 fl oz)	rice vinegar
85 g (3 oz)	granulated white sugar
1 teaspoon	sesame oil
⅓ teaspoon	cracked black pepper

Do not let the name of this dressing misguide you. The sweetness is imparted only to complement the heat of the ginger and balance the acidity of the vinegar. Used in dishes such as grilled asparagus with fermented bean curd (page 212), I learned this recipe during my time working for Christine Manfield at Universal.

1. Place all the ingredients in a bowl and whisk until incorporated.
2. The dressing should last for up to a week in the fridge in a clean glass jar. To extend its freshness, make the recipe without the lime juice, and add the lime just before using.

Giấm gừng ngọt
Sweet ginger vinegar

Makes about 1 litre (4 cups)

500 ml (2 cups)	rice vinegar
100 ml (3½ fl oz)	mirin
1 teaspoon	fish sauce
350 g (12 oz)	raw sugar
150 g (5½ oz)	ginger scraps (see note)

A vinegar made to take advantage of ginger scraps that come about in the kitchen. It is a zingy little number that can be used as a substitute where sweet acid or vinegar is called for. It is also a component of the sweet ginger dressing opposite.

1. Pour the vinegar, mirin and fish sauce into a saucepan. Add the sugar and stir until dissolved.
2. Add the ginger and bring to the boil, then set aside to cool to room temperature. Do not strain.
3. Stored in a clean airtight container in the fridge, the vinegar will keep for up to 6 months.

Note
If you don't have ginger peelings left over from other recipes, you can just use fresh ginger – you won't need to peel it, but do cut it down into small pieces.

Basic chicken stock

Makes 5 litres (169 fl oz)

5 kg (11 lb)	chicken bones
7 litres (235 fl oz)	water
2	brown onions, peeled and halved
200 g (7 oz)	ginger slices, unpeeled
1 tablespoon	whole white peppercorns, toasted (see page 268)
1 bunch	spring onion (scallion) tops (optional)
10	coriander (cilantro) roots (optional)

One of many chicken stock variations out there. As noted on page 16, clarity is king, so good stock management is crucial: do not let the pot boil over; skim, skim skim; ladle with care.

1. Place the chicken bones in a large pot and cover with water. Bring to the boil and skim to remove impurities.
2. Turn the flame down to low and simmer for 15 minutes, continuing to skim regularly.
3. Add the onions, ginger and peppercorns, as well as the spring onion tops and coriander root, if using. Continue to simmer for 4–5 hours. During this time, skim every now and then. Do not let the stock boil over. You want this to infuse rather than emulsify to get the most out of the bones.
4. Strain, let cool and set aside for later use. To achieve better clarity, ladle the stock out of the pot – avoid tipping it out. You can keep the stock in the freezer for up to 6 months.

Note
The stock is simmered for an extended 15 minutes before adding the aromatics to help with stock clarity. An alternative to extended simmering is to discard the water once the stock comes up to first boil. Empty the bones into a colander and wash the bones well to remove impurities clinging to the surface. Wash the pot thoroughly as well. Then repeat the first step: bones in pot, water to cover, bring to the boil. But this time, turn the flame down to low immediately and add the aromatics. Not the most efficient process with water restrictions.

Mỡ hành
Spring onion oil

Makes about 150 ml (5 fl oz)

100 g ($3\frac{1}{2}$ oz)	spring onions (scallions)
100 ml ($3\frac{1}{2}$ fl oz)	vegetable oil
1 teaspoon	salt
2 teaspoons	caster (superfine) sugar

The quintessential dressing used for almost everything. Most commonly found on charred corn cob, its application would not be lost on charred seafood, on noodle bowls or even grilled meats and vegetables for an additional dimension of brightness.

I love spring onion oil for its sweet and salty aspect. It is also quite forgiving. Too much oil to spring onion ratio? Drain it. Not enough oil? Just heat up more and pour over again. The trick is to find the 'goldilocks' ratio of oil to spring onion, so that there is enough oil to heat all the spring onion, but not so much oil that it takes too long to cool, and you end up with overcooked, jaundiced-looking spring onion. Aim for a vibrant green colour.

1. Wash and clean your spring onions. There are few things as disappointing as biting into a mouthful of dirt!
2. Slice the spring onions into thin rounds; I use both the green and white parts for this recipe. (For a gift that keeps on giving, do not discard the spring onion roots – stick them in some dirt and they will grow back again.)
3. Place the spring onion rounds in a thoroughly dry, heat-resistant vessel – I use a metal mixing bowl. (Make sure it is totally dry, or the oil may spit.)
4. Heat the vegetable oil in a small saucepan over medium–high heat until it starts to lightly smoke.
5. Pour the hot oil over the spring onion and stir well for about 10 seconds, until your spring onion rounds are coated and heated. Season to taste with the salt and sugar, then leave to cool.
6. Your spring onion oil is now ready to use. You can keep it refrigerated for a day and bring it back up to room temperature again before using, but the colour of the spring onion will be substantially less vibrant.

Dầu hạt điều
Annatto oil

Makes about 250 ml (1 cup)

50 g (1¾ oz)	annatto (achiote) seeds
200 ml (7 fl oz)	vegetable oil

The annatto seed leaches a naturally orange-yellow pigment when agitated. It was historically used within indigenous communities for dyeing, though it loses its brilliance quite quickly. When the annatto seed is cooked out with oil, it yields a vibrant vermilion colour and is used to enhance presentation in dishes like bún bò huế, xíu mại and bánh bột lọc (not chilli oil, as many assume). Annatto oil is typically neutral in flavour and imparts only a very subtle nuttiness to dishes.

1. Heat a small saucepan over medium–low heat. Add the annatto seeds to the pan and lightly toast for 2 minutes.
2. Pour the vegetable oil over the annatto seeds and allow to simmer in the oil over low heat for about 10–15 minutes. The oil will gradually take on a vibrant orange-red tinge, and the annatto seeds will darken in colour.
3. Remove from the heat and strain the infused oil into a sterilised glass jar, discarding the seeds. Allow the oil to cool completely before sealing the jar.
4. Stored in a cool dark spot, your annatto oil should last for months.

All roads lead to fish sauce

J.Y.

I remember once asking Thi where the salt was at home; I was cooking pasta and needed to salt the water. Amused, she told me to use a bit of fish sauce instead. I am not sure I was surprised when Thi first told me of her intention to brew her own fish sauce, as casually as one would propose baking cake for afternoon tea. Thi's mind is seldom idle; she is constantly thinking about the next idea, the next improvement, the next venture.

Thi and I had previously entertained the idea of making oyster sauce, while gorging ourselves along the oyster trail between Sydney and Melbourne over a Christmas break a number of years ago. A quick hashing of the manufacturing process and some maths had ruled that business idea out very quickly – a $50 bottle of oyster sauce was not going to be a sustainable business product in an environment where you can find oyster sauce for $8.

The seeds for brewing her own fish sauce were sown a while ago for Thi. She had noticed that her extended family in Cà Mau never bought their fish sauce, instead trading their dried prawns for fish sauce produced in the neighbouring town. As a chef, she has always been pickling and fermenting various bits of seafood in the kitchen. Perhaps brewing fish sauce was not that great a leap for her, especially in Australia. As a country, we are surrounded by a generous coastline containing pristine seafood resources, and there is generally an abundance of sun required for the fermentation process. The variation in annual temperature was but a minor detail; whisky production in Victoria and fish sauce production in Japan, we had reasoned, were two examples where temperature variation has introduced nuance to the products. Crucially, we realised that Japanese fish sauce – seeing both longer and slower ferments with the environment's lower ambient temperatures – yielded a more subtle and elegant product.

Provenance and locality was something we really focused on at the restaurant when we opened in 2015. Almost all our produce was sourced within 100 kilometres of the restaurant, and our pantry became the glaring outlier. The various condiments we used to build our base sauces – the fish sauce, soy and oyster sauces, the fermented bean curd and the rice wine, the various shrimp, fish and crab pastes – were produced overseas. Thi started to obsess over this detail, first making her own fermented bean curd (page 68), later her own cooking wine (page 254) and then ba khía, pickled shore crabs (page 50), a delicacy in Cà Mau.

The attempts at making ba khía had formed the foundation for fish sauce brewing, as it led her to an article alluding to historical Roman presence in An Giang in southern Vietnam. The conclusion of the article was never clear – did the Vietnamese introduce garum to the Romans or did the Vietnamese learn the technique from them? Regardless, it spurred Thi's obsession with sourcing anchovies in Australia as a base ingredient for fish sauce.

A cursory glance across the wares of Australian fishmongers and seafood suppliers show that anchovies are nigh on impossible to source here. They do exist in Australian waters, but their highly perishable nature and lack of market demand relegated them to the unwanted basket. It seemed like Thi had hit a dead end, until she came across a video of a woman in the mountains of northern Vietnam brewing vats of fish sauce from river fish. This opened up the idea that it was possible to make fish sauce without anchovies.

Thi's own fish sauce brewing attempts started with garfish, which yielded a mild and delicate brew. This was followed by variations with sardines and mullet. Then came another turning point, five years after the initial fish sauce idea, when Thi reached out to a contact she had met at a Slow Fish event quite a few years earlier. As a second-generation fisherman, Phil McAdam of Vancouver Fisheries had spent 45 years fishing around Melbourne's Port Phillip Bay, only half an hour away from our restaurant. The family fished primarily for sardines, both for human consumption and for recreational anglers as bait. Thi had rung Phil with intentions of sourcing sardines, but had been offered the opportunity to fish for anchovies in Port Phillip Bay instead. In fact, Phil was the only fishing business that still had the ability to use its commercial netting licence in the area ahead of a full ban on commercial netting instituted by the state government. The licence was due to expire in just six weeks.

The trip out to Port Phillip Bay with Phil and his family in late March was significant for two reasons: to source anchovies to make perhaps the first single-origin anchovy fish sauce from the bay, and, more importantly, the first and last time Phil's very young grandson would journey into the bay on the family charter, ending the multi-generational business.

Unlike the complicated journey of sourcing the anchovies, the production process of fish sauce is surprisingly straightforward: catch anchovies, salt immediately (while still on board the boat), place into lidded barrels, stir occasionally, wait for two years. Phil and his family were instrumental in helping us salt two seine nets' worth – roughly 800 kilograms of live anchovies. There were minor setbacks along the way, such as considering how to transport 800 kilos of salted anchovies, and learning to use a salinity tester.

After two and a half years, the fish sauce is being filtered as we are writing this book. Six passes through filters, and the result is a fish sauce that imparts the natural sweetness of anchovies. It lacks the sharpness of industrially produced fish sauce and instead smells and tastes like sea spray. If there is one major lesson Thi has learned from her fish sauce endeavour, it is that she enjoys the patience it demands from her.

'If there is one major lesson Thi has learned from her fish sauce endeavour, it is that she enjoys the patience it demands from her.'

Ba khía

Pickled shore crabs

Makes approximately 1 kg (2 lb 4 oz)

500 g (1 lb 2 oz)	live shore crabs
100 g (3½ oz)	table salt (20% by weight ratio for crabs; see notes)
375 g (13 oz)	toasted rice grains (75% by weight)

Toasted rice

375 g (13¼ oz)	jasmine rice
7.5 g (¼ oz)	fresh pandan leaves, roughly chopped
20 g (¾ oz)	lemongrass ends, roughly chopped
10	makrut lime leaves

Marinade

115 g (4 oz)	granulated white sugar (23% by weight)
60 ml (¼ cup)	freshly squeezed lime juice (12% by weight)
425 ml (15 fl oz)	fish sauce (85% by weight)
50 g (1¾ oz)	minced garlic (10% by weight)
15 g (½ oz)	minced bullet chillies

Camping along the eastern coast of Victoria one day, I was struck by the abundance of shore crabs in the area, later finding out they were invasive and considered pests in Australia. Hence, I decided to make my own ba khía. I adore ba khía in dressings and regularly use it as part of a carpaccio or a gỏi. It has a rounded depth, and the garlic and chilli become more subtle with time.

It would be easy to claim my experiments in ba khía as part of my sensibilities as a chef at a time when fermentation went mainstream, but in truth my interest had deeper roots, as I grew up adjacent to it. In Cà Mau, paddy crabs are plentiful and ba khía production is considered a craft. As a child, visiting the home of Mum's friend in Sydney, my curiosity was piqued by the saline aquatic smell coming from the various Styrofoam boxes that dotted their front yard; they were salting crabs for ba khía. I tried it so that none of you would have to: licking the salty concoction, wet with the juices of the still-live crabs. Not something I recommend.

I have found the process of making my own ba khía to be rewarding, although it really is a game of patience. The recipe takes approximately 9 days, and over that time it is easy to give in to the temptation to skip ahead and buy it from the shop. However, all home fermenters are familiar with the promise held by something that is so carefully nurtured.

Salt the crabs

1. Rinse the crabs under cold running water to remove any mud or debris. Sort through the crabs, discarding any dead crabs (even if bought from a live tank, a few dead crabs will often sneak in).
2. Place the crabs in a plastic container or glass jar, sprinkle with the salt and give them a good stir using a long-handled implement – taking care they do not pinch you! Place a weight over the vessel so they do not escape, but also leaving enough air so they can breathe.
3. Leave at cool at room temperature for 2 days.

Prepare the brine

4. After 2 days, take out the crabs, retaining any liquid and salt. If any crabs are covered in salt (a sign the salt was poorly mixed), scrape or brush it off – again retaining all the liquid and salt.
5. Add the reserved liquid and salt to a large pot and gently bring to the boil to dissolve the salt, ensuring you do not lose too much liquid to evaporation.
6. You will need enough brine to cover the crabs. If you do not have enough brine, make more brine using the same ratio of 20% salt – for example, for every 100 ml (3½ fl oz) water, use 20 g (¾ oz) salt.
7. Allow the brine to cool.

→

Toast the rice

8 Place wok over medium heat and toast the rice for about 5 minutes while constantly stirring. You want a light brown colour.
9 Add pandan leaves, lemongrass ends and makrut lime leaves and continue toasting until the colour is quite dark, almost burnt.
10 Remove from heat and let cool. Measure out 375 g (13 oz), or 75% by weight of the crabs, and wrap it in clean muslin (cheesecloth), enclosing the ends. Left-over rice can be stored in an airtight container for up to 6 weeks.

Brine the crabs

11 Remove and discard the abdomen of each crab by peeling it upwards and disengaging it from the body. (The abdomen is the triangular piece on the underside of the crab.)
12 Tightly pack the crabs into a large, clean, clear glass jar and wedge the sachet of toasted rice grains in with the crabs.
13 Pour the cooled brine over the crabs and weigh them down with a plate, so the crabs are completely submerged.
14 Seal the jar and leave for 7 days out of direct sunlight.

Drain the crabs

15 Drain the crabs, discarding the brine. Clean the glass jar the crabs were brined in, as you will be using it again shortly.
16 Capturing any liquid that is released, release the top shell from each crab by placing your thumb underneath the shell and separating it from the body; reserve the shells. Check the roe inside the crab: it should be bright and yellow – if it isn't, discard the crab.
17 Remove and discard the gills – the feathery structure on either side of the crab. You can simply pull these off with your fingers.
16 Split the body lengthways using a knife. Place the crab halves and the reserved shells in a large mixing bowl.

Marinate the crabs

18 Blitz together all the marinade ingredients.
19 Pour the marinade over the crabs and mix well. Taste the marinade: it should be spicy and mostly sweet, though the crab flavour should still come through.
20 Transfer the mixture to the jar you originally brined the crabs in, then seal the jar. The crab flesh and fermented sauce are now ready to use, and will keep refrigerated for up to 6 months.

Notes

- The ingredient quantities in this recipe can easily be scaled up or down according to the starting weight of the crabs, based on the percentages listed in brackets after each ingredient. For instance, if your crab starting weight is 1000 grams, for the brine you would need 20% table salt – which would be 200 g salt.
- The marinade ingredients are also based on the original starting weight of your crabs (rather than the combined weight of the crabs in the brine). So, if your crab starting weight is 1000 grams, for the marinade you would need 10% minced garlic to keep the ingredient proportions correct – which would be 100 grams of minced garlic.

'It would be easy to claim my experiments in ba khía as part of my sensibilities as a chef at a time when fermentation went mainstream, but in truth my interest had deeper roots.'

Tôm kho
Dried prawns

Makes approximately 400 g (14 oz)

1 kg (2 lb 4 oz)	whole fresh school prawns (shrimp), or other very small prawns
60 ml (¼ cup)	vodka
2 litres (8 cups)	water
50 ml (1¾ fl oz)	rice vinegar
a pinch	sea salt

These prawns need 2 days of sunshine to dry, so choose long days with the promise of continued sun and warmth. In Melbourne, where we are sometimes still in our down jackets at the start of summer, it is a project that we time carefully to maximise the solar cycle's potential. It's also best to avoid dusty or windy days. If you prefer, you can also use a dehydrator, drying the prawns on low overnight.

This recipe embodies the spirit of preservation and upcycling. My uncle's family in Cà Mau will routinely dry excesses from the day's catch – on rattan trays, baking racks and, yes, repurposed household appliances.

Enjoy the dried prawns as a snack or use them in your favourite stocks.

Clean the prawns

1 Trim the antennae off the prawns, leaving the shells on. Discard any prawns without a shell.

2 Rinse the prawns under cold running water, ensuring they're free of sand or grit, then drain well.

3 Place the prawns in a large bowl, pour the vodka over and leave to marinate for 15 minutes. The alcohol helps sterilise the prawns, removes any unpleasant smells and enhances the overall flavour by adding an aroma. Drain again.

Poach the prawns

4 Pour the water into a large saucepan, add the vinegar and salt and bring to the boil. Add the prawns and gently poach for 15 minutes; at this stage, they should be thoroughly cooked.

5 Remove from the water using a slotted spoon or spider strainer, then drain.

Sun-dry the prawns

6 Lay the prawns flat on a rattan tray in one even layer and leave them outdoors in the sun to dry for 2 days. (You may like to cover your prawns with fine mesh.) Check the prawns every 4 hours or so; you may need to flip them over to ensure even drying.

7 After 2 days in the sun, the prawns should be very dry. They should be dry enough not to be damp or feel moist in the mouth, but not so dry that they are brittle and crumble.

Shell the prawns

8 Place the prawns in a clean hessian bag or pillowcase and lightly bash them against a wall to remove the shells. (If the prawns aren't dry enough, the prawn shells will stick to the flesh, and you will damage the prawn meat.)

9 Your dried prawns are now ready to enjoy as a snack, or use with your favourite stocks.

10 Stored in an airtight container in a cool dark cupboard, they'll last for months, if not years.

'I grew up drying fish on a Hills Hoist clothesline in the backyard.'

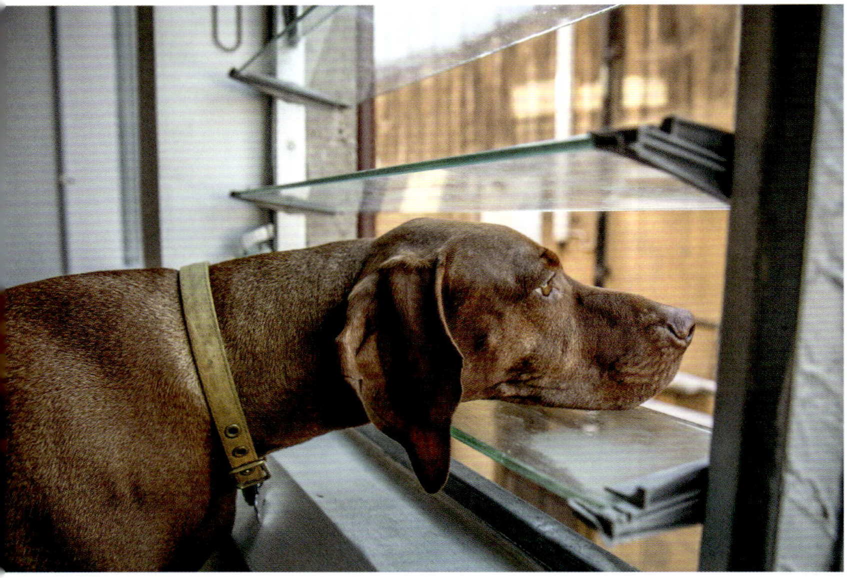

Cá kho
Dried fish

Makes a 1 litre (4 cup) takeaway container, for regular snacking

600 g (1 lb 5 oz)	whole garfish, or any small white-fleshed fish with delicate flavour, such as whiting

Curing mix

600 g (1 lb 5 oz)	coconut sugar
25 g (1 oz)	honey
25 ml (¾ fl oz)	fish sauce
15 g (½ oz)	cracked black pepper
1½ tablespoons	sea salt

Scooter around Vietnam and you will learn very quickly that dried fish is a way of life – rattans dot the periphery of houses, all layered with fish drying under the sun. Mum has not steered too far from that tradition in Australia; I grew up drying fish on a Hills Hoist clothesline in the backyard.

This recipe takes it a step further to create something like fish jerky – although it is way better than I can even describe. It is a fantastic way to use the fish you bought a few days ago but is now languishing in the fridge because you decided to go to the pub instead. It will take a couple of days, but the reward of fish jerky with your favourite chilli sauce, some hot steamed rice and beer will be worth it.

Clean the fish

1 Scale the fish (or ask your fishmonger to do it) by running a sharp knife over the scales, then slit the belly open and remove all the organs and bloodlines.

2 Butterfly the fish and remove all the bones, leaving in the dorsal spine bones to keep the fish intact. You should now have about 475 g (1 lb) cleaned garfish.

3 Give the fish a quick rinse and pat dry.

Cure the fish

4 Combine all the curing mix ingredients in a large bowl. Add the cleaned fish and toss gently until coated.

5 Cover and leave to marinate in the fridge overnight, or for at least 6 hours.

Dry the fish

6 Using fish hooks, hook each fish by the head and leave to sun-dry for 2 days. (Mum pegs the fish on her clothesline. At the restaurant, we dry the fish over our grill or hearth.) Alternatively, lay the fish flat in a single layer and place in a dehydrator or the oven on the lowest temperature for about 3 hours, until the fish takes on a leather-like quality.

7 At this point, the fish can be stored in an airtight container in the fridge for up to 2 months, until ready to serve.

To serve

8 Lightly grill or shallow-fry till crisp, about 1 minute.

Mắm tôm chua

Soured fermented prawns

Makes about 700 g (1 lb 9 oz)

1 kg (2 lb 4 oz)	whole school prawns (shrimp)
pinch of	sea salt
500 ml (2 cups)	vodka
200 g (7 oz)	young galangal, peeled
50 g (1¾ oz)	garlic cloves, peeled
50 g (1¾ oz)	red bird's eye chillies
100 g (3½ oz)	cooked white rice

Brine

500 ml (2 cups)	fish sauce
250 g (9 oz)	raw caster (superfine) sugar

Not to be confused with chẻo mắm tôm (page 37), this a ferment that is typically consumed as part of a wider meal or as a variation of a papaya salad.

Vodka is used in this instance to sterilise the prawns – a crucial process in food hygiene and safety. Resist the temptation to skip the sterilisation process or, worse, upcycle the vodka in other consumables. A rattan tray is used but a perforated tray is a reasonable substitute. Undertake when the sun is hot and the promise of daylight is sustained.

Prepare the prawns

1. Rinse the prawns under cold running water, then drain well.
2. Remove the heads and intestinal tracts from the prawns; the cleaned weight of the prawns should be about 660 g (1 lb 7 oz). Rinse the prawns under cold running water to remove any grit.
3. Toss the prawns with the sea salt and leave to drain for 5 minutes.
4. Place the prawns in a glass or plastic bowl. Pour about 350 ml (12 fl oz) of the vodka over, or enough to cover them. Cover and leave to marinate on the bench for 1 hour; the alcohol will sterilise the prawns, and turn them slightly orange and translucent.
5. Drain the prawns. Spread the prawns on a rattan tray in a single layer and leave on the bench for 3 hours to dry the prawns out a little and give them a firmer texture.

Brine and ferment the prawns

6. In a saucepan, bring the fish sauce and sugar to a gentle boil. Remove any scum from the top and set aside.
7. Using a mortar and pestle, pound the galangal, garlic and chilli to a coarse paste.
8. Place the prawns in a large mixing bowl. Add the pounded spices and cooked rice and mix thoroughly. Add the remaining vodka and leave to marinate for 15 minutes.
9. Drain the juices from the bowl. Add the cooled fish sauce brine and mix thoroughly. Transfer the mixture to a clean sterilised jar. Ensure the prawns are submerged using either a banana leaf, or some baking paper cut to size, then seal the jar.
10. Place the jar in the sun for 4 days, and up to 7 days. The prawns should start to deepen in colour – and the longer you let the mixture ferment, the more sour it should taste.
11. Your fermented prawns are now ready for you to enjoy, or you can store them in a cool, dark place and consume as required. They will keep for up to 1 month.

Bánh phồng tôm

Prawn crackers

Makes approximately 750 g (1 lb 10 oz)

500 g (1 lb 2 oz)	prawn (shrimp) heads, saved from making the prawn + papaya gỏi on page 114 (you can also use frozen ones you have stashed away in the freezer – just thaw before using)
2 litres (8 cups)	water
400 g (14 oz)	sago balls
2 tablespoons	caster (superfine) sugar
2	teaspoons sea salt

This recipe was developed to make use of the prawn heads obtained from making prawn and papaya gổi (page 114). Also, prawn crackers are one of my all-time favourite snacks, although this recipe does not yield the same smooth consistency that one might be more typically familiar with. The difference in texture is informed by the sago balls (small, fine, the size of bean-bag fillers), not to be confused by the substantially larger tapioca pearls that one would find in bubble tea.

This recipe calls for a dehydrator, though you can bake the crackers at a low temperature in an oven. Alternatively, time it for the height of summer when you can take advantage of the sun - lay your prawn crackers under the full heat of the summer sun for a day or two, taking care to flip the crackers at the halfway point.

Simmer the prawn heads

1 Place the prawn heads in a saucepan, pour in the water and bring to the boil.

2 Reduce the heat and simmer for about 10 minutes, until the prawn heads have changed colour.

3 Remove from the heat and leave to cool slightly, then coarsely blend the entire mixture using a stick blender.

Simmer the sago balls

4 Place the pan back over low heat and add the sago balls to the prawn mixture. Cook until they turn translucent, stirring frequently to ensure the mixture does not stick to the base of the pan.
The cooking time may vary depending on the brand of sago balls you are using, but will usually take about 30–40 minutes. You are looking for a mixture that is thick and sticky, where the sago balls are still maintaining their shape – thick enough that the mixture does not run, but pliable enough that it can still be shaped and spread.

5 Add the sugar and salt, adjusting to your taste.

Dry the crackers

6 Spread the mixture evenly across several pieces of baking paper and dehydrate for 12 hours at 50°C (120°F). A thicker spread will take longer to dry, but will yield a more satisfying crunch and stand up better when served with wetter ingredients. When dried sufficiently, the crackers should not stick to the baking paper – but you do not want them to be so brittle that they break. If you do not have a dehydrator, you can dry the crackers in the sun, checking them regularly and moving them indoors when the sun has set. The Vietnamese go by the arbitrary measure of *one sun* or *two suns* – on a hot day, one day's worth of sun is sufficient, otherwise go for two days' worth of sun.

7 The crackers will keep for up to 3 weeks in an airtight container, in a cool dark place. Try to keep the sheets whole so you can break them down later for different purposes, such as eating with the prawn and papaya gổi (page 114).

Dưa chua
Vegetable pickle

Makes 1 × 900 ml (30½ fl oz) jar

150 g (5½ oz)	carrot
150 g (5½ oz)	daikon (white radish)
150 g (5½ oz)	kohlrabi
100 g (3½ oz)	red Asian shallots
3 tablespoons	table salt
400 ml (14 fl oz)	rice vinegar
210 g (7½ oz)	granulated white sugar
2½ teaspoons	sea salt
1½ teaspoons	black peppercorns, toasted (see page 268) and coarsely cracked

A basic vegetable pickle for use with nước chấm (page 34) or to accompany a cuốn platter or part of a meal.

1 Peel the carrot, daikon, kohlrabi and shallots, then slice them about 3 mm (⅛ inch) thick. Place in a bowl, sprinkle with the table salt and leave to sit for 30 minutes.
2 Wash the vegetables to remove the excess salt. Shake them dry and place in a large sterilised jar.
3 Place the remaining ingredients in a saucepan and bring to the boil to dissolve the sugar and salt. Pour the pickling liquor over the vegetables.
4 Leave to stand overnight with the lid ajar. The pickles can be eaten the next day, but are best eaten after 3–4 days. After this time, seal the lid on the jar and keep in the fridge, where your pickles will last for up to 6 months.

Dưa muối vỏ dưa hấu

Watermelon pickle

Makes about 500 g (1 lb 2 oz)

1 kg (2 lb 4 oz)	whole watermelon
5 g (1/8 oz)	sea salt
	nước chấm base (page 34), for pickling
	banana leaves (optional)

A recipe to attempt when watermelon season is in full swing and you are faced with a mountain of watermelon rind. It is an exercise in flavour and texture – crunchy, sweet and salty in every mouthful.

Prepare the watermelon rind

1. Use a vegetable peeler to peel away the green outer skin of the watermelon rind, discarding the skin.
2. Roughly cut the white inner watermelon rind into 2 cm (¾ inch) strips. Rinse under cold running water and drain in a colander.
3. Sprinkle the watermelon rind with the sea salt and thoroughly mix. Leave to macerate for 1 hour, discarding any water that leaches out.
4. Wash the watermelon rind under cold running water to remove the excess salt. Squeeze the rind dry with a tea (dish) towel, until thoroughly dried.

Sun-dry the rind

5. Spread the watermelon rind on rattan trays in a single layer, allowing for air circulation.
6. Leave to sun-dry for 2 days; the watermelon rind should shrivel up to half its original size. If you would like a chewier result, continue dehydrating until the rind shrinks to about one-third of its original size. Alternatively, you can also dry the watermelon rind in a dehydrator on low for 12 hours.

Pickle the rind

7. Weigh the sun-dried watermelon rind, then place in a large sterilised jar.
8. Weigh out twice as much nước chấm base as the final weight of the rind. (For instance, if you ended up with 200 g/7 oz of watermelon rind, you will need 400 g/14 oz nước chấm base.)
9. Place the nước chấm base in a saucepan and bring to the boil, then pour over the watermelon rind. The rind should be fully submerged; if it isn't, simply boil up some more nước chấm base. Note that the rind will rehydrate at this point.
10. Use a few pieces of banana leaf (or baking paper cut to size) to help submerge the rind in the brine. Seal the jar and leave it in the fridge. The pickle is best consumed the next day, but will keep in the fridge for up to 1 month. The longer you leave it, the more flavour it will develop.

Cải xanh dưa chua

Pickled mustard greens

Makes 2.7 kg (5 lb 15 oz)

3 kg (6 lb 12 oz)	mature mustard greens
90 g (3 oz)	table salt (3% by weight brine ratio for mustard greens)
	rice vinegar (22% by weight)
	salt (1% by weight)
	caster (superfine) sugar (3% by weight; optional)

Note

If you like, you can add a toasted whole chilli and a few slices of fresh garlic cloves to each jar for an extra flavour dimension.

A staple of the Vietnamese pantry that goes alongside dishes such as thịt kho đậu. We have also used it in our bánh-strami (pastrami bánh mì) at our bánh mì shop, Cá Cơm. It yields the right amount of salty, pickled crunch and is lightly mustardy on the back palate, making it a perfect foil for something a little fattier and richer.

Pickling mustard greens is always a concerted effort at the restaurant, a bit like organising friends and family for passata making. We have to pick the right time of year when mustard greens are available in the wholesale market; weather and demand can make them difficult to find. We are after mature mustard greens for this recipe – they yield a more compact head, fleshy ribs or stalks, and a good heft when you pick one up in your palm. We have pickled younger mustard greens (known by the Cantonese name gai choy in Asian supermarkets) but they lack the crunch and mouthfeel. The key to this exercise is meticulous cleaning. There are few things as disappointing as sandy pickled mustard greens.

It is worth the effort making your own, but in the absence of such motivation, pickled mustard greens are quite readily available in Asian grocers. If you happen to be obsessive enough to plant your own mustard greens for this pickling journey, look for swatow mustard seeds for the correct variety of *Brassica juncea*.

Salt the mustard greens

1. Thoroughly clean and wash your mustard greens. Sprinkle them with the salt, then layer them in a plastic or glass container and close the lid.
2. Leave to sit for 24–48 hours at room temperature, out of direct sunlight. This step breaks down the mustard greens slightly, to help with brine penetration.

Brine the mustard greens

3. Wash the excess salt off the mustard greens.
4. Weigh the mustard greens, then calculate how much of each brine ingredient you will need. For instance, if your mustard greens now weigh 1000 grams, for the brine you would need 22% rice vinegar, 1% salt and 3% caster sugar – which would equate to 220 ml rice vinegar, 10 g salt and 30 g sugar.
5. Place the brine ingredients in a saucepan and bring to the boil; when the salt and sugar have dissolved, remove the brine from the heat and leave to cool.
6. Layer the mustard greens into sterilised jars, covering them with the brine. If you do not have quite enough brine to cover your mustard greens, make more brine using the same ingredient ratio.
7. Seal the jars and store in a cool dark spot, where your pickles will keep indefinitely. Once opened, reseal the jars and keep the pickles in a cool dark spot.

Đậu hủ
Tofu

Makes approximately 370 g (13 oz)

1 litre (4 cups)	unsweetened soy milk (page 69); see note
12 g (1/3 oz)	food-grade gypsum powder (available from Asian grocers)
60 ml (1/4 cup)	cool filtered water

Note

If you would prefer to buy rather than make your own soy milk, you need to find a brand with a high protein content – at least 4 g (1/8 oz) per 100 ml (3½ fl oz).

Tofu has been a part of Asian culinary traditions, including Vietnamese cuisine, for centuries. It is a staple ingredient in many iconic dishes like đậu hũ xào cà chua or bún đậu mắm tôm. I love tofu for the variety of textures, from silken to firm, and because it can be easily adapted to suit a variety of flavours and cooking methods. Think of it as a flavour sponge with high nutritional content. It is also a great source of protein for people on plant-based or vegetarian diets.

The tofu recipe provided yields silken tofu. Press it (see page 68) to remove moisture if you are after a firmer texture, which you will need for fermented bean curd (page 68).

1. In a saucepan, gently heat the soy milk to 80°C (175°F), taking care not to let it boil.
2. Meanwhile, mix the gypsum powder with the cool filtered water until smooth.
3. When the soy milk is at the right temperature, take it off the heat. Stir vigorously for 30 seconds and remove your spoon. You are trying to achieve a little whirlpool, so that when you add some of the gypsum mixture in the next step, it will self-integrate without the need to stir the soy milk again.
4. Pour one-third of the gypsum mixture into the centre of the whirlpool. Put the lid on the pan to retain the residual heat and keep the temperature constant.
5. After 3 minutes, remove the lid and gently stir the top of the mixture – do not let your spoon disturb the bottom.
6. Add another 3 tablespoons of the gypsum mixture. Put the lid back on and leave for 8 minutes.
7. Check to make sure the curds have set on top. If the mixture has chilled down considerably, and the curds haven't set, gently warm the mixture over low heat again to bring it closer to 80°C (175°F), before stirring and adding more gypsum mixture.
8. Once the curds have formed, use a thin-edged spoon or ladle to scoop all the curds into a perforated container lined with muslin (cheesecloth); I use a takeaway container, perforated with the help of a hot metal skewer. You can discard any left-over water in the mixture.
9. Fold the cloth over the top of the curds and press the curds down with a weight. (I use another takeaway container, placing it on top of the first one and weighing it down with a bag of rice, or the pestle from my mortar and pestle.) Use less weight if you prefer a softer tofu, and more weight if you prefer a firmer tofu, as it will expel more moisture from the block of tofu.
10. If not using it immediately, submerge the tofu in cool fresh water and keep it in an airtight container in the fridge. Change the water daily and use within 4 days.

Chao
Fermented bean curd

Makes 15 cubes

500 g (1 lb 2 oz)	medium–firm tofu, in one block
1 litre (4 cups)	water
20 g (¾ oz)	sea salt
5 tablespoons	toasted dried red bird's eye chillies, pounded or blended (adjust the quantity to suit your heat tolerance)
	sesame oil (to seal the jar)

Brine

350 ml (12 fl oz)	water
20 g (¾ oz)	sea salt
150 ml (5 fl oz)	rice wine or shaoxing wine

Fermented bean curd is a staple in various kitchens of historically Chinese influence. There are various brands available on the market, some just in brine, others in chilli, and others yet smothered in a red rice yeast. My family consumed a lot of fermented bean curd in all different forms, as condiments, marinades and accompaniments. I was always quite indifferent to it growing up; it did not bother me texturally, but I did find it salty. My turning point was having it with my uncles in Vietnam, as an accompaniment to grilled prawns (see page 98). Fermented bean curd, with its creamy saltiness, changed the nature of the prawn to enhance its sweet salinity.

My journey in making fermented bean curd was quite an interesting process. The initial attempts, while hilariously disheartening, were informative as lessons in colour naming - French violet and electric indigo, however pretty and vibrant, are colours one should be wary of in fermented bean curd.

The fermentation takes 2–3 weeks, and the options and flavours are endless once you get the hang of it. Take an easier route and make a green version with dried Vietnamese mint, reminiscent of herbed chèvre. A more ambitious undertaking would be to make your own rượu nếp or rice wine (page 254) before embarking on the fermented bean curd journey - the results are otherworldly.

As well as grilled prawns, use with lamb riblets (page 168), grilled asparagus (page 212) and vịt nấu chau (page 134).

Ferment the tofu

1. Place the tofu, water and salt in a saucepan and bring to the boil for 2 minutes. Boiling the tofu helps to sterilise the surface, while the salted water draws out more moisture.
2. Remove the tofu from the water. Firmly wrap the tofu in muslin (cheesecloth).
3. Find two plastic containers the size of your block of tofu. Pierce drainage holes in the base of one container, place the muslin-wrapped tofu inside it, then place the container on a draining rack. Stack the second container on top and weigh it down with something substantial (such as a bag of rice, or a pestle from a mortar and pestle).
4. Leave to drain overnight. (This will remove a fair amount of moisture, so you may be left with a very firm piece of tofu.)
5. The next day, cut your tofu into 4 cm (1½ inch) cubes. Place them on a plate lined with paper towel, place more paper towel on top, then cover the whole plate with plastic wrap.
6. Let the tofu ferment at 25–30°C (77–86°F). After 2–3 days, the tofu should have a slightly orange tinge. (The less smelly it is at this point, the milder the flavour will be once the tofu has been brined.)

→

Make the brine

7 Bring the water and salt to the boil in a saucepan. Leave to cool, then add the rice wine or shaoxing wine.

Brine the tofu

8 Without rinsing the tofu cubes, roll them in the chilli powder (at your discretion, to suit your chilli tolerance).

9 Place the tofu in a sterilised 1 litre (4 cup) jar. Pour the brine over, so the tofu is completely covered. Pour in enough sesame oil to cover the surface, then seal the jar.

10 Store in a cool dark place for 2–3 weeks before using. The tofu will become softer, creamier and stronger in flavour as it ages.

Sữa đậu nành

Soy milk

Makes about 2 litres (8 cups)

600 g (1 lb 5 oz)	dried soy beans
2.4 litres (80 fl oz)	cool filtered water

You can sweeten the soy milk with sugar or dried fruits, like raisins or longans. Alternatively, you can add vanilla or pandan for flavouring.

Soak the soy beans

1 Rinse the soy beans, place in a large container, cover with room-temperature water, cover and leave out overnight.

2 The next day, rinse the soy beans under cold water and drain again.

Blend and strain

3 Place the soaked soy beans in a large container with the cool filtered water. Using a blender or nutribullet, blend in batches until smooth.

4 Pour the blended mixture through muslin (cheesecloth) or a nut milk bag into a large bowl, squeezing to extract as much liquid as possible. Discard the pulp.

Cook

5 Pour the strained soy milk into a pot and boil over medium heat, stirring frequently. Let it simmer for about 5–10 minutes. Store in the refrigerator for up to a week.

Hành phi
Fried shallots

Makes 2 takeaway containers

500 g (1 lb 2 oz)	red Asian shallots, peeled
1.5 litres (6 cups)	vegetable oil, for frying

Fried shallots are a staple in Vietnamese cuisine. They make a great topping for salads, soups, sandwiches and plenty more. Frying your own shallots might sound painful – and will be painful if you burn the lot. However, it does reward you with a sweet, nutty flavour and crispy texture that well surpasses the store-bought alternatives, with their rancid oils and cardboard nature. My hot tips: slice them thin, do not burn the whole lot, and store when cool and dry. They are particularly good in gỏi (pages 114, 142 and 226).

1. Thinly slice the shallots lengthways, using a mandoline or sharp knife. Once sliced, ensure all the pieces are separated and not clumped together.
2. Line a few trays or plates with paper towels, ready to drain the freshly fried shallots. (Have some extra paper towel handy, as you will need to change the paper at least twice while cooking.)
3. In a deep pan or wok, heat the vegetable oil over medium–high heat. (You will need enough oil to submerge small batches of the shallots.)
4. Once the oil is hot, carefully add the shallots to the pan in small batches. Fry until they just turn golden brown, then turn the heat down and fry until crispy, stirring occasionally to ensure even cooking. This usually takes about 5 minutes per batch.
5. Using a slotted spoon or spider strainer, remove the crispy shallots from the oil and spread them out on your paper towels, to absorb any excess oil.
6. Allow the crispy shallots to cool completely before using or storing them. Once cooled, store in an airtight container lined with paper towel. They will last for 2 weeks if fried properly – otherwise, a flash in the oven will help refresh them.

Dooney + resilience

J.Y.

The camaraderie in a kitchen yields a lot of banter. One of the more regular topics in the Anchovy kitchen is upbringing, and how it can shape our actions and outlooks on life. Sore back and no stamina? Upbringing. Enthusiastic and always keen for the next project? Upbringing. Even how a chef irons their whites can be somehow related to their upbringing.

Thi's upbringing has undeniably shaped her mentality and outlook, forming the person and the restaurateur that she is today. While her palate and unending curiosity for history and geography might have influenced her as a chef, her iron-willed character and determination are a product of her life experiences.

When we first talked about this book, Thi had a strong vision of the opening paragraph. It would frame her as a primary school child, walking home with a friend, and having a conversation she remembers so clearly. The air is thick as it settles on hot suburban asphalt, void of shade from non-existent trees. The two girls are in conversation about their future, and Thi expresses in no uncertain terms: *I just want to get as far away from Dooney as possible*.

Doonside – or Dooney – is a small area approximately 40 kilometres west of Sydney's city centre, far away from the clusters of Sydney's Vietnamese communities. In the 90s, when Thi's mother was allocated a house there by the government, the landscape was largely commission housing surrounded by small farm plots, with horses, goats, cows and the odd alpaca or two. Front doors were always open, and kids milled about playing on the streets. Dooney had the suburban essentials: post office, pub, butcher, grocer, baker, hardware store, charcoal chicken shop, fish and chip shop, and the local Chinese restaurant. Thi's family was one of the very few Asian families in the area, and everyone assumed they ran the local Chinese restaurant.

The safety net of commission housing helped the family to break the pattern of upping and leaving to wherever work was available for the stepfather. However, the stability was not enough of a cushion for the fragile household. The family was not just poor but also broken. There were no motivational stories of migrant utility and innovation told within the house's walls. No happy-ending stories where the family was a tight unit despite the poverty. For Thi, the house in Doonside was the place of recurring nightmares.

Doonside was where Thi's character and resolve was regularly broken down – by the drunken tirades of the stepfather, who was no father figure; by the physical abuse of the same man, who thought nothing of colouring his partner black and blue and splitting her daughter's head open; by a man so controlling that Thi was screamed at for consuming a Cup-a-Soup in a bowl, having apparently made the mistake of not understanding that Cup-a-Soup is 'obviously' to be consumed from a cup.

It took years after I had been accepted into the fold of Thi's family for her to confess to me that she found returning to the house in Doonside traumatic. That there were triggering memories at almost each turn – the door that was once slammed shut with such force it fell off its hinges; the wall that she was thrown against like a rag doll; the room where she would lie still with fear under the covers each night. The recurring anxiety she would feel, waking up as an adult in that same room and feeling a warm body next to her, momentarily reliving the trauma experienced – by her eight-year-old self, her six-year-old self, or her ten-year-old self – before she dared to breathe again, because it was only me lying next to her.

Who did you first tell? This was the question I apprehensively led with when Thi first told me, out of the blue, about the transgressions she experienced at the hands of the stepfather. I was still processing what she had just said, so wanting to have heard incorrectly.

Thi was in Grade 2 when she shared her burden with her teacher; she does not quite remember what led her to. As a seven-year-old, she knew the concept of sex abuse was bad but did not have the vocabulary or the understanding to explain why. Her teacher stayed quiet for a few beats, perhaps in shock or deciding what to say next. Perhaps, like me, wishing that she had misheard. *Is he still living with you*? was her single question.

The series of events after the adults took charge remain both a blur and a source of bitterness for Thi. She was pulled out of class once a week to meet with someone, it was never explained who or why; it might have been a counsellor, but the sessions were not productive. Thi remembers sitting there, not being asked anything, with an expectation that she would just open up and share. She resented these sessions; returning to class became a source of dread because all everyone wanted to know was where she went. She was singled out in class just like she was singled out at home.

Eventually the police found out. The stepfather left and for a while there was markedly less violence at home. Her mother pressed charges, perhaps for domestic violence, and Thi found herself telling the police what had happened to her. She was taken to the hospital and physically examined by nurses.

In the end, nothing really changed. Her mother dropped the charges. The stepfather found his way back into their life and continued living with the family for four more terrible years.

Thi remembers walking home from school and, as she got closer, recognising a male silhouette washing the car in the driveway. He smiled at her, wordlessly. In that moment, with the devastation of betrayal, she recognised that she had only herself to trust.

+

This lost childhood is a part of Thi that she holds close. It is the reason she struggles to make it into the restaurant occasionally and we have had to cancel bookings some nights; the reason she sometimes cannot get out of bed in the morning. It has also led to her unshakable belief that change only happens if she instigates it, and her brutal impatience with those who refuse to change their own unhappy circumstances. Above all, it has given her a resilience that most people will never understand.

Our upbringing has been so different, mine and Thi's; our early fights as a couple could often be distilled to that difference. When pressure mounts within the business, I am often the one to cave first, while Thi will persevere. Thi sees a light, no matter the length of the tunnel, while my sheltered upbringing often advises against entering said tunnel in the first place. 'Against all odds' is a term that always comes to my mind, sometimes with admiration, other times with trepidation, as Thi launches into her next idea.

Thi joked once that she was like a peacock – peacocks absorb poison and oddly are not hurt by it; instead, they process it internally and exude it in vibrant colours on their feathers.

MUD CRAB
SPECIAL TODAY

Seafood

Seafood is a substantial part of my iteration of Vietnamese food. Some might say this reflects the general nature of the cuisine, or my family's background as fisher people along the banks of the Mekong Delta. The latter claim is a stretch considering I grew up inland in Sydney's west, some distance from the coast.

Really, seafood plays such a big part because I love eating it – the lightness seafood proffers as a complete meal without the heaviness of red meat, and how it retains the variety in saline flavour and the intricacy in textures. Despite my love for crustaceans, I am actually allergic to them. Regardless, I try not to let something as trivial as struggling to breathe stop me from indulging.

While this chapter focuses on the use of seafood as a star ingredient, it is worth remembering that the other dishes in this book are often marked by seafood – whether it's fish sauce or shrimp paste.

Bánh canh cua

Silver needle noodle + crab soup

Serves 5–6, with extra broth

1 kg (2 lb 4 oz)	live mud crab (preferably female)
1 kg (2 lb 4 oz)	live shore crabs

Silver needle noodles (see notes)

90 g (3 oz)	tapioca starch
45 g (1½ oz)	wheaten starch
45 g (1½ oz)	rice flour, plus extra for dusting
1 teaspoon	sea salt
3 teaspoons	vegetable oil, plus extra for coating
180 ml (6 fl oz)	boiling water
	ice bath

Broth

100 ml (3½ fl oz)	annatto oil (page 45)
1	whole lemongrass stem, roughly chopped
300 g (10½ oz)	brown onions, skin on, charred whole (see page 36)
100 g (3½ oz)	ginger, skin on, charred (see page 36)
1	whole garlic bulb, skin on, charred (see page 36)
4	dried longans
3.5 litres (118 fl oz)	chicken stock (page 43)
200 g (7 oz)	prawn (shrimp) heads (optional)
75 ml (2½ fl oz)	fish sauce
2 teaspoons	salt

→

Bánh canh cua has never been my first choice of noodles when visiting a suburban Vietnamese eatery in Australia. I have always found the dish to be too viscous and devoid of the crustacean flavour that ought to be its hallmark, as if the excess starch stirred into the pot has sucked out all the flavour, leaving behind a fluoro-orange oil spill. It also happens to be one of J.Y.'s go-to dishes.

In its optimum form, bánh canh cua is a dish that speaks of the freshness of the crabs and the supporting cast. It is about peak seasonality – cooked and consumed by those who live closest to the fresh source of flavour origin, and to be avoided at all costs when that source is replaced by a metallic tin of crab meat, absent in flavour and texture.

Bánh canh itself refers to a specific type of tapioca noodles that are thick and chewy. I have always preferred the pork-based versions of this dish that I grew up with, or the Laotian khao piak sen, imbued with so much chicken that it can renourish the sick. It was not until a recent trip back to Cà Mau that I really found an appreciation for bánh canh cua. I stayed next to a bánh canh restaurant on that trip and was curious to know how different an iteration of bánh canh cua would be offered in the land of its origin. In a single bowl, it painted a picture of Cà Mau: its prawn-farming and crabbing inhabitants, the laid-back cadence of life, and optimistically, the restaurant's young, gay proprietor taking over the family business from Mum.

The recipe I have provided here is actually for bánh lọt or silver needle noodles, also known as rat tail noodles in some circles for their resemblance to their namesake. Found in the cuisine of Cambodia, Malaysia and Brunei, these noodles share a similar starch make-up to bánh canh. I find their shorter length makes the act of eating this soupy dish all the more delightful.

Prepare the noodles

1 Combine all the noodle ingredients, except the boiling water and ice bath, in a large bowl.
2 Add all the boiling water to the bowl at once. (It's important to use boiling water, to activate the starch.)
3 Mix well until a dough forms, using a wooden spoon if the dough is too hot. It should come clean off the bowl and your hands. Cover the bowl with plastic wrap and leave to rest for 10 minutes.
4 Lightly dust your bench and a tray with extra rice flour.
5 Portion the dough into 10 equal parts. Roll each part out into long logs on the floured bench.
6 Cut the logs into 5 g (⅛ oz) pieces, roughly the size of your fingernail. Rigorously roll each piece back and forth between your palms, until you form a strand of noodle. The ends of each

→

Toppings

poached prawns (shrimp)
chả chiên or chả lụa (meatloaf), sliced
cooked blood jelly (available from Asian butchers), sliced
fried shallots (page 71)
sliced spring onions (scallions)
coriander (cilantro) sprigs
blanched mustard greens
lime or lemon wedges
cracked black pepper

strand should be pointy. Place the strands of noodles onto your lightly floured tray. Repeat the process until finished.

7 You can use the noodles straight away, or keep in an airtight container in the fridge for up to 2 days.

Cook the noodles

8 Bring a large saucepan of water to the boil, and have the ice bath ready.

9 Gently boil the noodles in batches until they float; this usually takes 2–3 minutes.

10 Scoop them out with a spider and place them into the ice bath to stop them from cooking.

11 Drain the noodles and leave in the colander, lightly tossed with a coating of oil to stop them from sticking. Set aside.

Prepare the crabs

12 Place the mud crab in the freezer for about 1 hour to put it to sleep. You can remove it from the freezer once it stops moving – but take care not to freeze it.

13 Rinse the mud crab and shore crabs thoroughly under cold running water to remove any mud or debris.

14 Lightly crack the mud crab claws, using the blunt edge of a cleaver or a rolling pin, and set aside. If using a female mud crab, remove and reserve the roe, to serve alongside the noodles as part of the final assembly.

For the broth

15 In a large stockpot, heat the annatto oil, then fry the lemongrass over medium heat for a minute or two, until aromatic.

16 Add the charred onion, ginger and garlic (you can leave the skins on, just remove any loose bits), along with the dried longans, chicken stock and prawn heads, if using. Bring to a gentle boil.

17 Add the mud crab and shore crabs and bring to a gentle boil for 20–25 minutes, skimming off any impurities during cooking.

18 Remove the mud crab from the pot. Leave the shore crabs in the broth and allow to simmer over low heat for 2 hours to keep infusing the stock with flavour – but do not let the broth boil or reduce in volume.

19 Strain the broth, then add the fish sauce and salt. The broth should now taste like shellfish.

Extract the mud crab meat

20 While the broth is simmering, prepare the crab meat. If the mud crab is still warm, rinse under running cold water to cool it down. Remove the top shell by firmly holding the crab down with one hand, and gently pulling from the top left-hand corner towards the bottom right-hand corner with your other hand.

21 Do not extract the meat from the claws. Set aside.

22 Using a crab picker, remove the meat from inside the body and legs, ensuring there are no bits of shell. Set the meat aside.

→

Assemble the soup bowls

23 Blanch approximately 150 g (5½ oz) of the noodles and the crab claws in a large saucepan of boiling water to refresh for about 30 seconds, then strain straight into individual bowls.

24 Pour about 400 ml (14 fl oz) of the hot strained broth over the noodles, then garnish with crab meat and your choice of toppings.

25 Repeat for each additional serving bowl and serve with the blanched mustard greens, lime or lemon wedges and pepper.

Notes

- If you would prefer the bánh canh noodles traditionally included with this recipe, they can be bought fresh from your Asian grocer.
- There are two styles of this broth. One version is thick and slightly gloopy, and the other, clean and light. If you prefer the gloopy version, cook the fresh noodles in the broth for the starch.

Bún mắm

Fermented fish noodle soup

Serves 4–6

1.5 litres (6 cups)	water
1	lemongrass stem, smashed
175 g (6 oz)	firm white fish fillets, such as barramundi, sliced
2	prawns (shrimp) per person
200 g (7 oz)	squid, cleaned and scored in a cross-hatched pattern
45 g (1½ oz)	pork belly per person, either poached or roasted (see pages 196 or 174–75), then sliced
1 kg (2 lb 4 oz)	fresh vermicelli noodles

Broth

2 tablespoons	vegetable oil
30 g (1 oz)	garlic cloves, minced
80 g (2¾ oz)	ginger, sliced
30 g (1 oz)	galangal, sliced
2	lemongrass stems, bruised, then cut into 8 cm (3¼ inch) lengths
1	brown onion, sliced lengthways
6	makrut lime leaves
1 teaspoon	sea salt
1 teaspoon	cracked black pepper
250 g (9 oz)	mắm cá sặc, no bones (see notes)
2.5 litres (85 fl oz)	water
1 litre (4 cups)	young coconut juice (or unsweetened coconut juice)
100 g (3½ oz)	Japanese eggplant (aubergine), sliced into thick coins

To serve

120 g (4¼ oz)	morning glory stems, shredded into curls (see notes)
35 g (1¼ oz)	garlic chives, chopped into 5 cm (2 inch) batons
	lime wedges

To claim this noodle dish is too pungent is to admit that your palate is insufficiently adventurous. I love this dish for the miscellany of surf-and-turf toppings, the greenery and herbage, and the absolutely addictive broth that pulls you in while those around you start diving for cover.

Make the broth

1 Heat the oil in a large saucepan over medium heat. Fry the garlic for 1–2 minutes, until fragrant, then add the ginger, galangal, lemongrass and onion and fry for another minute.

2 Add the lime leaves, salt, pepper and mắm cá sặc. Pour in the 2.5 litres (85 fl oz) of water and the coconut juice, stirring well.

3 Bring to a gentle boil, skimming off any impurities. Turn the heat down to low and leave to infuse for 30 minutes.

4 Add the eggplant to the broth. Cook for a further 5 minutes, or until the eggplant is tender.

Organise the toppings

5 While the broth is simmering, bring the 1.5 litres (6 cups) of water and the smashed lemongrass to the boil. Gently poach the fish, prawns and squid for 3–4 minutes, until cooked, and remove from stock. Set aside.

6 Also prepare your pork belly and other serving garnishes.

7 Just before serving, warm the vermicelli noodles in boiling water for 10 seconds and drain.

Assemble

8 Transfer the noodles to individual serving bowls. Arrange the seafood, pork belly and eggplant in each bowl, then ladle the broth over the top and garnish with morning glory, garlic chives and cut lime.

Notes

– Mắm cá sặc is pickled or fermented gouramy fish, available in jars from Asian grocers.

– Your Asian grocer should sell morning glory shredders. Once shredded into curls, keep the morning glory in cool water until needed.

Ăn lẩu – eating the Vietnamese way

J.Y.

It is easy to employ the tourist's eye for detail when it comes to describing a location. The alleyways, the vendors, the wares they are peddling and the colours that surround them. I love travelling with Thi because our surroundings are almost always narrated by her nose, often leading us to barbecue pits or small vendors.

We first came across this particular bò nhúng dấm joint in Hanoi when we stopped to dine at the bánh cuốn place across the road. It was quite the spectacle: diners hunched over roiling pots for as far as the eye could see, and that was not an exaggeration. They had taken over three shop fronts and the adjacent footpath, as well as the footpath of neighbouring shops on either side, and the equivalent scope of footpath across the road. The turnover of tables was chaotic, involving much yelling and hand gestures to direct the whisking away of meal remnants, the ushering of new guests to knee-high tables, and the orchestration of dishes, baskets and portable hot pot cookers.

We wandered back a few nights later and found ourselves caught in the middle of the chaos. Having a minimal grasp of the language, I had no idea what was going on, relying on the ever-handy sign language to denote that, *Yes, we would like a table for two*. It turned out that Thi's own rudimentary grasp of Vietnamese and its southern twang was only slightly more useful. They pegged us as tourists almost immediately, sat us down and popped a basket of vegetables and meat on the table along with the requisite poaching liquid, having failed to determine the specificities of what we wanted. Honestly though, I was not quite sure what the specificities were either at the time. Based on an assessment of tables around us, we concluded that we had missed out on the enoki mushrooms, Chinese doughnuts and perhaps a more superior selection of beef available for poaching.

The poaching liquid was delicate, infused with pepper and rice vinegar rather than the more abrasive white vinegar, and it was studded with pieces of onion, pineapple and the surprise of coconut flesh. It got progressively sweeter through the meal. Eventually, the lines between poaching liquid and broth blurred sufficiently and I started drinking it, an act that would no doubt be deemed sacrilegious by the purists. (See page 192 for a bò nhúng dấm recipe inspired by this meal.)

Perhaps it was the din of the experience, or the delicious poaching liquid, or perhaps it was the dips – salt, pepper and green calamansi, and a mean version of mắm nêm – in any case, it was one of my more memorable meals in Hanoi. At the end of the meal, one of the (possible) owners had a friendly chat with Thi. I did not understand much but caught the words 'viet kieu' being bandied around.

It is easy to typecast lẩu, Cantonese steamboats and Chinese hot pots as one and the same – unidimensional, easy-to-prepare events; the brothy equivalent of fried rice, an opportunity to get rid of or employ any ingredients that catch your fancy. The similarities are easy to spot: a communal meal around a cooking vessel in the middle of the table, a seasoned or flavoured broth, proteins and vegetables prepared to be cooked in said vessel and the accompanying dipping sauce. This familiarity takes away from the nuance of lẩu, which is as intricate and as varied as Japanese nabemono.

The various lẩu in Vietnam are informed by regional specialities and can also be ingredient-driven, although few things are as important as how well the soup base is seasoned. There are bases soured by tamarind or fermented rice, thickened through the use of fermented bean curd or naturally sweetened with coconut juice. For Thi, lẩu embodies the principles of Vietnamese dining – that hot food is always eaten hot and never tepid; that the proteins and vegetables should always be fresh; that the ingredients should be prepared in abundance and with variety.

There are a smattering of lẩu recipes in this book. Some are more readily recognised in Vietnamese culinary pop culture, for example canh chua (page 86), also often known as 'Vietnamese sweet and sour soup.' Some, such as lẩu bò nhúng dấm (page 192) or lẩu vịt nấu chau (page 134), are readily accessible for an accomplished home cook or someone with a knack for entertaining.

Others, such as lẩu cơm mẻ (page 176), have been included to showcase the depth and traditions in the Vietnamese kitchen. The development of cuisine that is specifically Vietnamese began in 939 BCE. It is a cuisine that has existed just shy of three thousand years, and longer if you consider that Vietnamese legends reference sites and agricultural achievements going back to 2000 BCE.

Putting all the jargon and technicalities aside, lẩu has the ability to bring people together. It encompasses the Vietnamese ethos of shared meals, of organising the best produce the family can afford, and the duality of lẩu and nhậu – to eat and to drink.

Lẩu recipes	
Canh chua chanh dây (sweet + sour fish soup with passionfruit)	page 86
Lẩu vịt nấu chao (duck with fermented bean curd)	page 134
Lẩu cơm mẻ (fermented rice hot pot)	page 176
Lẩu bò nhúng dấm (Beef dipped in vinegar hot pot)	page 192

Canh chua chanh dây

Sweet + sour fish soup with passionfruit

Serves 4–6

500 g (1 lb 12 oz)	murray cod fillets
150 g (5½ oz)	morning glory, cut into 5–7 cm (2–2¾ inch) lengths
1 stem	elephant ear, cut on an angle into thumb-sized chunks
150 g (5½ oz)	okra, kept whole if small, or cut in half if large
150 g (5½ oz)	bean sprouts
2 stalks	Chinese celery, cut on an angle into 1 cm (½ inch) slices
2	tomatoes, each cut into 6 wedges
200 g (7 oz)	ripe pineapple flesh, cut into chunks (you can also use tinned unsweetened pineapple here)

Broth

12–14	passionfruit (or 7–8 large panama tropical passionfruit)
30 ml (1 fl oz)	vegetable oil
1	brown onion, peeled, thickly sliced lengthways
1	red bird's eye chilli, split down centre, but left whole
2 litres (8 cups)	water
60 ml (¼ cup)	fish sauce
1 tablespoon	sugar
1 teaspoon	salt

Garlic oil

40 g (1½ oz)	garlic cloves, finely chopped
100 ml (3½ fl oz)	vegetable oil

→

Canh chua translates to sour soup – a clear broth typically made from fish, soured with the addition of tamarind and tomato, and balanced in sweetness with pineapple. Rice paddy herb and sawtooth coriander each lend a distinctive earthy, citrusy note that I have always associated with canh chua. It is eaten in a style of a lẩu, a communal hot pot, with associated ingredients ranging from elephant ear stems to okra and morning glory cooked in the broth and fished out at varying levels of doneness depending on the eater's care and/or cooking prowess.

This version of canh chua is made with passionfruit pulp in place of tamarind, a variation I have only ever seen in Cà Mau. Stylistically, it is lighter and a touch fruitier. I have used Murray cod fillets in place of the oft called-for catfish. Any firm white-fleshed freshwater fish can be used as a substitute.

Make the broth

1. Set a fine-meshed sieve over a bowl. Cut each passionfruit in half and scoop the pulp into the sieve. Push the pulp through the sieve to strain out the seeds; you will need about 200 ml (7 fl oz) of passionfruit juice. Set the juice aside.
2. In a large saucepan, heat the vegetable oil over medium heat, then sauté the onion and chilli for 2–3 minutes, until fragrant.
3. Pour in the water and passionfruit juice. Stir in the fish sauce, sugar and salt, then adjust the seasoning to your taste. The broth should be slightly sweet, sour and salty.

Simmer the fish

4. Cut the fish fillets into bite-sized pieces, being sure to remove any bones.
5. Carefully add the fish to the broth. Simmer the fish for about 3–4 minutes, until cooked three-quarters of the way through; be careful not to overcook the fish, to maintain its tenderness. Remove the fish with a slotted spoon and set aside.

Make the garlic oil

6. Place the garlic in a small saucepan and pour in enough oil to submerge the garlic. Stir over medium heat until the garlic starts to turn colour. Do not crank up the heat or leave the garlic unattended; if you would like it to be golden, take it out of the oil just before that point.

→

Dipping sauce (per person)

1½ tablespoons	fish sauce
1–2	fresh chillies (or to taste), chopped

To serve

- sawtooth coriander (culantro), cut into 1 cm (½ inch) lengths
- rice paddy herb, cut into 1 cm (½ inch) lengths
- steamed rice or rice vermicelli noodles

Make the dipping sauce

7 Combine the dipping sauce ingredients in small individual serving bowls.

Assemble and serve

8 Arrange all the vegetables and pineapple on a platter.

9 Return the fish to the broth to finish cooking.

10 Pour the garlic oil over the broth just before serving and garnish with the coriander and rice paddy herb.

11 Serve with steamed rice or rice vermicelli noodles, and individual bowls of the dipping sauce.

Assembling a lẩu hot pot

In some circles, the broth is the star, and in others, the proteins and vegetables shine brighter, which is all to say spare some love and attention across every aspect of the assembly.

The hot pot The stock or poaching liquid should always be hot. Any heating base will do – such as a camper cooktop or an electric wok – so long as the heat levels are adjustable. It is not necessary to start with a very well-seasoned broth, as the act of cooking and poaching will flavour the broth throughout the meal. Do have a large pot of broth available to top up the hot pot throughout the meal as required.

The proteins and vegetables Arrange the sliced proteins and vegetables on plates around the pot. They can be of different sizes and they can be frozen. I prefer not to use anything too starchy or at least par-cook starchy items, so that their introduction into the broth does not thicken it too much.

The tools A ladle for the broth and a perforated ladle for chasing down ingredients. Some use serving chopsticks to side-step the debacle of double dipping.

The dipping sauces Arrange separate dipping sauces and bowls for each person at the table.

The cooking Wait for the broth to come up to the boil before adding the proteins and vegetables. Each person can choose what they want to eat and cook. Avoid the urge to dump everything into the pot – the broth goes tepid, the ingredients take longer to cook, and there is uncomfortable conversation around the table while everyone silently curses the culprit.

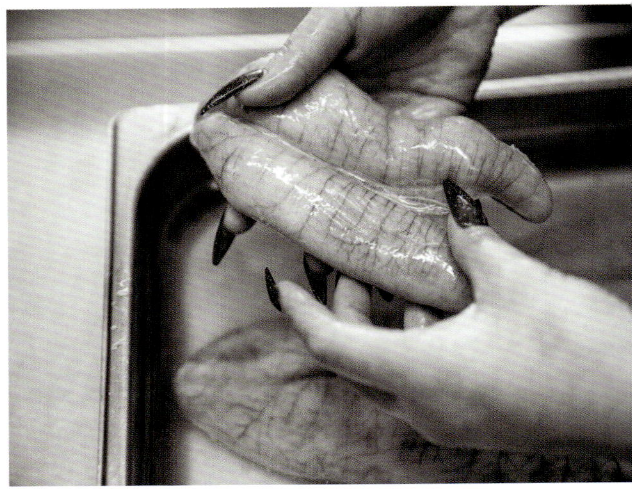

Canh cá nấu ngót

Fish roe sac soup

Serves 6–8

650 g (1 lb 7 oz)	fresh whole trevally roe sacs (see note)
100 g (3½ oz)	Chinese celery stalks and leaves, cut into 4 cm (1½ inch) lengths
½ bunch	dill, roughly chopped
	cracked white pepper (optional)

Broth

1 bunch	spring onions (scallions)
2	red bird's eye chillies, stems removed
30 ml (1 fl oz)	vegetable oil
2.2 litres (77 fl oz)	water
15 g (½ oz)	rock sugar
250 g (9 oz)	ripe tomatoes, cut into wedges

A recipe from fellow viet kieu Kim Tran, who once gifted us this meal during the pandemic. This soup is best attempted over winter when trevally roe sacs are in season. Ask for these, or large roe sacs with small beads, as opposed to larger roe beads such as those belonging to trout. They are usually on display in Asian fish markets – just point! Do also take care to soak the roe sacs overnight and bleed the bloodlines so that the flavour of the broth is not tainted.

Soak and clean the roe sacs

1. First, ensure the membrane surrounding each egg is intact, discarding any that aren't.
2. Place the roe in a large bowl, cover with cool water and leave to soak overnight in the fridge.
3. The next day, change over the water and continue to soak. While the sac is in the water, remove the bloodlines from the roe sacs by gently pushing the blood out of the veins towards the central channel, then 'milking' the blood out through the central channel. Take care not to puncture the egg sacs, or the roe will spill out.

Prepare the broth

4. Cut the spring onion whites into 4 cm (1½ inch) lengths. Cut half the spring onion greens into 4 cm (1½ inch) lengths and reserve them for serving.
5. Using a mortar and pestle, pound together the spring onion whites and chillies.
6. Warm the oil in a large heavy-based saucepan over medium heat. Add the spring onion and chilli mixture and stir-fry for a minute or two, until fragrant.
7. Add the water and bring to the boil, then add the rock sugar, tomatoes and fish sauce to taste. The stock should be lightly seasoned at this stage.

Simmer the roe

8. Add the fish roe to the broth, bring back to the boil, then reduce the heat and simmer for 15 minutes, until the fish roe is firm and the tomatoes are cooked out. Do not let the stock reduce during this time.

To serve

9. Check the seasoning and adjust to taste. Just before serving, add the reserved spring onion greens, Chinese celery and dill – and a pinch of cracked white pepper if you like.
10. You can enjoy this soup with rice noodles or steamed rice, and small individual bowls of fish sauce for dipping.

Note

Trevally roe is in season over winter. In its absence, feel free to substitute fish roe from any firm fish.

Viet-Cajun seafood boil-up

Serves 6–8

2	blue swimmer crabs, or Dungeness or Jonah Crabs, halved straight down the middle
500 g (1 lb 2 oz)	periwinkles
500 g (1 lb 2 oz)	pipis (or clams of your choice)
500 g (1 lb 2 oz)	tiger prawns (shrimp)
500 g (1 lb 2 oz)	yabbies (or crayfish)
500 g (1 lb 2 oz)	mussels, beards removed
250 g (9 oz)	new potatoes
2	corn cobs, cut into 5 cm (2 inch) pieces, husks reserved for the broth
250 g (9 oz)	okra
1 bunch	Thai basil

Spice mix (see note)

100 g (3½ oz)	hot or smoked paprika
60 g (2¼ oz)	cayenne pepper
60 g (2¼ oz)	lemongrass powder
60 g (2¼ oz)	ground ginger
60 g (2¼ oz)	onion powder
60 g (2¼ oz)	garlic powder
20 g (¾ oz)	Chinese five spice
30 g (1 oz)	fennel seeds, blitzed or crushed
1	green cardamom pod, crushed
20 g (¾ oz)	sea salt
10 g (¼ oz)	granulated white sugar

Broth

3 litres (100 fl oz)	chicken stock (page 43)
500 ml (2 cups)	coconut water (no added sugar, if using a commercially packaged version)
2	corn husks, tied
8	oranges, juiced, skin reserved
150 g (5½ oz)	ginger, peeled and chopped
2	lemongrass stems, cut into 5 cm (2 inch) lengths
1	onion, quartered

→

This dish takes inspiration from my cousins in the US. Mum has told me a few iterations of how she ended up in Australia – one was because my biological father had been sent to Australia rather than the US after leaving the refugee camp; another because she heard Australia was a much nicer place; the last was because apparently, back in the day, applicants would need to recite parts of the Bible before passage into the US was granted. Mum bombed out on the Bible recital, so while my cousins made it to the US to meet up with the other relatives, Mum found her way into Australia.

In any case, the idea of crawfish boils sent me down a Viet-Cajun rabbit hole. It is the ultimate viet kieu story – migrants and naturalised Vietnamese forced to find a living in a new area (Houston from Louisiana as a result of Hurricane Katrina), then adapting a local dish by amping it up with Vietnamese condiments: lemongrass, orange wedges, spring onion oil, ginger, butter, muối tiêu chanh (salt, pepper and citrus). The practice of boil-ups is hardly foreign to generations of Vietnamese regardless of location – fresh seafood hauled onto land, boiled, seasoned and enjoyed with lots of beer and a healthy dose of shit-talking.

This recipe should give you the starting point for your own Viet-Cajun party. The beauty of Australia is the seafood – instead of the crawfish of our Viet-American cousins, we have used prawns, mussels, shore crabs, calamari, fish and mud crabs. Do not forget the side dishes: corn doused in spring onion oil (page 44), collard greens and okra, blanched beans, as well as egg noodles and bread to soak it all up.

This undertaking is best enjoyed in a grassy backyard. Historically, we have tipped everything onto a table, hoed into the lot, and proceeded to hose down the entire table after a quick clean-up.

Prepare the spice mix

1. Combine all the spice mix ingredients in a bowl, mixing well.

Make the broth

2. Place all the broth ingredients – including the orange skins – in a stockpot, along with 100 g (3½ oz) of the spice mix. Bring to the boil and leave to infuse over low heat for 30 minutes.

Prepare the seafood

3. Clean the seafood, depending on the types you have selected.
4. If using crabs, turn them over, pry off and remove the belly plate, and chop the body in half with a cleaver.
5. If using periwinkles and/or pipis, purge them of sand using the method on page 122.
6. If using prawns, you can remove the shells and intestinal tract. I like to keep the heads on for extra flavour during cooking.
7. Rinse all the seafood under cold running water and leave to drain.

→

1	garlic bulb, halved
8	fresh bay leaves
6	star anise
1	cassia bark stick

Sauce

50 ml (1¾ fl oz)	vegetable oil
75 g (2 oz)	garlic, peeled
50 g (1¾ oz)	ginger, peeled and roughly chopped
50 g (1¾ oz)	lemongrass, very finely chopped
25 g (1 oz)	red bird's eye chillies, very finely chopped
125 g (4½ oz)	unsalted butter
50 ml (1¾ fl oz)	fish sauce

To serve

1	orange, juiced
	salt, pepper and citrus (page 40) or hot sauce

Cook the seafood and vegetables

8 Bring the stock back to the boil with the lid on.

9 Add the crab, periwinkles, potatoes, corn and Thai basil to the stock and cook rapidly for 10 minutes, covered.

10 Add the okra, pipis, prawns, yabbies and mussels and cook for a further 5 minutes, covered.

Make the sauce

11 While the seafood is simmering, heat the oil in a large wok over high heat. Add the garlic, ginger, lemongrass and chilli and fry for 1 minute. Add the butter and let it melt. Bring to a bubble and stir in the fish sauce and 150 g (5½ oz) of the spice mix.

12 Check the seasoning; the sauce should be spicy and buttery, with a hint of sweetness on the back palate. Once you are happy, turn off the heat.

Serve the boil-up

13 Once the seafood is cooked, scoop it out of the broth and add it to the wok. Give the seafood a good toss to ensure it is evenly coated in the sauce.

14 Check the seasoning, and add more spice blend to your liking.

15 Stir the additional orange juice through the seafood to lighten the sauce. Toss in a good handful of Thai basil leaves, then empty the contents of the wok into a large vessel, like a paella pan, or straight onto a table covered in plastic wrap.

16 Serve with salt, pepper and citrus, or your favourite hot sauce.

Notes

- You can use any combination of seafood here – just aim for a combined weight of 2.5–3 kg (5 lb 8 oz–6 lb 12 oz).
- Store left-over spice mix in an airtight container for several weeks.

Morning, moonshine + the Mekong

Thi

At 16, I spent two months in Cà Mau, at the southern-most tip of the Mekong. I had essentially been deported by my mother, from the familiarity of my outer Western Sydney environment to the province where she grew up, where her family home still remains, and where I could be stewarded by my uncles – her brother and cousins.

Mum thought it would do me good to leave Sydney for a short while, to experience the world around me. I was more than a handful at home. Our relationship balanced uncomfortably along an invisible precipice. Mum fought with me, often – over my companions, my dalliance with hard drugs and my consummate relationship with the recreational variety, my *choice* to be queer. I fought back, incensed that she would judge me for any and all of my choices, knowing how her nightmare of choices the decade prior had stained my life.

My anger regularly led to destruction, and the drug-induced paranoia only heightened the wrath. My fragile relationship with my mother and my environment reminded me of my lost childhood, of my vulnerability. I would sometimes see flashes of abuse suffered by a facsimile of my childhood self while my adolescent self stood by, watching, unable to do anything. My mother was often at a loss when my rage seethed beyond the white burn of charcoal. Sometimes I blacked out from the pure weight of emotions. She called the police once, when I was irreconcilable; I spent the next few days in a psychiatric ward and was given sleeping pills to relax.

In contrast, the three months I spent in Cà Mau passed by generally uneventfully. I eased into the experience, spending time with my extended family and honing my grasp of the language. There were plenty of distractions, and I was distantly aware that my general happiness and quality of life had improved away from Sydney. My uncles were more than happy to welcome a young charge into the fold of their lives, and I found comfort in their occasional alcohol-induced trash-talking.

One morning, my uncle dragged my 16-year-old frame out of bed. At 9.30 am, the air was already hot from the equatorial sun and heavy with the automotive fumes of yet another workday. We walked, chattering benignly, criss-crossing the paddy-fields and prawning ponds, towards the house of another uncle.

Our arrival was met with raucous cheers from the other uncles and some aunties, nine of them on the patio, already merry with beers and thimbles of moonshine in hand. They settled me into their circle on the ground. Someone pushed a glass of juice into my hands, apparently finding the clarity during their mid-morning shenanigans to realise I should not be partaking in a 10 am booze session. A metal tub sat in the centre, already burning hot with local mangrove charcoal and coconut husks.

I asked: *Aren't any of you working today?* Oh, we're all done for the day, we have already worked. *It's only ten o'clock.* We all woke up really early this morning to work. A murmur of laughter bubbled up from the edge of our circle and everyone took a drink. Who was I to judge?

Out came prawns, their bodies taut and firm, their bluish-green-grey bodies transforming to a vibrant orange from the gentle heat beneath. The chatter continued as fermented bean curd was presented and prepared. The soft, milky cubes were mashed with a spoon, and into the pulp went minced garlic and a slug of moonshine. *It's like cooking wine but better,* one of the uncles offered with a wink.

The prawns – most lightly charred and perfectly cooked, the odd one nearing the brink of cremation when the drinking distracted – were a wonderful foil for the creamy, salty bean curd mixture. I delighted in the moment, peeling prawns and fishing their sweet bodies through the moonshine-tinged concoction, almost forgetting that I was allergic to crustaceans.

The conversation took a sombre turn at one point – or perhaps it was always headed in that direction, given the morning fuel of alcohol and our eating of prawns, which represented the modest livelihoods of a handful of my uncles and many residents of the province. Circumstances were never quite the same since the war; I was one of the lucky ones, someone pointed out, because my mother had the courage to leave.

I found out that day that Mum was on one of the very last boats out of Cà Mau. She had not intended to leave at all, while my uncle had been an active boat organiser. Her decision to leave had upset her parents. *She almost stayed*, chimed an aunty, *but the soldiers were looking for her. We knew it was time and she had to go. We hid her in a rice hut that night. We piled paddy rice over her, you could not tell there was someone hiding, and she spent the night in there.* The next night, my mother took my two older sisters and her two nephews with her to board the boat.

I felt foolish at that moment, as everyone was recounting their memory of the circumstances. Mum had rarely spoken about her life or journey out of Vietnam. She had summarised the experience with a few vague words: *I got on a boat and I came to Australia*. The sentiment was always so casual; it was easy to overlook the illegitimate nature of the exercise or the anxiety and terror of it.

The odds were stacked against her – she had four dependants with her; she might have been raped or killed or both; they might have been caught before making it to the open sea; the boat might have capsized or been targeted by pirates. Years later, I would learn from my eldest sister that the boat actually had been boarded by pirates. Mum risked her life, and the lives of her daughters and nephews, for an unknown opportunity for a better life, one less bitter and less fraught by poverty.

The information I learned about my mother that morning, over grilled prawns and fermented bean curd, gave me a different perspective. I used to get upset that Mum could not afford to buy me a Nintendo, or horrified that our school holidays were always embarrassingly *ethnic*, spent prawning by the beach with other Vietnamese families in the area. Regardless, our commission housing in Australia yielded mechanical properties that would easily outperform the straw huts that still dotted the Cà Mau landscape. I had the opportunity to go to school and indulge in technical drawing classes, just because it interested me. Infant mortality rates were lower in Australia. Getting to the next major town did not require a 12-hour drive along a weaving dirt road lined with poverty.

My new perspective pacified a lot of resentment I held against my mother, although our relationship took many more years to really improve. Perhaps 20 years later, I would recount the lessons I learned that day to my younger sister and my nephew, both of whom were at a crossroads with their careers. Neither of them wanted to take a leap and instead spent an inordinate amount of time and energy working out the endless possibilities of what might go wrong. Yet my own mother, the woman who I had harboured a multitude of grievances against, saw a sliver of opportunity and took it.

Prawns and fermented bean curd still remind me of my uncles and their 10 am booze session, but it also reminds me of the time I started to forgive my mother.

Tôm nướng chao

Grilled prawns with fermented bean curd

Serves 3–4 as part of a shared meal, or 1–2 as a snack

6	very large tiger prawns (shrimp), about 500 g (1 lb 2 oz) in total

Marinade

2 cubes	fermented bean curd (page 68), mashed
1 tablespoon	shaoxing wine
2	garlic cloves, minced
1 tablespoon	minced fresh ginger
1 tablespoon	sugar
2 teaspoons	sesame oil

To serve

Vietnamese mint leaves
salt, pepper and citrus (page 40)

This moreish marinade works its charms on any seafood or protein for that matter; see page 168 for use with lamb ribs. Serve this hot as an appetiser or main dish with muối tiêu chanh (salt, pepper and citrus).

Marinate the prawns

1. Rinse the prawns under cold running water. Pat them dry with paper towels and set aside.
2. If you like, you can trim the antennae using scissors, to stop them catching on fire during grilling. You can also trim away the rostrum (the sharp spike), so it does not catch on the back of diners' throats, for those who like to suck on the heads.
3. Mix the marinade ingredients in a bowl until smooth. Add the prawns and gently toss until coated, then cover and marinate in the fridge for at least 30 minutes.

Heat your grill

4. Prepare a barbecue grill or chargrill (see page 104) to medium heat.

Grill the prawns

5. Place the prawns directly on the hot grill.
6. Grill the prawns for 2–3 minutes on each side, or until they turn pink and opaque, brushing them with any remaining marinade for added flavour. Avoid overcooking, so they do not become tough and rubbery.
7. Transfer to a plate and garnish with Vietnamese mint leaves. Serve hot as a delicious starter or main dish, with salt, pepper and citrus.

Mực nướng xốt ớt xanh

Grilled squid with green chilli

Serves 2–3 as part of a shared meal

350 g (12 oz)	whole squid, cleaned
30 ml (1 fl oz)	olive oil, for brushing
pinch of	sea salt
100 ml ($3\frac{1}{2}$ fl oz)	green chilli and lime dressing (page 42)
	Thai basil leaves, to garnish

This recipe is an ode to the ubiquitous bottles of Dasavi Lemon Chilli Sauce for Seafood that you find offered as a condiment by almost all street food vendors in Ho Chi Minh City. Thi proffered her unrequited love to this sauce the very first time she had it, with grilled calamari from a road-side vendor somewhere along Bùi Viện Street.

Clean the squid

1 In one hand, hold the bottom of the squid (head and tentacles). With your other hand, hold the hood (triangular piece on the other end) and gently pull it away from the body. If necessary, trim any connective tissue to completely detach the hood. Set aside.

2 Locate the beak at the centre of the tentacles, where they meet the body. Cut off the beak with a sharp knife and discard.

3 The hard rings are the firm, circular sections found along the length of the tentacles. Slice through each ring with your knife to remove, and discard.

4 The slimy black outer layer is the skin of the squid. The easiest way to remove it is to gently peel it off by starting at one end and pulling it away from the flesh.

5 Clean the hood, tentacles, body and wings (the flat, triangular extensions on either side of the body, which add texture and flavour) using a paper towel to remove any debris.

Grill the squid

6 Prepare a barbecue grill or chargrill (see page 104) to medium heat.

7 Brush or spray the squid, including the hood and tentacles, with oil and sprinkle with sea salt.

8 Place all the squid on the hot grill, pressing it down with tongs. Cook on each side for 2–3 minutes until the flesh turns opaque.

9 Remove from the heat and leave to rest for 1 minute.

To serve

10 Cut the squid into thick slices and transfer to a plate. Dress with the green chilli and lime dressing and serve topped with Thai basil.

Ốc xào me

Clams with tamarind + native lime

Serves 2–3

500 g (1 lb 2 oz)	clams (vongole)
25 ml (¾ fl oz)	vegetable oil
1	lemongrass stem, smashed and cut into 5 cm (2 inch) batons
100 g (3½ oz)	red Asian shallots, finely diced
75 g (2½ oz)	garlic cloves, minced
15 g (½ oz)	red bird's eye chillies, minced
8	makrut lime leaves

Tamarind and native lime dressing

10 g (¼ oz)	galangal, peeled and roughly chopped
22 g (¾ oz)	garlic cloves, roughly chopped
6 g (⅛ oz)	red bird's eye chilli, roughly chopped
55 g (2 oz)	whole desert (native) lime
300 g (10½ oz)	tamarind base (page 38)
	lime juice, to taste

To serve

roasted peanuts
fried shallots (page 71)
Vietnamese mint sprigs

A big part of respecting Vietnamese cuisine is understanding its deference to local and seasonal produce. Australian desert or native limes add a tactile pop to this sauce while also offering a very understated intensity to underscore the savoury acidity. In the event that you are unable to find a suitable substitute for desert lime, you can still proceed with this recipe with just the tamarind component.

This sauce is very versatile. I have found great success with prawns or pipis, and with vegetables such as brussels sprouts.

Make the dressing

1. Using a mortar and pestle, pound the galangal, garlic and chilli to a coarse paste.
2. Add the desert lime and pound lightly, ensuring the lime retains its texture.
3. Stir in the tamarind base. Check for tartness, adjust with a squeeze of lime juice if needed, and set aside. You can store any left-over dressing in an airtight container in the fridge for up to 1 month.

Steam the clams

4. Rinse the clams under cold water to remove sand and debris, discarding any damaged ones. Drain and set aside.
5. Add about 2.5 cm (1 inch) of water to a steamer.
6. Place the clams in the steamer basket, cover with the lid and steam for about 3–4 minutes, until just cooked. Reserve the clam juices.

Stir-fry the clams

7. Heat the oil in a wok over medium heat. Add the lemongrass, shallot, garlic and chilli, frying for 1–2 minutes until fragrant.
8. Add the clams and their juices, then toss and stir in 150 g (5½ oz) of the dressing, until the clams are well coated, and cook for a further 2–3 minutes.
9. Add the lime leaves.

To serve

10. Transfer the clams and sauce to a large serving plate. Pour the dressing from the wok over the top, and garnish with roasted peanuts, fried shallots and Vietnamese mint. Serve immediately for the best flavour.

Building a barbecue

I use a Weber kettle drum to grill. Charcoal introduces a consistent heat source but imparts very little flavour. Firewood burns at a less predictable heat range, depending on the wood variety, but it is still my preference. Source dried or aged firewood that is double split (approximately 12 cm/5 inches wide, and 30 cm/12 inches long).

The grill Make sure the grill is clean and free from old ash. Open the vents on the bottom of the drum for airflow.

The wood Place two pieces of firewood parallel to each other in the drum, approximately two fist widths apart to allow airflow. Place the next pieces of firewood perpendicular on top of the first layer, creating a cross pattern – think tic-tac-toe. Add one more layer, running the same direction as the first. Then place one or two handfuls of kindling in the spaces you left for airflow between the firewood, and 3–4 firelighters or some sheets of newspaper at the bottom.

The fire Using a match or long lighter, light the firelighters or newspaper. Fan lightly at the base of the fire, to help ignite and increase the intensity of the flame. My younger sister's cheat tip – a hairdryer can speed up the ignition and intensity of the flame. Let the fire catch and establish.

The cooking When half of the firewood has caught, knock the firewood to spread the embers. This will give you a good balance of heat and smoke to grill over. Place the grill grate on top and allow to heat up for 3–4 minutes. You can now start cooking. Introduce additional pieces of firewood at regular intervals and in moderation for sustained heat. Remember that you want to cook with hot embers, not flame. White embers provide a steady heat source ideal for cooking. Close the lid or keep a spray bottle of water nearby to help slow down the burn of the wood (and to generate more smoke).

The smoke If you are looking to smoke your proteins, bring them to room temperature first, and get them smoking on the grill grate before the wood catches. Shuffle any flaming firewood aside to keep the fire at a lower temperature – you need a mixture of smouldering embers and smoking wood. Look for a regular column of smoke that is quite thin. Avoid dense, dark black smoke (an issue with combustion) and billowing white smoke (too much moisture in the wood).

Marrons + bơ sa tế

Serves 2–3

4	live marrons, about 200 g (7 oz) each
100 g (3½ oz)	unsalted butter
130 g (4½ oz)	sa tế (page 41)

Marrons are freshwater crayfish that are unique to Western Australia - do not confuse them with chestnuts of the French tradition! With their sweet, large tails, marrons are great for eating. Their thicker shells provide the flesh a little more protection from the direct heat of the grill, and once split also form a lovely little boat for the sa tế butter to be spooned over. In the absence of marrons, any crustacean would work.

1 Prepare a barbecue grill or chargrill (see page 104) to medium heat.
2 Using a dry tea (dish) towel, firmly hold the marrons and spike them through the throat using a sharp knife. Split the marrons lengthways using a sharp knife or cleaver.
3 In a small saucepan, melt the butter and stir in the sa tế until well combined. Keep warm.
4 Place the marrons on the grill, shell side down. Grill for about 3 minutes, or until cooked to your preference, spooning the lemongrass butter over the marrons as they cook. For larger marrons, I have a kitchen blowtorch handy to torch some of the head juices if the tail is already cooked, but the head needs a bit longer.
5 Serve warm off the grill.

'The thicker shells of the marrons provide the flesh a little more protection from the direct heat of the grill, and once split also form a lovely little boat for the sa tế butter to be spooned over.'

'Cua. Tôm hùm. Ốc. Mud crab. Lobster. Shellfish. All of these are words that my family and I associate with good times.'

A bathtub of crabs

Thi

Cua. Tôm hùm. Ốc. Mud crab. Lobster. Shellfish. All of these are words that my family and I associate with good times. These were not ingredients that appeared regularly on the dining table. However, when celebratory circumstances called for it and financial circumstances allowed for it, we would indulge in some form of crustacea or expensive fish. We had a particular penchant for mud crab. Perhaps it is in the family's DNA, with my mum and two older sisters having grown up in Cà Mau, where the palm trees sway, the air is clammy and sticky, and the mud crabs scutter about in abundance across the alluvial plains.

In Cà Mau, crabs are king. The province's geographical position at the mouth of the Mekong estuary, with the sweeping sea along the cape, nurtures an ideal ecosystem for various species of crabs and the equally various manner in which they are consumed. Charcoal grilled crabs, steamed crabs, braised, roasted, dunked in a hot pot; from specialty to everyday dishes, prepared and eaten at any time of the day.

Imagine a bathtub in a suburban family home out in Western Sydney in the early 2000s. Now imagine that same bathtub filled to the brim with mud crabs. A-grade female mud crabs, all trussed up, alive and struggling against their ties, soon scheduled to meet the cleavers and woks of a restaurant.

The bathtub at my mum's house was off limits the weekend of my older sister's wedding. It was simultaneously inconvenient – being the only bathtub for the entire household – and thrilling, with the anticipation of the upcoming feast. A Vietnamese wedding feast was always a tantalising prospect for my younger self, and this event was no exception. In fact, the excitement might have been enhanced by the fact that I was, for the first time, attending such a wedding feast as family, and therein lay the promise that I might actually get a second helping of whichever delicious dish my 12-year-old self desired. My soon-to-be brother-in-law's family were a crabbing family up in Darwin with roots from the Delta. The bathtub of crabs was their wedding gift.

The extended family's connection to the Darwin crab industry would serve me later on in life as a chef. We occasionally got crabs through the restaurant – sand crabs, spanners, shore crabs and muddies. When the pandemic lockdowns hit, we threw many takeaway menu ideas at the wall, and one that stuck was wok-tossed seafood. Seafood was surprisingly cheap at that time, because the international markets had closed their doors. I felt that the dreariness of winter lockdowns could partially be answered by the joy of mud crab, with its sweet shellfish aromas and complex nuttiness imparted by a life in the mangroves. I was also obsessed by the luxury of ripping into a mud crab in the privacy of one's home, dressed to the nines or in PJs – no one cared either way.

The only thing thwarting my grand lockdown plans was my inability to source mud crabs in the local market. Cue: my brother-in-law's family and their respective contacts. After talking to my sister, I was given a number and a specific set of instructions. *Give this sister a call at this time. Tell her who gave you this number. Tell her what you need. Good luck.* It was all quite thrilling! I was not in the business of helping crabs break out of jail, but it really did feel like I was dabbling in the underworld.

I duly followed said instructions and received my delivery of crabs, as well as many subsequent lots. I cooked many mud crabs over that lockdown and found much joy in feeding those within the restaurant's radius such tasty sauce-smothered crustaceans.

Cua xào tiêu núi

Mud crab with mountain pepper

Serves 1–2

1 kg (2 lb 4 oz)	live mud crab
40 g (1½ oz)	cornflour (cornstarch), for coating
775 ml (26 fl oz)	vegetable oil
80 g (2¾ oz)	minced red Asian shallots
40 g (1½ oz)	minced garlic
40 g (1½ oz)	minced fresh ginger
100 g (3½ oz)	unsalted butter
15 g (½ oz)	red peppercorns, ground
9 g (¼ oz)	mắc khén or mountain peppercorns, ground
10 g (¼ oz)	curry leaves
50 ml (1¾ fl oz)	fish sauce
1	lime, halved

One of my younger sister's favourite dishes is mud crab dry-roasted in salt; the thick, white braids of flesh flourish in saline cookery. This dish reminds me of one of the best lessons – that the duality of simple but quality ingredients allows for maximum flavour. The dish is always best during garlic season, when there is an array of local garlic to choose from. I pair the garlic with quality sea salt, giving a bright and clean flavour of the ocean, just as the sweet, firm mud crab gives a flavour of the mangroves.

There is nothing quite like licking the salty, crispy, garlicky bits off your crab shell and dunking the meat into fresh lime juice. Perhaps only the prospect of another mouthful.

Prepare the crab

1. Place the mud crab in the freezer for about 1 hour. This is a humane way to kill mud crab; the chill numbs it and results in a quick, painless death. You can remove it from the freezer once it stops moving – but take care not to freeze it.
2. Rinse the crab thoroughly under cold running water to remove any mud or debris.
3. Remove the top shell by firmly holding the crab down with one hand, and gently pulling from the top left-hand corner towards the bottom right-hand corner with your other hand.
4. Using a cleaver, split the crab in half down the spine and chop the claws off. Lightly crack the claws with the back of your cleaver and set aside.
5. Remove the gills and digestive gland. (The gills look like a feathery structure on either side of the crab; you can simply pull these off with your fingers.) Cut the crab in half again, down the spine, to give you four pieces.

Fry the crab

6. Dredge the crab, including the claws, in the cornflour, ensuring the pieces are well coated, and shaking off any excess.
7. In a wok, heat 700 ml (24 fl oz) of the vegetable oil to 180°C (350°F). Fry the crab pieces and claws in batches until the shell turns red, which will take about 2 minutes. Drain on a wire rack and set aside.

To finish the dish

8. Discard the frying oil and wipe the wok clean. Heat the remaining oil in the wok and stir-fry the shallot, garlic and ginger over medium heat for 1–2 minutes, until fragrant.
9. Add the butter, ground peppercorns and curry leaves and cook to the 'burnt butter' stage, being careful not to burn the butter. This should take about 5 minutes, and the butter should have a nutty aroma, mingling with the fragrance of the pepper and curry leaves.
10. Add the fried crab to the wok and toss until evenly coated in the sauce. Season with the fish sauce, transfer to a platter and serve with the lime halves.

Ốc nấu nước dừa

Periwinkles poached in coconut milk

Serves 3–4 as part of a shared meal

500 g (1 lb 2 oz)	periwinkles
50 g (1¾ oz)	lemongrass, roughly chopped
50 g (1¾ oz)	red Asian shallots, roughly chopped
10 g (¼ oz)	ginger, peeled and sliced
10 g (¼ oz)	garlic cloves, minced
2	red bird's eye chillies, split down the middle
2–3	makrut lime leaf, roughly torn
400 ml (14 fl oz)	fish or chicken stock (page 43), or water
120 ml (4 fl oz)	coconut milk
2–3 teaspoons	fish sauce
1 teaspoon	sugar
good pinch of	sea salt
	salt, pepper and citrus (page 40), to serve

A recipe that can be thrown together relatively quickly for a mid-week dinner as it leans on fridge and pantry staples. Swap the periwinkles out for meaty pipis or a bag of mussels if it is easier for you.

1. Wash the periwinkles under cold running water to remove any sand and debris. Drain and set aside.
2. Put all the ingredients, except the periwinkles, in a large clay pot or stockpot. Bring to a simmer and leave to infuse over low heat for 20 minutes.
3. Add the periwinkles and poach over a gentle heat for 20–25 minutes, with the lid on, until the periwinkles' little caps (the operculums) come off.
4. Serve with salt, pepper and citrus.

Gỏi tôm đu đủ

Prawn + papaya gỏi

Serves 3–4

300 g (10½ oz)	raw king prawns (jumbo shrimp); see notes
250 g (9 oz)	green mango, peeled and julienned
210 g (7½ oz)	green papaya, peeled and julienned
50 g (1¾ oz)	red Asian shallots, thinly sliced
35 g (1¼ oz)	finely sliced lemongrass
1	green scud chilli, sliced at an angle (see notes)
2	makrut lime leaves, centre vein removed, leaves finely julienned
12	lime slices, skin on, very thinly sliced
10 g (¼ oz)	coarsely chopped sawtooth coriander (culantro)
10 g (¼ oz)	finely chopped mint
10 g (¼ oz)	finely chopped Vietnamese mint

Dressing

80 g (2¾ oz)	nước mắm base (page 34)
4	garlic cloves, minced
2	red bird's eye chillies, minced

To serve

crushed roasted peanuts
fried shallots (page 71)
prawn crackers (page 60)
lime wedges

One of the few things that never fails to summon a disproportionate amount of rage in me is coming across recipes by food personalities with their take on an 'Asian-style salad' – inspired by the apparently monolithic entity that is Asia. Wombok or cabbage. Carrots and coriander. Heaven forbid they include bean sprouts. Sesame seeds. Noodles. And the obligatory fish sauce.

A gỏi or nộm (in southern- and northern-Vietnamese parlance respectively) shares some characteristics of a coleslaw, with shredded vegetables dressed in some variation of nước mắm. They are not to be confused with the Vietnamese sa lát, which aligns more closely with the global concept of a salad – a greener, leafier number. A gỏi or nộm typically stars locally accessible produce, running the gamut of banana flowers through lotus stems, sea snails through jellyfish and calamari, thinly sliced pork through chicken feet, green mangoes through jackfruit and water spinach.

There is no star in this gỏi. The prawns might be the reason your guests dig into this dish, but they are staying for the rest of the cast – the subtle pops of lime slices; the textural crunch proffered by the green mango; the oh-so-familiar flavour that leaves them second-guessing their knowledge of herbs.

A note on the green papaya and green mango: taste your produce before going ahead. You can use equal amounts of each if the green mango is not very sour.

Peel and poach the prawns

1 Peel the prawns and remove the heads, saving the shells and heads for the prawn crackers on page 60. Remove and discard the intestinal vein.
2 In a large saucepan of simmering water, poach the prawns for 30 seconds, or until cooked to your liking.
3 Scoop them out using a slotted spoon and leave to cool, then slice the prawns in half lengthways.

Assemble the salad

4 Place the prawns in a large mixing bowl with the mango, papaya, shallot, lemongrass, chilli, shredded lime leaves and lime slices.
5 Combine the dressing ingredients in a small bowl, mixing well, then use to lightly dress the vegetables. The vegetables should just be coated, rather than swimming in dressing
6 Taste the salad to check the seasoning, adjusting to taste. Once you are happy, add the herbs and lightly toss.
7 Transfer the salad to a serving plate and serve with the garnishes.

Mì xào đồ biển
Crispy egg noodles with seafood

Serves 1–2

200 g (7 oz)	fresh egg noodles
60 ml (¼ cup)	vegetable oil, plus 1 teaspoon for noodles
20 g (¾ oz)	ginger, peeled and sliced
2	red Asian shallots, sliced
2	garlic cloves, minced
6	spring onions (scallions), white parts cut into 5 cm (2 inch) batons (reserve the greens for the spring onion oil on page 44)
150 ml (5 fl oz)	chicken stock (page 43) or water
60 g (2¼ oz)	squid, cleaned, cut into chunks and lightly scored in a cross-hatched pattern
2–3	prawns (shrimp), shelled and deveined
60 g (2¼ oz)	firm white fish fillets, such as John dory or barramundi, cut into chunks
70 g (2½ oz)	broccolini (tenderstem broccoli), cut into chunks
30g (1 oz)	Chinese celery, cut into 5 cm (2 inch) batons

Slurry

1½ tablespoons	cornflour (cornstarch)
3 tablespoons	cool water

Sauce

1 tablespoon	soy sauce
1 teaspoon	fish sauce
1 teaspoon	oyster sauce
pinch of	raw sugar
pinch of	cracked white pepper

A staple dish across the menus of Melbourne's Viet-Chinese eateries. The good versions are stuff that dreams are made of, and the questionable versions are very much questionable. I like my egg noodles straddling the apex of crisp and just softened by the heat of the sauce between the time it was spooned over the noodles to the time the dish was walked to the table. I like the sauce with just enough gloop to coat but not so much to glue. I love my seafood fresh and just cooked. I have bitten into mouthfuls of cold (sometimes still frozen) imported seafood, ammonia- or chemical-laced, often texturally lifeless. I will take the natural sweetness and the tactile snap of a wok-licked local prawn any day.

Prepare the noodles

1 Loosen the fresh noodle pucks, then blanch in boiling water for about 50 seconds. Rinse under cold water until cool, vigorously shake out any excess water, and let drain. Set aside.

Make the slurry

2 In a small bowl, combine the cornflour and cool water, mixing well until smooth. Set aside.

Make the sauce

3 Combine all the sauce ingredients in a bowl, stirring until dissolved. Set aside.

Fry the noodles

4 Heat the 1 teaspoon of oil in a large wok or frying pan over high heat, then reduce to medium. Add the cooked noodles, spreading them out evenly. If they start to stick, add another splash of oil.

5 Once the noodles start to char, flip them to char the other side. Be careful not to burn them.

6 Transfer the crispy noodles to a plate and keep warm. Rinse and wipe out the wok.

Cook the seafood and vegetables

7 Heat the 60 ml (¼ cup) of oil in the wok over medium heat.

8 Add the ginger, shallot, garlic and spring onion batons; stir-fry for 1 minute until fragrant.

9 Add the stock and bring to the boil. Add the squid, prawns and fish, stirring occasionally for 2 minutes.

10 Add the slurry and sauce mixture, along with the broccolini. Stir fry for 2–3 minutes until the broccolini is just cooked.

11 Remove the wok from the heat and toss in the Chinese celery.

To serve

12 Serve the seafood and vegetable mixture over the fried noodles.

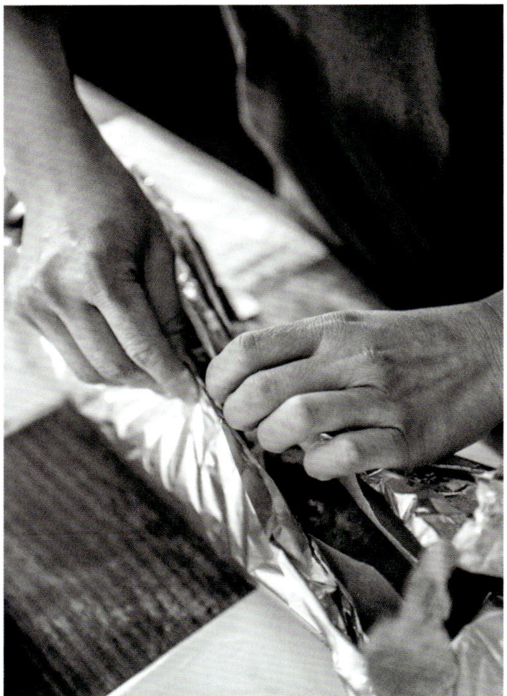

Cá hấp
Steamed coral trout

Serves 2–4 as part of a shared meal

100 g (3½ oz)	dried glass noodles
30 g (1 oz)	dried wood ear mushrooms
30 g (1 oz)	dried lily flowers
1 × 800 g (1 lb 12 oz)	whole coral trout; if you like, ask your fishmonger to scale and clean the fish for you before taking it home
70 g (2½ oz)	ginger, peeled and julienned
3	spring onions (scallions), whites cut into 5 cm (2 inch) batons, greens reserved
	ice bath
	handful of coriander (cilantro) sprigs, to garnish

Sauce

80 ml (⅓ cup)	shaoxing wine
50 ml (1¾ fl oz)	oyster sauce
30 ml (1 fl oz)	soy sauce
25 ml (¾ fl oz)	sesame oil

Garlic oil

100 ml (3½ fl oz)	sunflower oil
50 g (1¾ oz)	garlic cloves, minced

There are a couple of key things to remember with steamed fish. Whole fish is preferable for flavour, but otherwise I prefer cutlets over fillets. Use fresh fish – I cannot stress this enough. If you can't find coral trout, substitute another white, firm-fleshed fish with good fat content: kingfish, Murray cod, rock cod or barramundi. Do not use salmon or ocean trout.

Soak the dried ingredients

1 Soak the glass noodles in cold water for at least 20 minutes or until ready to use.

2 Meanwhile, in separate small bowls, soak the wood ear mushrooms and lily flowers in enough warm water to cover for 15 minutes. Drain them both, then take the lily flowers and tie knots in each individual strand. Set aside.

Steam the fish

3 Clean and scale the fish, if your fishmonger has not already done this for you. Using a sharp knife, score the fish by making three incisions, about 5 cm (2 inch) deep, on both sides.

4 Line a large sheet of foil with baking paper. Place the fish on top. Place the ginger and the white spring onion batons inside all the fish incisions.

5 Mix all the sauce ingredients together and pour the sauce over the fish. Seal the foil into a parcel around the fish.

6 Half-fill a wok or large saucepan with water and place over high heat. Place a steaming basket inside the wok, or on top of the saucepan, and put the lid on. When the water starts boiling vigorously, place the foil-wrapped fish in the steamer basket and put the back lid on. Steam the fish over high heat for 30 minutes, taking care to top up the water level when it gets low. (Alternatively, you can place the foil-wrapped fish in a baking dish and bake in a preheated 200°C/400°F oven for 50–60 minutes.)

Cook the noodles

7 Drain the glass noodles and place in a heatproof bowl. Cover with boiling water and leave for about 5 minutes, or until cooked. Rinse and drain.

8 Unwrap the fish and check it is cooked – it should come away from the bone quite easily. When the fish is cooked, place the glass noodles on top and steam for a further 1–2 minutes.

Prepare the garlic oil and garnishes

9 Just before serving, add the oil and garlic to a small saucepan and fry over medium heat for a few minutes, until the garlic starts to turn colour. Turn off the heat.

10 Using a sharp knife, julienne the reserved spring onion greens, then place in the ice bath until they curl; this will take less than a minute.

To serve

11 Remove the fish from the steamer and unwrap it. Garnish with the green spring onion curls and coriander and pour the hot garlic oil over. Serve with hot steamed rice.

Cá mòi sống và gỏi dừa

Sardines + coconut salad

Serves 4–6

250 g (9 oz)	raw sardine fillets
2 bunches	rice paddy herb, roughly chopped
1 bunch	Vietnamese mint, roughly chopped
50 g (1¾ oz)	fresh flaked coconut (see note)
¼	lime, skin on, thinly sliced

Onion pickle

100 g (3½ oz)	brown onion, thickly sliced
⅓ cup (80 ml)	rice vinegar
25 g (1 oz)	sea salt
1 teaspoon	caster (superfine) sugar
½ teaspoon	cracked black pepper

To serve

fried shallots (page 71)
galangal and nut dressing (page 41)
rice paper sheets (optional)
lettuce leaf cups (optional)

It has always made sense to me that sardine rice paper rolls should exist, particularly in Australia. We have access to trays of wild-caught South Australian sardines in the supermarket, perfectly lined in their clear plastic caskets, cleaned and filleted, 'ready to be cooked', as the packaging proudly declares. I look at these trays of sardines occasionally while I wander the aisles of the supermarket and imagine biting into a sardine rice paper roll. The rice paper would resist for a split moment before releasing the moreish, oily sardines and a tangy dressing. I like letting the obscenity of this linger in my mind for more than a moment before moving on.

This salad can be assembled into rice paper rolls, or lettuce cups, or just be enjoyed on its own.

Pickle the onion

1 Place the onion in a mixing bowl with the remaining pickle ingredients. Mix well and leave to pickle for at least 10 minutes, to soften the onion. Drain.

Assemble the salad

2 Arrange one-quarter of the onion pickle on a large plate.
3 Fan one-quarter of the sardines over the bed of onion.
4 Sprinkle with one-quarter of the herbs and lime slices.
5 Repeat the onion, sardine and herb layers, until all the ingredients are used.

To serve

6 Sprinkle fried shallots over the salad, and either drizzle with dressing to enjoy on its own, or make into rice paper rolls or lettuce cups to dip in dressing.

Note

You can buy fresh frozen flaked coconut from an Asian grocer.

Pipis, cải xoong và mắm tép dầu giấm

Pipis + watercress with mắm tép

Serves 2

500 g (1 lb 2 oz)	large pipis (or clams of your choice)
1–2	bullet, birds-eye or green scud chillies, roughly sliced
300 ml (10½ fl oz)	fish stock or water
50 g (1¾ oz)	watercress, washed and picked
70 ml (2¼ fl oz)	mắm tép vinaigrette (page 32)

To serve

olive oil
Vietnamese baguette (optional)

This recipe came about when I was out camping near Mount Baw Baw in Victoria's High Country at the old Chinese Gardens Campground. I have never been one to chance my dining luck on a cup of noodle soup, nor do I plan my camping meals too strictly, lest I come across something exciting along the way. Additionally, I have always preferred to bring along something versatile (an errant container of mắm tép, in this instance) and a bit of protein, just in case.

A freshwater stream runs adjacent to the Chinese Gardens Campground and we chanced upon an abundance of watercress growing there. A quick rummage through the car yielded some solid campervan pantry staples and a tasty meal was had.

Purge the pipis

1. Rinse the pipis under cold water and transfer to a clean bowl.
2. Cover with water and add the cut chillies, then let sit for at least an hour before cooking. The oils in the chillies will help stimulate the clams to expel sand.
3. Just before cooking, remove the pipis from the chilli water (the chillies and water can be discarded). Rinse them and drain them again.

Steam the pipis

4. Heat a heavy-based saucepan over medium heat. Add the pipis and stock, cover with a lid and steam for 2–3 minutes, until the pipis pop open.
5. Remove the open pipis from the pan. You can either continue steaming the closed ones until they pop, or discard them.

To serve

6. Place the open pipis back in the pan, along with the watercress and mắm tép vinaigrette, and stir to combine.
7. Check the seasoning and add more vinaigrette if you prefer. Finish with a good swirl of olive oil and serve hot, with crusty slices of Vietnamese baguette.

Chả cá lã vọng
Turmeric + dill fish

Serves 4

500 g (1 lb 2 oz)	rockling fillets or other white fish, diced into large pieces
1½ tablespoons	vegetable oil, for frying
100 g (3½ oz)	dill stems and fronds, chopped into 4 cm (1½ inch) lengths
	spring onion (scallion) batons, to garnish

Marinade

2 tablespoons	vegetable oil
25 g (1 oz)	cơm mẻ (fermented rice, page 243)
10 g (¼ oz)	mắm tôm bắc (fermented shrimp paste)
10 g (¼ oz)	lemongrass, minced
9 g (¼ oz)	fresh turmeric, peeled and minced
3–4	garlic cloves, peeled and minced
½ teaspoon	ground turmeric
1 teaspoon	raw sugar
1 teaspoon	fish sauce

To serve

250 g (9 oz)	fresh rice vermicelli noodles (or 150 g/ 5½ oz dried noodles, prepared according to the packet instructions)
½ bunch	perilla, leaves picked
½ bunch	spearmint, leaves picked
½ bunch	lemon balm, leaves picked
	crushed peanuts
½ head	lettuce, leaves separated
30 ml (1 fl oz)	mắm tôm bắc (fermented shrimp paste), per person
2 wedges	calamansi, per person to taste

We often cook this on a camper cooktop, so we can keep it warm while eating, but feel free to do the same on your stove. The fish will need to marinate overnight.

Marinate the fish overnight

1. Combine all the marinade ingredients in a mixing bowl. Add the fish and gently mix until the pieces are well and evenly coated with the marinade. Cover and leave in the fridge overnight.

Fry the fish

2. Bring the fish to room temperature for cooking. Meanwhile, have all your accompaniments ready.
3. Heat the oil in a frying pan over high heat.
4. Place the marinated fish in the pan with half of the dill and fry until it starts to sear, then turn the heat down to medium until cooked.
5. Garnish with the remaining dill and spring onion batons.

To serve

6. Arrange the noodles, herbs, nuts, lettuce and mắm tôm bắc around the fish, so that people can serve themselves.
7. Toss the mix in your bowls before eating, and add a squeeze of calamansi to taste.

Hunger

J.Y.

Thi's first distinct memory of cooking with her mother was when she was 28 and well into her career as a professional chef. Thi was preparing for a pop-up dinner the next day; her mother and younger sister were in Melbourne to attend the dinner.

One of the components of Thi's dish was yuba – bean curd skin. A tray of soy milk sits over a low heat, waiting for a skin to form, at which point a quick trace of the perimeter with a sharp knife will loosen the skin from the tray. Deftly, Thi lowers a second smaller tray onto the loosened piece of yuba and lifts the whole piece out intact. The bean curd skin dries very quickly in the surface of the smaller tray before it is peeled off and added to the growing pile.

Thi's mother sidled up to the stove in curiosity as Thi worked quietly on this process. Enamoured, she quickly took over the task from Thi, methodically loosening and drying bean curd skins for the dish.

There is a romantic eagerness to trace a chef's cooking roots to the family kitchen, particularly a maternal influence: memories of being attached to mum's apron strings; lessons in recreating childhood-favourite dishes. Thi was never close to her mother by any stretch of the imagination. Her mother's difficult experience as a boat person, coupled with her need to work and spend time with the new man and baby in the household, meant Thi was often lower down the list of priorities.

Instead, Thi learned to cook because she had to learn to cook. There was not always food at home. The family had no money – what little they had, the stepfather would keep to himself to feed his vices of gambling and drinking. Thi grew to be both wary of hunger and familiar with it. Early school lunches consisted of white bread clumped together with rock-hard margarine and sugar. Thi laughs that her mother did not quite know what she was doing, packing a school lunchbox.

There were instances where the stepfather forbade Thi to eat for reasons unknown to her; perhaps it made him feel better about himself to wield such power over a child. Thi meant nothing to him, and he made it known, regularly and often. On occasion, closer inspection of the aforementioned margarine sandwiches revealed green spores on the bread chosen for her, because he had insisted. Thi would sneak instant noodles into bed at night, to eat under her covers – a crunchy puck of dehydrated wheaten starch given life by a sachet of savoury powder. She is oddly still quite partial to that specific brand of noodles, making me buy them over what I deem the more superior brands.

The stepfather once brought a lamb kebab to school for Thi, an uncharacteristic gesture and a welcome surprise for an uncynical child. Perhaps she had done something right and it was a reward, or perhaps it was *just because.* As it turned out, the kebab was a trade. Thi told me the story under the too-bright fluoro lights of a kebab shop after a long day in the restaurant. The shadows that were cast barely allowed me to see the emotion in Thi's eyes, and I felt my breath catch as she said he'd asked her to take something off in return – it was her necklace, probably to trade at a pawn shop, making her promise not to tell her mum. *It's why I do not wear jewellery*, Thi continued quietly. *It's all fake and it means nothing. If you do not have anything, they can't take it away from you*.

> 'Thi started cooking for herself to stave off the hunger, and as she learned to cook, she learned to appreciate the shapes in which flavours form on the palate.'

Thi does vaguely remember being enlisted to help her mother cook to entertain guests of the stepfather. A celebration meant the presence of many other adults and free-flowing beer. The former meant Thi knew she was safe for those few hours. The latter, however, meant that the calmness that preceded these parties would almost always be followed by violence after everyone left.

Thi's childhood was not punctuated by hunger, like a comma in a sentence – it was defined by hunger. The complex and gnawing hunger that creeps up on you when there is no food in the fridge; the miserable hours tracked only by the shadows inching across the empty dining room table as the sun rises, sets, and rises again, without a meal or a kind word provided.

Thi started cooking for herself to stave off the hunger, and as she learned to cook, she learned to appreciate the shapes in which flavours form on the palate. Eventually, she found that food saved her and that cooking became her life, metaphorically and literally.

Birds

In Vietnam, the true answer to the question, *Why did the chicken cross the road?* is perhaps, *Because it could*. Hens, roosters and other birds roam the streets across the country: in its urban centres, among the ever-moving sea of legs and wheels, pecking through the morning's delivery of mustard greens; scratching along the dusty and construction-heavy thoroughfares; or preening in sleepy towns, backed by the verdant valleys of rice fields and mountain scapes of country Vietnam.

The quality is radiantly clear in a plate of half a chicken, chopped up into chopstick-friendly pieces and sauteed with fresh, young ginger, yielding the heat of chilli and a nose of vanilla. However, it is not the aromas that the mind focuses on, but on just how tasty this plate of chicken looks. With its glossy, taut skin a deep marigold in colour and its firm, heat-inflected flesh curling gnarly around the bones, this chicken was clearly not barn-raised or even free-range. It was inadvertently pasture-raised, with freedom to cross the road whenever it wanted.

Similarly, a bowl of chicken *phở* in Mỹ Châu, with broth so intensely imbued with chicken flavour, belies the isolated nature of this most unexpected experience. Maybe the clean mountain air or lush green backdrop had an impact, but this was chicken essence distilled.

Chicken in Australia is so different from chicken in Vietnam. The birds are so much larger, the colour of the flesh is so much paler, the flavour is less intense, and the mouthfeel softer, mushier. Perhaps the cause of difference is breeding variety rather than the variety in breeding. In any case, I often use cockerel bought from the market instead of a chicken. The flavour is richer and more concentrated; it yields a firmer bite and just has better texture overall. I prefer pasture-raised ducks for the same reason – firmer bite and better texture as well as more developed flavour, particularly if the duck has an opportunity to live a fuller life at 14 weeks before being processed.

Súp nui

Pheasant + short pasta soup

Serves 4–6

1 × 1.5 kg (3 lb 5 oz)	pheasant (or substitute duck, chicken or pork ribs)
4 litres (135 fl oz)	chicken stock (page 43)
1 bunch	spring onions (scallions), white and green parts separated
100 g (3½ oz)	ginger, peeled and sliced
75 g (2½ oz)	salted radish (sold in packets and jars), rinsed
5–7	dried longans
pinch of	sea salt
3 teaspoons	fish sauce
400 g (14 oz)	dried macaroni or small shell pasta

To serve

spring onion (scallion) greens (saved from the broth above), cut into rounds
sawtooth coriander (culantro), roughly chopped
fried shallots (page 71)
lime wedges
fish sauce
fresh chopped chillies
pickled garlic (see note)

Note

To pickle garlic, add peeled and thinly sliced garlic cloves to white vinegar, using 2 parts white vinegar to 1 part garlic. Store in an airtight container in the fridge overnight before using. The pickled garlic will keep for up to 4 months in the fridge.

My younger sister and I grew up eating macaroni and chicken soup – always home cooked; this dish is rarely, if ever, found in Vietnamese eateries. Evidently, it is a dish that my sister still finds comfort in, as she continues to demand Mum cook it when we get together. Mum does not understand why we love it so much and will always put up a fight before relenting. If my sister had her way, this dish would be on high rotation for her mid-week dinners. I wanted to include this recipe for her sake, as she is not much of a cook.

Feel free to sub out pheasant for another bird or even pork ribs. The key to this dish is to buy the best bones you can get your hands on, as the soup is the backbone of the dish.

This soup also offers one of the few occasions one would find me enjoying overcooked pasta. Nui, macaroni, ended up in the Vietnamese repertoire via the French, with the origins of the word coming from nouille, noodles.

Cook the soup

1. Rinse the bird under cold running water, inside and out, and pat dry with paper towel.
2. To make the broth, bring the chicken stock to the boil in a large stockpot. Slice the spring onion whites, reserving the green parts for serving, and add to the pot with the ginger, salted radish and dried longans.
3. Place the whole bird in the broth, ensuring there is enough liquid to submerge it. Return to the boil, then turn the heat down to low and simmer for 10 minutes.
4. Turn the heat off, cover the pot and leave the bird to poach in the hot broth for 40 minutes, until cooked. You can check the bird is cooked by removing it from the broth and inserting a meat thermometer into the thickest part of the thigh; it should read 75°C (167°F). Alternatively, make a small incision between the leg and body; the juices should run clear, not pink.
5. Set the bird aside to cool. When cool enough to handle, shred the meat into bite-sized pieces and set aside.
6. Season the broth with the salt and fish sauce, adding more if needed; at this point you want the broth to be well seasoned, to serve with the finished dish.

Cook the pasta

7. Just before serving, cook the pasta following the packet instructions. I like to cook my pasta shells al dente, but my mother insists on overcooking hers. Your choice, your journey.

To serve

8. Drain the pasta and place in individual serving bowls. Add a small handful of shredded pheasant. Ladle the scorching-hot stock over the top, then add a good handful of spring onion greens, sawtooth coriander and fried shallots.
9. Serve with lime wedges, fish sauce, chilli and pickled garlic for diners to flavour their own bowls as they wish.

Lẩu vịt nấu chao

Duck with fermented bean curd

Serves 4–6

1 × 2.2 kg (5 lb)	duck (see note)
300 g (10½ oz)	fermented bean curd (page 68), mashed
50 g (3½ oz)	ginger, peeled and minced
500 g (1 lb 2 oz)	taro root, peeled and cut into 5 × 3 cm (2 x 1¼ inch) chunks
50 g (1¾ oz)	bean curd knots (sold in packets)

Paste

125 g (4½ oz)	red Asian shallots, peeled and roughly chopped
100 g (3½ oz)	lemongrass stems, roughly chopped
75 g (2½ oz)	ginger, peeled and roughly chopped
25 g (1 oz)	garlic cloves, peeled

Stock

2 litres (8 cups)	chicken stock (page 43)
1 litre (4 cups)	coconut water (no added sugar, if using a commercially packaged version)
500 ml (2 cups)	coconut cream
1 tablespoon	black peppercorns, crushed
7 g (5–7)	makrut lime leaves
4	red scud chillies, stems removed

Dipping sauce

4 cubes	fermented bean curd (page 68), mashed
30 g (1 oz)	garlic cloves, minced
30 g (1 oz)	lemongrass stems, finely chopped
2	red bird's eye chillies (optional), finely chopped
2 teaspoons	caster (superfine) sugar
2 tablespoons	lime juice

→

Duck hot pot was the first dish I cooked for my family after I moved out of home and started cooking professionally. It seemed like a good idea; it had always been one of my favourite dishes. As the clock ticked down and dinnertime drew closer, however, my nerves started to get to me. I am one of four sisters, and my eldest sister was notoriously difficult to impress. Fifteen years older than me and regarded as the cook of the family, she also held the opinion that I could not cook.

I first had this dish – or a variation of it – at my aunt's house in Ho Chi Minh as a 16-year-old. I remember the hubbub of dinner as lẩu dê nấu chao, goat hot pot, was served. The uncles sat around, bottles of beer in hand. The accompaniments, the steam and the distinct fragrance in the air. To this day, my preference is to have this dish on a cool autumnal night.

The main flavour component that binds this dish is fermented bean curd: creamy, savoury and nutty. It is an absolute delight.

This dish is so dear to me that it was on our opening menu in Anchovy. I despaired when I learned it was not to the taste of some customers – one called the rich broth 'gluggy'; another denounced the taro as 'furry', while across the table his Asian dining companion mocked his inability to open his mind to foreign ingredients and textures. Six years later, I put it back on the tasting menu. It was a hit. The same customer who had pushed the dish away for its 'furry' ingredients now slurped it up and decreed it one of his favourite dishes.

Chop up the duck

1. Rinse the duck under cold running water and pat dry with paper towel.
2. Place the duck on a chopping board, on its back. Using a cleaver, remove the neck at the point closest to the wishbone, then remove the head from the neck.
3. Cut the neck into 4 cm (1½ inch) pieces and set aside.
4. Cut the feet off the duck at the first joint from the webbing and set aside.
5. Where the wing tip meets the mid-wing, separate the mid-wing from the drumstick and set aside.
6. Remove any errant feathers, then repeat on the other side.
7. Place the duck on its back. Make an incision where the thigh and body meet. Gently pull the thigh away from the body to locate the joint where the thigh connects to the body.
8. Use your knife to cut through the skin around the thigh joint, exposing the joint itself, and firmly pull the thigh away from the body to dislocate the joint. You may hear a pop as it separates.

→

To serve

300 g (10½ oz)	fresh egg noodles
1 bunch	mustard greens, sliced
½ bunch	chrysanthemum leaves (also known as tong ho or shungiku), sliced
½ bunch	morning glory, cut into 6 cm (2½ inch) pieces
	okra, sliced
	shiitake mushrooms, sliced

9 With the thigh pulled away, cut through the joint with your knife to completely remove the thigh from the body. Repeat for the other thigh.

10 Use your cleaver and cut the thighs into 5 cm (2 inch) pieces, keeping the bone in as it helps keep the duck from going dry. Set aside.

11 Remove the breast fillet from the crown and cut into 5 cm (2 inch) pieces.

12 Using a pair of scissors or a cleaver, cut against the backbone from the neck to the tail (on both sides). You can discard this bone or cut into 4 cm (1½ inch) pieces and set aside.

Marinate the duck

13 Place the duck pieces in a large bowl with the fermented bean curd and ginger, tossing well to coat. Cover and set aside in the fridge to marinate for 4–8 hours.

Fry the duck

14 Remove the duck from the fridge and bring back to room temperature.

15 Place the paste ingredients in a food processor and blend into a smooth paste.

16 In a large heavy-based stockpot, sauté the paste over medium heat for 4–6 minutes, until fragrant.

17 Turn the heat up to medium–high. Working in batches, sear the marinated duck pieces to evenly colour them all over.

Poach the duck and taro

18 Return the duck to the stockpot and add all the stock ingredients. Bring the mixture to the boil, skimming off any impurities.

19 Reduce the heat to low, cover the pot and simmer for 1 hour.

20 Add the taro and bean curd knots and simmer for a further 15 minutes, or until the taro is tender.

To serve

21 Combine all the dipping sauce ingredients and pour into small individual ramekins for each diner.

22 Transfer the duck and broth to a hot pot and arrange on the table with the egg noodles, raw vegetables and dipping sauce, ready for diners to cook and eat. See page 87 for more on hot pot assembly.

Note

If you prefer not to cut up a whole duck, you can use duck leg quarters instead and skip the first section.

Gà rô ti
Grilled spatchcock

Serves 1–2

1 × 400 g (14 oz)	spatchcock (Cornish game hen)

Marinade

100 g (3½ oz)	red Asian shallots
20 g (¾ oz)	fresh ginger
20 g (¾ oz)	fresh turmeric
20 g (¾ oz)	garlic cloves
30 ml (1 fl oz)	fish sauce
30 ml (1 fl oz)	light soy sauce
1 tablespoon	vegetable oil
2 teaspoons	raw sugar
1 teaspoon	cracked white pepper
1 teaspoon	Chinese five spice
1 teaspoon	măc khén or native Australian pepper

To serve

glutinous (sticky) rice
vegetable pickle (page 62)
chẩm chéo (page 37)

Roasted chicken is a simple joy. When I first considered starting my own business, I intended to open a chicken rotisserie – something I could manage on a small scale, with really delicious roast chickens. I was only deterred by the difficulty of acquiring an inexpensive rotisserie.

The irony of gà rô ti is that the chicken is actually pan-fried, not roasted. The name is borrowed from the French poulet rôti, but households in Vietnam did not traditionally own an oven. (This deficit is the reason flans in Vietnam have typically been steamed rather than baked.)

I like using a spatchcock for this dish. In this instance, spatchcock refers to both the noun, a younger bird, and the verb, with the bird splayed out flat.

Prepare the spatchcock

1 Pat the spatchcock dry with paper towel. Place the bird, breast side down, on a chopping board, with the neck facing towards you. Using a pair of kitchen scissors, split the spatchcock into two pieces, down the breastplate and backbone.

Marinate the spatchcock

2 Peel the shallots, ginger, turmeric and garlic cloves and roughly chop. Place in a blender or food processor and blitz until smooth. Transfer to a large bowl, add the remaining marinade ingredients and mix together well.

3 Add the spatchcock, gently tossing to coat. Cover and leave to marinate in the fridge for at least 4–6 hours.

Cook the spatchcock

4 Start a barbecue using wood (see page 104). While bringing the grill up to medium heat, I like to smoke my meats for 20–25 minutes to impart a smoky flavour. After smoking, the bird's skin starts to dry and show a light amber colour.

5 When the spatchcock is smoked and the barbecue is at medium heat, grill for 8–10 minutes, flipping the spatchcock to ensure even cooking on the surface. Probe the meat to check it is done – it should reach 76°C (169°F) at its thickest part.

6 Rest for 20 minutes before serving with the sticky rice, vegetable pickle and chẩm chéo.

Taking from the land

Thi

I know Allen from my art days; he is now a shaman in the Amazon. He has been living off the land and I have been thinking about something he said to me: that for me to be a chef, I need to be able to take from the land. So yeah, I think I need to slaughter a chicken. Mum told me I could buy a happy chicken from the chicken people down the road.

J.Y. looked simultaneously confused but supportive – in the way that a caring partner would be when you are saying something to them with conviction that makes very little sense. She sat silently and nodded slowly; characteristically, I ploughed on.

What Allen said made complete sense to me. As a chef, my line of work requires me to end the life of a being, whether it be plant or animal. I felt I needed to be able to use a sacrifice from the land in the same way that my ancestors did; it was not good enough to just have a chicken delivered to me via a slaughterhouse. I needed to be able to slaughter the chicken myself, to understand and experience the process.

×

Soon enough, we were speeding down the backroads of Eastern Creek in Western Sydney in my little Astra hatch, on our way to find two happy chickens. If I was going to prove my mettle as a chef from paddock to plate, then I was going to do it on my terms; I wanted assurance of the welfare of these chickens. We have had it drummed into us as consumers that the tastiness of a morsel correlates positively with their happiness throughout their growth cycle. I wanted healthy chickens that had lived a contented life. Mum had said these chickens lived in a big house with a lot of sunlight – a north-facing mansion, possibly. I wanted two chickens, because I thought that it would be too obvious for a solo hen that she would be that night's dinner. These chicken friends would inevitably sit calmly in the boot of my Astra for the 15-minute ride back to Mum's, where they could then peck around the veggie patch before the deed was done. I did hold a small bud of doubt, mainly because my grasp of the Vietnamese language is shaky when it comes to discussing the nuance of pasture-raised, free-range, barn-raised or caged hens.

As we drew closer to the address Mum gave us, the agrarian, trellis-speckled landscape gave way to a more industrial scene of imposing transmission towers. We turned the corner and saw a large shed, the afternoon sunlight gleaming off its industrial, Colorbond-ed form, in a shade of orange not dissimilar to the yolk of a happy chicken. These were not going to be happy chickens.

It was quiet as we pulled up the dirt driveway; a small part of me hoped they were already closed for the day. Then a man came out, and proceeded to answer my questions about procuring two hens. *Yes, we sell direct to the public*. Great. *These are barn chickens, not caged.* OK. *We are all out of hens for the day*. Oh. *But we can sell you two roosters*. Done. He offered to put the two roosters in a box for me for the ride home, and laughed when I suggested they just hang out in the boot.

In my urban naiveté, I failed to consider the real change in circumstance. Roosters, historically, are actors in cock fights. Roosters lead their flock and, in oriental mythology, represent bravery and strong character. Two roosters were not going to be the same as two hens.

It all went pear shaped the moment we let the roosters run free in Mum's backyard. Rather than preen and make happy chicken sounds as I had narrated in my head, the roosters puffed their big chests and opened their giant wings. Then someone let the dog out of the house. My gentle little white, fluffy dog was completely unprepared to be chased by two enormous fowls, nor were we prepared for the commotion of barking and crowing, with family starting to arrive for dinner and neighbours observing over the fence with great interest, beers in hand.

We felt the circumstantial stress levels would not benefit these roosters – and by extension, their taste and texture. A decision was passed to proceed with the ritual sooner rather than later. We had not considered exactly how to catch the roosters again and attempted to corner one with a milk crate. Mercifully or regrettably, Mum decided this was the moment she would take charge, although not before telling me I was pathetic.

It was a very cinematic moment when Mum walked up to one rooster still splaying its full wingspan; in a swift motion, she had trussed it up with nothing else but its own wings. She did the same with the second rooster while we watched, mouths agog, then she handed me a warm and now docile fowl with a very casual direction: *The knife is over there.*

Allen's words continued to stream through my mind as I held the rooster down: *As a chef, you have to be able to take from the land.* I tried to recall the YouTube videos I had watched in advance of this moment, and their instructions to nick the neck humanely and bleed it. I held the cleaver in my right hand while my left brushed the rooster's feathers, still soft, smooth, downy in parts and brilliantly coloured. At that moment, with the rooster's warm neck still in my hands, I unfortunately tuned into the instructions both my mum and older sister were offering in the characteristic Vietnamese way: unnervingly loud, blasé and blunt. I lost my concentration and I lost my nerve.

I remember walking around the corner to a cooler, shadier side of the house, away from my sister's well-meant advice in Vietnamese, which now sounded like emotionally charged jeers: *This is not a game; it's another being's life; what are they teaching you chefs in the city?*

J.Y. always recalls this as my older sister's bad-ass moment: in my absence, she squatted next to an upturned ceramic bowl on the sun-drenched concrete and started sharpening the cleaver on the unglazed portion of the bowl's foot. Imbued with the type of confidence that only practice can offer, she took from the land and bled the roosters. We made chicken congee for dinner.

Cháo gà trống + gỏi gà trống

Cockerel congee + cockerel salad

Serves 6–8

Congee

200 g (7 oz)	glutinous (sticky) rice
25 ml (¾ fl oz)	vegetable oil
50 g (1¾ oz)	ginger, peeled and sliced
2	garlic cloves, skin on, smashed
1.5 litres (6 cups)	chicken stock (page 43)
	sea salt, to taste

Poached cockerel

1 × 1.8 kg (4 lb)	cockerel (or chicken leg quarters)
4 litres (135 fl oz)	water
100 g (3½ oz)	ginger, peeled and sliced
1	onion, peeled and quartered
15 g (½ oz)	sea salt
1 teaspoon	sugar

Salad

1	fennel bulb, thinly sliced
1	white onion, thinly sliced
100 ml (3½ fl oz)	rice vinegar
1 teaspoon	sea salt
2 teaspoons	raw sugar
1 tablespoon	cracked black pepper
1 bunch	young Vietnamese mint, roughly chopped, including stems
2 bunches	sawtooth coriander (culantro), roughly chopped
50 ml (1¾ fl oz)	ginger nước mắm (page 36)

To serve

fried shallots (page 71)
crushed nuts (optional)
spring onion (scallion) rounds
coriander (cilantro) sprigs
ginger nước mắm (page 36)

Cháo is a dish that goes by many names across the Asian diaspora: congee, rice porridge, jook, cháo. There are as many variations of it as there are names, ranging from the thick and starchy variety to the thin and runny gruel-like versions. In many circles, congee is the go-to dish when one is feeling under the weather – hot and comforting, a reminder of childhood, and easy on the stomach, with no strong flavours to hamper digestion.

Congee is now undergoing a gentrification in Australian cafes – a multi-grain, multi-textured affair, doused with soy sauce and chilli oils, tricked-up with as many intensely flavoured ingredients as one would find fruits on a fancy acai bowl. However, a good cháo gà is typified by its simplicity – poultry, rice, ginger, spring onion, and its accompanying sidekick, a salad or gỏi gà.

I always associate cháo gà with my mum or eldest sister slaughtering a chicken in the backyard. A whole chicken or cockerel yields two wholesome dishes – cháo gà and gỏi gà – that can be eaten together or separately. Chicken leg quarters can be used in the absence of a whole bird.

What I love about eating this congee is its lightness, that I can go back for bowl after bowl. Dunking the cold, textural and acidic gỏi gà into the piping hot congee adds another dimension to the dish.

Prepare the congee

1 Rinse the rice under cold running water until the water runs clear, then drain.

2 Heat the oil in a large stockpot, then toast the rice over medium heat for about 5 minutes, stirring frequently. Add the ginger and garlic and fry for another 10–12 minutes, until the mixture turns golden brown and fragrant. Be careful not to burn it, and keep scraping the pan so the rice does not stick to the bottom.

3 Add the stock and bring to the boil. Reduce the heat to low and let the rice simmer, stirring occasionally to prevent sticking, for 1–1½ hours, until the rice breaks down and the congee thickens. If it becomes too thick, stir in more stock or water to reach your desired consistency. Season the congee with a little sea salt to taste; it should not be well seasoned.

Poach the cockerel

4 Rinse the bird under cold running water, inside and out, and pat dry with paper towel. Set aside.

5 In a stockpot, combine the water, ginger, onion, salt and sugar. Bring to the boil, then reduce the heat and simmer for 10 minutes to infuse the liquid.

6 Place the bird in the pot, breast side down. The liquid should fully submerge the cockerel.

→

7 Bring the liquid back to the boil, then reduce the heat to low and cover the pan. Leave over low heat for 15 minutes, then turn the heat off and leave the bird to gently poach in the residual heat of the broth for about 30–40 minutes.

8 Check the bird is cooked by removing it from the poaching stock and inserting a meat thermometer into the thickest part of the thigh; it should read 75°C (167°F). Alternatively, make a small incision between the leg and body; the juices should run clear, not pink.

9 Set the bird aside to cool. When cool enough to handle, roughly shred the meat and set aside.

For the salad

10 Soak the fennel and onion in separate bowls of cold water for no more than 1 hour.

11 Drain the fennel and onion, then marinate in a large bowl with the vinegar, salt, sugar and pepper for 15 minutes.

12 Add the Vietnamese mint and sawtooth coriander and toss together. Drizzle with the ginger nước mắm and toss to lubricate the salad.

To serve

13 Arrange the cockerel on top of the salad. Garnish with fried shallots, and crushed nuts if desired.

14 Ladle the hot congee into serving bowls and top with spring onion and coriander.

15 Serve immediately, with individual bowls of extra ginger nước mắm for diners to flavour their dish as they wish.

Vịt tiết canh

Duck blood pudding

Serves 5–8 as a drinking snack

100 ml (3½ fl oz)	fish sauce (choose a brand containing no additives such as sugar or colourings)
100 ml (3½ fl oz)	cold water
1 × 2.8 kg (6 lb)	live mature duck
2	lemongrass stems, bruised, then cut into 6 cm (2½ inch) lengths
8	young papaya leaves; if you can't get these, increase the total lemongrass quantity to 8–10 stems
50 ml (1¾ fl oz)	vegetable oil
150 g (5½ oz)	brown onion, finely diced
2 teaspoons	cracked black pepper

Poaching liquid

4.5 litres (152 fl oz)	water
100 g (3½ oz)	old ginger, bruised but not peeled

To serve

1 bunch	sawtooth coriander (culantro), thinly sliced
125 g (4½ oz)	roasted peanuts, skinned and crushed
1 bunch	rice paddy herb
1 bunch	coriander (cilantro)
1 bunch	spearmint
1	lemon, cut into small wedges
5	puffed coconut rice crackers
120 ml (4 fl oz)	ginger nước mắm, per person (page 36)

→

There are several words that can be used to describe this undertaking. Ambitious and controversial quickly come to mind. I prefer the words conservation or documentation. It was important to me that this dish be part of this book – while acknowledging it is not for all readers – because I did not want it to be lost to history. Tiết canh is a blood pudding dish attributed to northern Vietnam but can also be found in Laos, Cambodia and northern Thailand. It is likely rooted in the traditions of an ethnic group traversing these borders.

Duck blood and fresh duck have been used in this instance, although pigs and goats can also be used. It is a true offal-focused dish in that the prime cuts are the giblets, livers, intestines and the blood. The remainder of the duck – the carcass and the meat – is typically used to prepare duck congee. As the dish requires fresh blood, it is important to source a healthy animal of provenance and of the required hygiene standards.

Dispatch the duck

1 Mix the fish sauce with the cold water in a large bowl, and set aside.

2 Pluck some feathers from the neck of the duck to reveal the jugular vein. Hold the duck still – you may need the assistance of another person. Working quickly and using a sharp knife or cleaver, slit the duck neck along the jugular.

3 Collect the blood in the fish sauce bowl, for your blood jelly. Stir thoroughly and set aside in a warm spot in the shade while you continue preparing the duck.

4 Rinse the blood dribbles off the duck.

Feather the duck

5 Fill a large stockpot with water. Add the lemongrass and papaya leaves and bring to the boil. These ingredients are thought to reduce the gaminess of the duck.

6 When the water has come up to a rapid boil, remove from the heat and add the duck to poach for 1 minute.

7 Remove the duck from the stockpot and, while it's still hot, pluck out all the feathers, plucking downwards towards the feet.

Break down the duck

8 At the lower belly, underneath the breast plate, cut the duck open lengthways using a cleaver.

9 Remove and discard the organs and fat, keeping the livers, gizzards and heart. Rinse the offal clean.

10 Clean the internal cavity of the duck, rinsing and pat dry. Pluck any errant feathers and pat dry.

11 Place the duck on a chopping board on its back. Remove the neck at the point closest to the wishbone, then remove the head from the neck. Separate the wing tips from the mid-wing by cutting through the joint. Keep the breast, leg and wing in one piece.

→

Poach the duck and offal

12 Place the poaching liquid ingredients in a large saucepan and bring to the boil, then reduce the heat to low.

13 Add the duck pieces and poach for about 25 minutes, until the meat is just cooked, or the internal temperature reaches 78°C (172°F).

14 Remove the duck pieces from the poaching liquid and set aside to rest for 10 minutes.

15 Add the offal to the poaching liquid and poach until cooked to your preferred doneness: liver about 10–15 minutes, heart about 20 minutes and gizzard about 30–40 minutes. Remove from the poaching liquid and rest for about 20 minutes, then thinly slice and set aside.

16 Skim the poaching broth of scum that rises to the top and keep warm for the blood jelly. Do not allow to reduce.

Mince and sauté the duck

17 Meanwhile, once the duck has rested, remove the meat from the bones. Using a cleaver, very finely chop the meat and skin.

18 Heat the vegetable oil in a frying pan or wok and sauté the onion over medium heat for about 3 minutes, until fragrant. Add the minced duck and sauté for about 6–10 minutes, until cooked. Stir in the pepper.

Make the blood jelly

19 Take your reserved bowl of blood and fish sauce.

20 Into a separate bowl, measure out 1 part of the blood mixture to 3 parts warm poaching liquid, approximately 250 ml (1 cup) of each.

Assemble the dishes

21 Lay the cooked duck mince thinly over your serving plates. Arrange the offal over each plate.

22 Ladle the blood jelly mixture over in a thin layer, to completely cover the meat.

23 Chill in the fridge for 30 minutes, or until the blood mixture has set into a wobbly jelly.

To serve

24 Garnish each dish with sawtooth coriander and crushed roasted peanuts.

25 Serve with the herbs, lemon wedges, rice crackers, ginger nước mắm and your choice of hard liquor. This dish is a drinking dish, after all.

'... the head of the bird also forms a significant part of Vietnamese drinking culture at the end of a meal – spin the head of the bird and have a shot of hard liquor if the beak lands on you.'

The whole bird

J.Y.

It was 10 pm in Cà Mau; we were in town visiting Thi's relatives, and Thi's cousin expressed his desire to eat cà ri gà, chicken curry, cooked by Thi's mother. I idly wondered where we could get a chicken of the required size to feed the hungry, boozed-up cousins. In any case, phones were pulled out around me, and my very basic grasp of the language suggested to me that someone was getting the curry delivered. Excellent. I was just getting peckish.

Cà ri gà finds its origins bedded in the second half of the nineteenth century, when primarily Tamil migrants moved to Saigon in search of work via a pathway of French colonial rule. There was a gradual evolution of the term 'curry' in its gravied form and the spices used in its Tamil root 'kari' to variations appreciated by the French in Pondicherry. It found its way into Vietnamese households, hastened by Indian spice sellers now localised in Saigon and an emerging Vietnamese middle class embracing a taste for foreign cuisine. Anecdotes from the turn of the century suggested the use of curry powder in Vietnamese home kitchens, although the composition of ingredients and spices would be different from that used for cà ri chà (Vietnamese for Indian curry).

On that balmy Cà Mau night, I was almost ready to forgo the promise of chicken curry for sleep, when suddenly someone pulled up on a motorbike, bag in hand, and sticking out of the bag was a pair of feet belonging to a chicken. Something Thi once said to me now rang true: *You can get anything you want in Vietnam*. Delicious street food, visas organised for you while you sip juice by a roadside stand, and apparently a freshly killed and plucked chicken at 10.30 pm.

The presentation of whole birds is so different in Australia – almost censured. At markets in Hanoi, I have encountered whole chickens with cockscombs on their heads, feet folded elegantly underneath their pâté-stuffed bodies; likewise in Paris, I have seen birds in their full-feather regalia in refrigerated cabinets. In Australia, they are featherless and oddly pumped up in their heavily decorated plastic cocoons; we are hardly able to tell if the head is still intact.

For a brief period, we were sourcing whole quails into the restaurant. These were magnificent quails: rich in flavour, generous in size, head on and feet intact. Thi could barely contain her glee when the first batch arrived. They ended up on the menu roasted with barberry sauce.

We kept the quail on the menu even when there was some pushback, with a well-followed Instagram account running a poll on whether the dish was 'barbaric' and some customers asking in advance for the head to be taken off. Thi was always ready to give any member of the dining room team an earful for accommodating this request. It's a symptom of our industrialised food system that we are happy to consume meat but don't want to be reminded that it was once a sentient being.

Serving birds intact symbolises unity within Confucian values. More to the point, however, the head of the bird also forms a significant part of Vietnamese drinking culture at the end of a meal – spin the head of the bird and have a shot of hard liquor if the beak lands on you. Thi was always keen to know whether any customer spun the head of the quail whenever we ferried the remains of the whole carcasses back into the kitchen.

Gà giả cầy

Chicken masquerading as dog

Serves 6–8

1 × 2.2 kg (5 lb)	cockerel (see notes)

Curry

200 ml (7 fl oz)	vegetable oil
200 g (7 oz)	red Asian shallots, minced
80 g (2¾ oz)	lemongrass stems, very finely chopped; retain tops and cut into 8 cm (3¼ inch) batons
70 g (2½oz)	garlic cloves, minced
30 g (1 oz)	fresh turmeric, peeled and very finely chopped
10 g (¼ oz)	red bullet chillies, stems removed, very finely chopped
30 g (1 oz)	curry powder (ideally, Vianco Bot Cari curry powder)
350 g (12 oz)	fresh galangal, peeled and very finely chopped
1 litre (4 cups)	young coconut water (no added sugar, if using a commercially packaged version)
25 ml (¾ fl oz)	fish sauce
3 teaspoons	raw sugar
pinch of	cracked white pepper
270 g (9½ oz)	cơm mẻ (fermented rice, page 243; see notes)
170 g (6 oz)	salted soy beans (tương hột), rinsed and mashed (see notes)
50 g (1¾ oz)	shrimp paste (mắm ruốc)
500 ml (2 cups)	coconut milk
10	makrut lime leaves

→

I first came across the dish while researching the cuisine of Miền Tây or the Mekong Delta area, where Mum is from. While it is historically prepared with dog meat, cockerels are the protein of choice these days and the name suggests as much – chicken masquerading as dog.

This dish stood out to me because it was not something I had previously seen or tasted. Mum had never cooked it for us, neither had the extended family ever prepared it when we were back in Cà Mau. Imagine my surprise when Mum casually mentioned that she does in fact regularly cook this dish for the Vietnamese church she attends in Sydney – and that she makes one of the better versions around.

The other reason that this dish appealed to me was because of the ingredients. Salted soy beans (tương hột), shrimp paste (mắm ruốc) and, to a lesser degree, fermented rice (cơm mẻ) are common ingredients in the Vietnamese kitchen, but they are seldom used all together in a single recipe. This recipe also employs a substantial amount of galangal, in ratios that are more commonly seen with lemongrass. As it were, galangal is one of the spices that goes hand-in-hand with dog meat.

I like to think that this dish is best prepared by the campfire. The outdoor setting lends a less daunting, less messy feel to the act of charring a whole cockerel. One is also less likely to set off the smoke alarm. The charring of the cockerels may be related to the historical nature of the dish, when dog meat was the protein of choice and skinning was involved.

Mum insists that the consistency of the dish is entirely up to the cook. I prefer mine closer to a loose curry, with blitzed-up lemongrass to give body and mouthfeel.

Char the cockerel

1. Rinse the internal cavity of the bird under cold running water and pat dry with paper towel.
2. Char the cockerel over a flame or charcoal grill, for 3–4 minutes each side. The bird should just be seared.
3. Remove from the heat and leave until cool enough to handle.
4. Using a cleaver, and leaving the bones in, chop the bird into 5 cm (2 inch) chunks.

Make the curry

5. Heat the oil in a large heavy-based saucepan. Add the shallots, lemongrass, garlic, turmeric and chilli and sauté over high heat for 3–4 minutes, until fragrant. Add the curry powder and fry for another minute.
6. Add the charred cockerel pieces and galangal to the curry base and continue stirring for 1–2 minutes until everything is well mixed.

→

Dipping sauce

4 cubes	fermented bean curd (page 68), mashed
40 ml (1¼ fl oz)	lime juice
30 g (1 oz)	garlic cloves, peeled
30 g (1 oz)	lemongrass stems, very finely chopped
2	red bird's eye chillies (optional), finely chopped
2 teaspoons	raw sugar

To serve

steamed rice
rice paddy herb
Vietnamese mint (optional)
roasted peanuts (optional), smashed

7 Add the coconut water and stir to deglaze the pan.
8 Stir in the fish sauce, sugar, pepper, cơm mẻ, salted soy beans, shrimp paste, coconut milk, lime leaves and reserved lemongrass batons.
9 Bring the mixture to the boil and skim any impurities that rise to the top. Retain the oils in the pot.
10 Check the seasoning – it should be light and a little acidic.
11 Simmer, uncovered, over low heat for about 40 minutes, allowing the liquid to reduce by a third. After the 40 minute mark, turn the heat off and let the mixture continue to infuse in the pot from the residual heat.

To serve

12 Combine all the dipping sauce ingredients and pour into small individual ramekins for each diner.
13 Bring the curry back up to heat. Serve the curry piping hot with bowls of rice, ripping the herbs over each bowl, and liberally scattering the peanuts over the top if desired.

Notes

- Instead of a whole cockerel, you can use chicken leg quarters in this dish.
- As an alternative to cơm mẻ, you can use a mix of milk kefir and lemon juice. As a general guide, try mixing 1 tablespoon of lemon juice with 100 ml (3½ fl oz) milk kefir, adjusting the quantity to suit the tartness of your lemons.
- If you are unable to find whole salted soy beans, you can use soy bean purée, but halve the amount (85 g/3 oz).

Mì vịt tiềm

Duck in medicinal noodle soup

Serves 6

6	duck leg quarters
60 ml (¼ cup)	cooking wine
100 g (3½ oz)	ginger, charred (see page 36), then sliced
2 tablespoons	mushroom soy sauce
1 tablespoon	soy sauce
2½ tablespoons	Chinese five spice
1½ teaspoons	sea salt
1½ teaspoons	cracked white pepper

Broth

1½	cinnamon sticks
2	star anise
3	whole cloves
2 teaspoons	coriander seeds
1.5 litres (6 cups)	chicken stock (page 43)
¼	onion, charred (see page 36), then sliced
100 g (3½ oz)	ginger, charred (see page 36), then sliced
10 g (¼ oz)	dried longans
150 g (5½ oz)	small daikon (white radish), peeled and cut into finger-thick half-moons
2 bunches	coriander (cilantro) roots, scrubbed well
40 g (1½ oz)	spring onion (scallion) tops
20 g (¾ oz)	dried shiitake mushrooms
6	dried red dates
10 g (¼ oz)	dried goji berries
2 tablespoons	light soy sauce (Pearl River brand)
2 teaspoons	sea salt

To serve

450 g (1 lb)	mustard greens, chopped
	ice bath
900 g (2 lb)	fresh thin egg noodles per person, cooked to packet instructions

A medicinal soup that I consider to be more invigorating and comforting than a bowl of phở. The gentle sweetness of dried fruits tends to dominate the front palate, but it is very quickly chased by a mid-palate warmth of ginger.

Marinate the duck overnight

1 Rinse the duck legs under cold running water and pat dry with paper towel. Place in a large bowl with the cooking wine and ginger. Cover and leave to marinate in the fridge for 30 minutes.

2 Mix together the soy sauces, five spice, salt and pepper, then rub all over the duck legs. Place in a large zip-lock bag and leave to marinate in the fridge overnight.

Make the broth

5 In a dry frying pan, toast the cinnamon sticks, star anise, cloves and coriander seeds over medium heat for a few minutes, or until fragrant. Place in a spice infuser or wrap in muslin (cheesecloth).

6 Bring the stock to the boil in a large stockpot, skimming off any scum from the surface.

7 Add the toasted spices, onion, ginger and longans, then leave to infuse over medium–low heat. A gentle bubble is adequate here, as you do not want the stock to reduce.

Pan-fry the duck

8 While the stock is infusing, pan-fry the duck in batches over medium–high heat for 2 minutes on each side, just to seal the meat; you are not aiming to cook the duck at this point. Set aside.

Finish the soup

9 After the broth has infused for about 1 hour, add the daikon, coriander roots, spring onion, shiitake mushrooms, dates and goji berries. Stir in the soy sauce and salt.

10 Add the duck legs and simmer for another 30–45 minutes. (I like my duck legs to still have some texture to them. You can cook them further, if you wish – in which case, I would start cooking the duck legs in advance of the daikon, dates and goji berries, as these will fall apart with longer simmering.)

11 You are aiming for a clear stock, so ensure the broth does not come to a rapid boil at any point, as this will introduce impurities and turbidity.

To serve

12 Blanch the mustard greens, refresh in the ice bath and divide among the serving bowls, along with the cooked noodles.

13 Ladle the hot broth over the noodles, together with a duck leg, and some daikon and shiitake mushrooms. Serve immediately.

Note

If you have them, you can use confit duck legs for this recipe. You may just want to tweak the amount of soy sauce used, as the confit duck will be more salty.

Thi Le, the chef

J.Y.

In August 2022, Thi went on stage to accept the *Gourmet Traveller*'s Chef of the Year award, a peer-voted honour. In her acceptance speech, she said, *This is for all the ethnic, Asian girls who wanted to be chefs and did not want to be accountants.*

Her quip was met with much supportive laughter, and would also have hit home for a subset of the Asian diaspora in Australia, and around the world, whose parents placed substantially more value on white-collar jobs than skilled vocational work. It took Thi's mother many years to accept Thi's decision to drop out of her forays into higher education in favour of cheffing, and many more years after that to openly share with her social circle that she did in fact have a daughter in the trades.

In contrast, it was cheffing that gave Thi the confidence and structure to get through her days, after years of struggling with the demons of drugs and depression. When she began working in the hospitality industry, first as a source of casual income and later as a career, she found that the kitchen helped build her confidence and became a safety net where she felt she was part of a family. The hospitality industry was a different world: where adults were mentors and peers; where the kitchen was a platform for creativity. It allowed Thi to feel like she was good at something, and appreciated for what she was doing. It gave her an escape that was not in her own head. In short, it was cheffing that helped Thi survive being a survivor.

×

Thi's journey into cheffing started very unintentionally. She took up home economics in school because her intended elective, technical drawing, was unavailable. When higher education came a-knocking, she somewhat combined the two interests – planning to arm herself with a diploma in interior design with the intention of designing bars and restaurants.

As she studied, she spent a number of years working in pubs around Sydney's business district, learning the art of banter and beer pulling, dealing with a miscellany of colourful characters and earning short stints in the kitchens. A decision to take a gap year to see the world would change the course of her career.

Travel opened Thi's eyes. The smell of whole and powdered spices in the many kedai runcit around Penang reminded her of being offered salted pumpkin seeds from the Middle Eastern proprietors in Auburn. Spilling out of a nightclub in the middle of a chilly Chongqing winter's night, she was greeted by carts of steaming dumplings and spicy meat skewers prepared to order while snow fell around her. Then, a meal cooked as a quid pro quo for free accommodation in Leeds led to an offer for Thi to work at the host's Thai restaurant back in Australia after her year away.

On her return home, Thi's unfinished design school ventures were cast aside in favour of the opportunity to cook at the Thai restaurant. It was a short-lived adventure – kicked off by the chef at the restaurant returning to rehab within the first week of Thi's arrival, followed by a disastrous first solo service. Thi soon realised she needed qualifications in the industry and thus turned to obtaining a certificate in commercial cookery, while working in a catering company and later at a Japanese sushi train.

Thi was employed as an apprentice at Aqua Dining, then a hatted Italian restaurant. It was here that she was exposed to the ethos of simplicity in produce, a guiding light that would go on to inform her own cooking. She embraced the industry, including through cooking competitions (no apprentice from her restaurant won; the judges valued sous-vide cooking; her head chef was livid) and mentorship programs. In Tasting Success, an all-women mentoring program, Thi was paired with her future mentor Christine Manfield, dubbed Australia's Spice Queen. Thi would eventually gain a spot in Chris's powerhouse kitchen at Universal, where she honed her palate. A crisis in Thi's personal life saw her uproot her life in Sydney to move to Melbourne, first working at contemporary restaurants like Cumulus Inc. and then briefly at the Town Mouse and Luxembourg Restaurant. Until we opened Anchovy, she did not work in a Vietnamese kitchen.

+

As a student, Thi took part in a cookery competition in Toowoomba. The year was 2008 and pork belly was a sudden favourite among Australian consumers. Unsurprisingly, it was the star ingredient in that year's cookery competition.

Thi had settled on thịt kho tàu as her dish. Her reasoning was sound – it was a pork belly dish that showcased both cookery technique and her own heritage. It is essentially a braise where the primary skill lies in achieving a stock or sauce of a specific turbid clarity, like the brackish water in estuaries that the tàu in the name alludes to. The secondary skill is in achieving the sweet–salty profile that references the meeting of freshwater and marine water. Incidentally, Thi's mum has a volume of thoughts relating to the specifics of thịt kho tàu, as well as the role of nước màu in the dish.

Thi did not fare very well in the competition. The judges said: *It was too simple a dish and did not require enough technique to execute for a cooking competition*. This comment lived with Thi rent-free for many years. Twelve years on from that cooking competition, a comment that triggered that same memory was made on a nationally broadcast Australian reality-TV cooking competition: *Asian food does not lend itself to fine dining*.

Both comments hinted at a similar premise of failure – that we, as the Asian diaspora living in places of occidental roots, while having been successful in communicating a level of academic prowess, have been substantially less fruitful in communicating the legacies of our culinary history and their associated techniques. This realisation is somewhat painful, given our collective acknowledgement of the significant roles that both food and mealtimes play in our cultural identity.

Meat

Going back to my mother's house as an adult gives me the chills – not always necessarily because of my memories associated with it, but because her fridge and freezer is often a disaster.

Her fridge and freezer combo in the kitchen is fitting for a matriarch – over 500 litres in capacity, filled to the brim with takeaways and fresh produce. Three packs of feta cheese, all open and all with more than three-quarters of themselves to offer; four heads of lettuce, crisp and fresh but not for long, because their rightful spot in the crisper is filled with random jellies and a pumpkin whose rightful spot would be in the compost bin; always some form of liquid inebriation chilling and waiting to go, except neither inhabitants of the house drink. Then there are the countless kilos of chicken wings and sausages and pork belly, all frozen into rock-solid hunks that have not been reportioned into servings suitable for a household of two.

The kitchens I am used to function in a slightly different way. Deliveries are always packed down properly. Everything is labelled and dated, a discipline that helps us know what arrived and when. I lose this battle in Mum's kitchen.

A random bag of something has taken on an odd trapezoid shape because Mum has Tetris-ed the bag into the freezer; it is impossible to interrogate the contents without removing the two other miscellaneous frozen chunks on either side of it. As it were, the bag of interest contained pork mince, all five kilos of it. Incidentally, one of the other two bags also contained pork mince, two kilos' worth, bought in a separate transaction. I later found another scant half kilo in the fridge.

The invention of the refrigerator and its subsequent accessibility has meant that Mum has the luxury of hoarding seven and a half kilos of pork mince, seven of which was frozen solid, together with countless other bags (kilos) of miscellaneous meats and animal parts. It was because of the lack of this luxury that some of the recipes in this section exist, designed to use up all parts of the animal before it spoiled – and their unfortunate loss in popularity also correlates with the advent of such technology.

Bánh patê sô

Pâté chaud

Makes 15

Filling

3 teaspoons	vegetable oil
50 g (1¾ oz)	red Asian shallots, finely diced
1½ teaspoons	minced garlic
100 g (3½ oz)	duck legs, bone off, skin on, minced (ground)
100 g (3½oz)	minced (ground) pork with 20% fat
50 g (1¾ oz)	chicken livers, minced (ground)
2	coriander (cilantro) roots, washed well, finely chopped
25 ml (¾ fl oz)	brandy
1 teaspoon	oyster sauce (Megachef brand preferred)
½ teaspoon	fish sauce
½ teaspoon	sesame oil
2 teaspoons	coarsely cracked white pepper
½ teaspoon	sea salt
½ teaspoon	caster (superfine) sugar
1½ teaspoons	cornflour (cornstarch)
pinch of	curing pink salt #1
50 g (1¾ oz)	water chestnuts, roughly chopped

Pastry

2 × 375 g (13 oz)	packets full butter puff pastry sheets (do not use pastry containing vegetable shortening; I have used the Carême brand of puff pastry)
1	egg
1 teaspoon	cool water

I have been hoovering up these little parcels of puff pastry for as long as I can remember. In Australia, patê sô is typically found in the local Vietnamese bakery; disappointingly, the pastry is often substantially less flaky, having been sitting in a pie warmer for quite a few hours. Patê sô was on the restaurant's opening menu in 2015, and it amused me when these nostalgic pastries were such a hit with food critics.

The filling of a patê sô is based on a basic terrine recipe. Making terrines was a skill I picked up while working at Cumulus Inc., a Melbourne institution that was integral in my formative cheffing years. My version contains pork mince, shallots and water chestnuts, encased in house-made puff pastry, perhaps served with pickled fennel and dijon mustard. The authenticity police will come after me with a pitchfork, but all I can say is that I am paying homage to the dish's French roots. The water chestnuts should not be chopped too finely. Their addition gives the terrine a variation in texture – a light crunch.

This recipe is best attempted across 2 days, to allow the filling to firm up in the fridge overnight. It can also be staged in steps, if you would like to prepare and freeze the uncooked pastries in advance, and bake them just before serving (see note).

Prepare the filling

1 Heat the vegetable oil in a frying pan. Sauté the shallot and garlic over medium heat for about 2–3 minutes until fragrant. Set aside to cool to room temperature.

2 Place the remaining filling ingredients, except the water chestnuts, in a large mixing bowl. Mix together well, then mix the water chestnuts and shallot and garlic mixture through.

3 Check the seasoning by frying a small amount of the mixture in a pan. Adjust the seasoning if required – the mixture should be well seasoned and flavourful, to account for the dilution of salt when consumed with the pastry.

4 Cover and place in the fridge overnight to let the mixture firm up.

Prepare the pastry rounds

5 Preheat your oven to 180°C (350°F) conventional.

6 Lightly flour a clean work surface, and an 8 cm (3¼ inch) round cookie cutter or the rim of a glass. (Flouring will aid in the release of the pastry in the next step.) Line a baking tray with baking paper.

7 Lie the puff pastry sheets flat on the floured surface, then cut out circles using the cookie cutter or glass.

8 Place half the pastry circles on the baking tray, leaving space between each one.

→

Assemble the pastries

9 Prepare an egg wash by beating the egg in a small bowl with the water.

10 Spoon 25 g (1 oz) of the chilled filling into the centre of each pastry round on the baking tray. Brush the egg wash around the pastry rims. Place another pastry circle on top of each.

11 Gently crimp the pastry edges with a fork, or the blunt edge of a 5 cm (2 inch) pastry cutter, while using your finger to push excess air or air pockets from the puff pastry parcel.

Bake the pastries

12 Brush the tops of each pastry with more egg wash.

13 Bake for 22 minutes, or until the pastry is golden brown and crispy. The pastries are ready when the internal temperature hits 78°C (172°F).

To serve

14 Once baked, let the pastries cool for a few minutes before serving.

15 I like to eat mine with some dijon mustard and thinly sliced pickled vegetables on the side.

Note

If you are freezing your pastries to bake at a later date, don't preheat your oven at step 5. Instead, after step 12, place the assembled pastries in an airtight container for up to 4 weeks. The pastries will take approximately 28 minutes to bake from frozen.

Bánh ướt

Steamed rice noodles with egg + meatloaf

Serves 1

120 g (4¼ oz)	bánh ướt (see note)
1	poached or soft-boiled egg
100 g (3½ oz)	chả (meatloaf), cut into thick batons
40 g (1½ oz)	mixed herbs, such as coriander (cilantro), perilla, mint and Vietnamese mint, leaves picked and roughly chopped
30 g (1 oz)	cucumber, cut into batons
20 g (¾ oz)	blanched bean sprouts
60 ml (¼ cup)	nước chấm Hanoi style (page 35)

To serve

pinch of	fried shallots (page 71)
pinch of	cracked black pepper
	pickled garlic (optional)
	fresh chilli slices (optional)

This is my go-to dish for feeding the team for breakfast. It is light, filling and delicious. It also has the added benefit of being quick to whip up, especially since we often have most of the ingredients on hand.

Bánh ướt are essentially bánh cuốn (page 252) sheets that are rolled and not filled (see note). Chả is an umbrella term for the myriad Vietnamese meatloaves, where ground meat is shaped and then steamed or fried. The steamed varieties are often wrapped in banana leaves, which impart a distinct aroma and flavour. Deli alternatives I would employ for this dish include mortadella or pressed tongue, which is to say something less salty. Remember to cut the meat into thick batons to maximise the tactile quality.

1. Refresh the bánh ướt in a steamer for 2 minutes, then transfer to a plate. (It can also be reheated in a microwave on high; cover and check every 30 seconds.)
2. Top the plate with the egg, chả, herbs, cucumber and bean sprouts. Garnish with fried shallots and black pepper and drizzle with nước chấm Hanoi style.
3. Serve immediately, with pickled garlic and fresh chilli if desired to add a lovely kick to an otherwise mild dish.

Note

Bánh ướt are available at some Asian grocers, or if you want to make your own, you can refer to the bánh cuốn recipe (page 252).

'I worry that these styles of dishes – typified by whole animal butchery and the need to use all the parts – might one day disappear.'

Bì cuốn bánh tráng

Pork skin rice paper rolls

Serves 4-6

Pork skin

250 g (9 oz)	raw pork skin or pre-shredded pork skin
1 tablespoon	white vinegar
	ice bath

Marinated pork

175 g (6 oz)	pork leg or shoulder, in one piece
1 tablespoon	fish sauce
3 teaspoons	raw sugar
1 teaspoon	cracked black pepper
2	garlic cloves, minced
50 ml (1¾ fl oz)	vegetable oil
125 ml (½ cup)	young coconut juice (or unsweetened coconut juice)

To assemble

80 g (2¾ oz)	toasted rice powder (see note)
1 × 150 g (5½ oz)	packet rice paper sheets
1 head	lettuce, leaves separated
2 bunches	mint, leaves picked
2 bunches	sawtooth coriander (culantro), leaves picked
2 bunches	coriander (cilantro), leaves picked
250 g (9 oz)	fresh rice vermicelli noodles (or 150 g/5½ oz dried noodles, prepared according to the packet instructions)

Dipping sauce (per person)

120 ml (4 fl oz)	nước chấm ớt (page 34)

Note

The distinct flavour in this dish is from the toasted rice powder – it should not be omitted. It is available from Vietnamese and Thai grocers, or instructions for toasted rice are available on pages 50–51. Blitz into a fine powder before using in this recipe.

A dish that epitomises the paddock-to-plate philosophy before it was even trendy. I worry that these styles of dishes – typified by whole animal butchery and the need to use all the parts – might one day disappear. You can skip the first stage if you are able to procure shredded pork skin from your local Vietnamese butcher.

Prepare the pork skin

1 Skip this stage if using pre-shredded pork skin. Otherwise, wash the pork skin under cold running water and scrape off any hairs with a sharp knife.

2 Place the pork skin in a saucepan of boiling water, ensuring the pork is immersed. Add the vinegar (it stops discolouration). Bring back to the boil, then reduce the heat to medium and poach for 35 minutes, removing any scum that rises to the surface. Do not overcook the pork skin; it is ready when you are able to just pierce the skin with a chopstick.

3 Remove from the heat. Working quickly while the skin is still hot, quickly scrape off any remaining fat.

4 Dunk the pork skin into the ice bath for at least 1 minute to stop the cooking process.

5 Drain the pork skin and pat dry. Roll the skin tightly into a log, then use a sharp knife to slice into very thin strips (the width of vermicelli noodles).

Marinate and cook the pork

6 Cut the pork leg or shoulder into two or three pieces. Place in a bowl with the fish sauce, sugar, pepper and garlic, coating evenly. Cover and marinate for 30 minutes.

7 Heat the vegetable oil in a heavy-based saucepan over medium heat. Cook the pork for a minute or so on each side to allow the sugars to caramelise.

8 Pour in half the coconut juice, stirring to deglaze the pan. Bring to the boil, then reduce the heat to medium. Cover and simmer for 3–5 minutes, until the coconut juice has evaporated or caramelised.

9 Check the pork for doneness. If the pork mixture looks too dry, add more coconut juice. Check the seasoning if you do add more coconut juice, as it will dilute the flavours and sweeten the pork.

10 Remove from the pan and leave to cool, then cut the pork into strips.

Assemble and serve

11 Place the pork skin and pork meat in a large mixing bowl and toss to coat with the toasted rice powder.

12 Dunk a rice paper sheet in a bowl of cool water and place on a clean flat surface. The rice paper will continue to hydrate as you assemble the roll.

13 Place a piece of lettuce on top, followed by the herbs, the vermicelli noodles and about 20–30 g (¾–1 oz) of the pork mixture; try a bit less depending on your skill with rolling.

14 Start rolling the sheet up tightly towards the top. Half-way through, fold the sides in, and continue rolling until you have a complete roll.

15 Repeat with the remaining ingredients, and serve the rolls immediately with the dipping sauce.

Thịt sườn cừu ướp chao

Lamb riblets with fermented bean curd

Serves 3–4

1 kg (2 lb 4 oz)	lamb riblets

Marinade

4 cubes	fermented bean curd (page 68), mashed
2 tablespoons	shaoxing wine
4	garlic cloves, minced
2 tablespoons	minced fresh ginger
2 tablespoons	sugar
2 tablespoons	sesame oil

Chẻo xanh (green chẻo)

2–3	garlic cloves, peeled
2	green scud chillies, stems removed
1 teaspoon	cracked white pepper
1 handful	coriander (cilantro) leaves
1 handful	Vietnamese mint leaves
1 tablespoon	coriander seeds, toasted and ground
2 teaspoons	fish sauce
25 ml (¾ fl oz)	calamansi or lemon juice, to taste

This recipe has been included if only to demonstrate the function of this book – to be creative and combine two base sauce recipes with any protein in order to come up with a dish that is equally delicious in any iteration. Pork ribs are another good alternative.

Marinate the lamb

1 Mix the marinade ingredients in a bowl until smooth. Add the lamb and coat it all over with the marinade. Cover and marinate overnight, or for at least 6 hours. Bring to room temperature for grilling.

Grill the lamb

2 Place the riblets on a hot grill (see page 104 for more on barbecue cooking) and gently cook over low heat for at least 25–30 minutes. You want to render all the fat, and cook the riblets so they are tender.

Prepare the chẻo xanh

3 Using a mortar and pestle, pound the garlic and chillies with the pepper until smooth. Add the coriander and mint leaves and pound to a smooth paste.

4 Mix in the ground coriander seeds, fish sauce and calamansi juice to taste. This chẻo should be quite spicy and zingy, with the savouriness coming through on the back palate – salt should not be the initial taste.

To serve

5 Transfer the cooked lamb ribs to a plate and serve warm, with the chẻo xanh.

Blood pudding + other delicacies

J.Y.

My first memory of eating blood pudding was at Cumulus Inc., where Thi was then working as a chef. After two months of texting, Thi and I had only just met each other face to face the week prior. Having just finished work one Melbourne spring afternoon, I received a message to come sit at the marble bar at Cumulus Inc. So I did.

The blood pudding I tried that day was all at once light and decadent, an exercise of textures and contrasts, with a smoky but vegetal lure of tomato – a single, moreish bite of deliciousness. It was almost a before-blood-pudding and after-blood-pudding experience.

This blood pudding would go on to inspire Thi's rendition that later made its way to the Anchovy menu. Blood as food has always been prominent in Vietnamese cuisine – in its coagulated form in a variety of noodle soups, used as a thickener for yet other broths, and in rituals involving the killing and bleeding of animals for tiết canh (page 146).

Thi's blood pudding was an amalgamation of two very different methods. The first follows the French tradition, which uses cream and eggs, similar to a custard. However, rather than using rice or breadcrumbs as a filler, it was all herbs, which lightened the product and is consistent with the Vietnamese approach.

I have one other special memory of blood pudding. It was my birthday and Thi had driven us to a secluded park spot for a simple birthday picnic that involved just us and a camper cooker. I remember looking at the cooker and wondering whether it was okay to use it in a park. This moment exemplifies a common theme throughout the course of our relationship, where Thi's delight at trespass is mirrored by my ever-increasing panic.

In any case, out came a deli package of morcilla, Spanish blood sausage, along with a bundle of herbs, cos leaves, ginger pickle and a small handful of scud chillies. Thi busied herself frying the little block of morcilla and assembling other bits and pieces on the back of a plastic lid while I busied myself looking around, trying to make out a park ranger idling among the leafy eucalypt shadows.

Then she handed me an assembly of food, held together on a cos leaf, and all was forgotten in the rolling spice of ginger, the pungency of Vietnamese mint, the light crunch of cos leaf, and the hot, savoury mouthful of blood pudding.

Anchovy's blood pudding would go on to define much of the restaurant, and spoke to a turning point in modern Australian cookery, with younger first- and second-generation migrant chefs using food as an expression of their cultural self. It was also just a monumentally delicious snack.

The divergent contemporary approach to organ meats across Asian cuisines interests me: prized by some and actively avoided by others, used as a measure of food adventure by those who can afford it, and as the only source of affordable protein by others again. In Australian cities, the prices of some offal varieties have soared in the past few years – beef tongue and large pork intestines, for example – inadvertently making delicacies of these historically humble foods.

The thrall of intestines lies in their chewy yet tender texture – redeeming to some, off-putting to most. The texture is not dissimilar to the steamed skin of coral trout or the fatty bit from a lamb cutlet, the latter of which Thi enjoys and the former she detests. It is completely different in texture from other components of animal offal – chicken giblets, chewy-crunchy or chewy-stringy; pork or chicken liver, grainy; solidified blood, jelly-like. I often find that my eagerness to bite down into a piece of pork intestine is tempered by a cautious sniff for the unmistakable smell of urea. It is the large intestine, after all.

One day, we visited Thi's older sister for a meal, and walked into a wall of boiling pig intestine smell. The smell of pig intestines being boiled in a pot is so distinct – it always hits me first on the back of the throat, as if there was such intensity in its rich, meaty and uric core that my front palate steps aside.

Thi's sister spent a long time cleaning the intestines with care. She rinsed them over and over, turning them inside out and repeating the process. I had learned about villi in high school biology – the finger-like projections on the inside surface of the large intestine that increases the surface area available for nutrient absorption. It was the villi she was also scraping off the surface of the intestines, along with other matter, digested or otherwise. *Scrape it off or it will smell,* she had advised, *but it takes a lot of time so not many places do it; that is why it always smells at restaurants*. Wise words.

Another nugget of information Thi's sister shared: always go with the large intestines. It is an easy temptation to succumb to small intestines, being half the cost of large intestines. Small intestines are also less fatty than large intestines, which may feel like a win for the health-conscious among us. It is, however, the fat in the large intestines that help with the crisping of the morsel and its overall mouthfeel and texture. Enjoy a serve of flaccid fried small intestines at your own risk.

I first ate Thi's older sister's take on pork intestines while on holiday with the family in the beachside region of Jervis Bay. Thi's sister had driven the two and a half hours south of Sydney with fresh pork intestines in tow and fried them up with pickled mustard greens. It was one of my favourite dishes from that holiday.

Lòng heo xào

Stir-fried pickled mustard greens + intestines

Serves 4 as part of a larger meal

35 g (1¼ oz)	rice flour
1 kg (2 lb 4 oz)	large pork intestines (see note)
35 ml (1¼ fl oz)	vinegar
2 teaspoons	table salt
4 tablespoons	vegetable oil
25 g (1 oz)	garlic, minced
300 ml (10½ fl oz)	coconut water (no added sugar, if using a commercially packaged version)
200 g (7 oz)	pickled mustard greens (page 64)
3	spring onions (scallions), cut into 4 cm (1½ inch) batons
2	bullet chillies, sliced
2 tablespoons	sweet soy sauce (ABC brand preferred)

Marinade

45 ml (1½ fl oz)	rice wine
1 tablespoon	sweet soy sauce (ABC brand preferred)
3 teaspoons	annatto oil (page 45)
2 teaspoons	light soy sauce (Pearl River brand preferred)
1 teaspoon	cracked black pepper
3	star anise
1	cinnamon stick
1½ teaspoons	Chinese five spice
1½ teaspoons	caster (superfine) sugar

There are several ways intestines can be cooked and served. Chopped into smaller pieces, dredged through flour and deep-fried. Stuffed with prawn mousse, flattened and deep-fried. Boiled and served with a dipping sauce of some description. Shallow-fried with pickled mustard greens remains one of our all-time favourites.

Clean the intestines

1 Mix the rice flour and the intestines in a bowl to coat well.
2 Turn the intestines inside out, rinsing constantly under running water. Continuing to rinse, remove the villi (the finger-like projections) on the inner surface of the intestines by scraping them off with a spoon, but do not remove the fat.
3 Return the intestines to the bowl, then add the vinegar and salt. Mix and coat well.
4 Repeat the process of turning the intestines inside out and running under cold water. Continue repeating until the water runs clear and all traces of flour, vinegar and salt are removed.

Marinate the intestines

5 Combine the marinade ingredients in a large bowl.
6 Add the washed intestines, mix to coat well, and set aside for at least 45 minutes on the bench.

Cook the intestines

7 Heat 2 tablespoons of the oil in a saucepan and sauté half the garlic over medium heat for 1–2 minutes, until fragrant.
8 Add the marinated intestines and cook, covered but with the lid ajar, for 20 minutes, so that the flavours can absorb.
9 Add the coconut water and cook for another 15 minutes. The intestines are ready when you can poke a chopstick through them.
10 Remove the intestines from the pan and set aside to cool. Slice diagonally into 2 cm (¾ inch) thick chunks.

Finish the dish

11 In a wok over high heat, heat the remaining oil. When the wok is smoking, stir-fry the remaining garlic over medium heat for 1–2 minutes, until fragrant.
12 Add the pickled mustard greens, spring onion, chilli and sweet soy sauce. Stir-fry for another 2–3 minutes.
13 Add about 250 g (9 oz) of the cooked intestines, turn the heat down to medium and quickly braise for 2–3 minutes.
14 Serve immediately.

Note

It is difficult to buy intestines in less than 1 kg (2 lb 4 oz) portions. You will only need about 250 g (9 oz) of the cooked marinated intestines for this dish, but once properly prepared, the remainder will keep in an airtight container in the fridge for up to 3 days to use in other dishes. If you are looking to freeze, do not clean or marinate the intestines until after you thaw and are ready to use them.

Bánh hỏi và heo quay

Pressed vermicelli with suckling pork

Serves 6–12 as part of a larger meal

1 × 7–8 kg (15 lb 7 oz–17 lb 10 oz) suckling pig
10–15 litres (340–510 fl oz) boiling water

Marinade

3 tablespoons fine sea salt
2 tablespoons Chinese five spice
2 tablespoons rock sugar, blitzed
2 tablespoons sweet bean paste
2 cubes fermented bean curd (page 68), mashed

Maltose wash

2 tablespoons maltose
2 tablespoons white rice wine
250 ml (1 cup) red rice vinegar

Salted coconut cream

250 ml (1 cup) coconut cream (Aroy-D brand preferred)
1 teaspoon salt
2½ teaspoons caster (superfine) sugar

Noodles

16 pieces dried fine rice vermicelli (bánh hỏi), cooked to packet instructions
125 ml (½ cup) spring onion oil (page 44)
70 g (½ cup) roasted peanuts, lightly crushed

Note

At the time of writing, it is no longer possible to commercially procure suckling pigs in Victoria due to abattoir politics. Perhaps you are in a better position to gain access to a suckling pig wherever you are – I hope you find joy working through this recipe.

→

I have Chef Cheong Liew to thank for the suckling pig recipe in this dish. He and his ground-breaking Neddy's restaurant is one of the reasons Southeast Asian cuisine has a seat at the fine-dining table in Australia. Chef Cheong Liew has been a fantastic resource for me and all my suckling pig-related questions. Once over lunch, he almost convinced me to build my own duck oven. It is rare to find such a kindred spirit driven by impulse and an excitable energy.

There are two parts to this recipe: the roasting of the pig, which is the hype up for the party, and the actual party itself. A suckling pig frame or hanger can typically be bought from specialty Chinese kitchenware shops. Some helpers and a large outdoor space are required. The steps here also ask for a very large fridge and a few days of lead time. If you have neither, the skin will not be as crispy. For a smaller version, try half a belly instead, adjust the quantities accordingly and go nuts!

Prepare the pig

1. Use a cleaver to split the pig from the belly through the sternum.
2. Run the cleaver down the centre of the mouth and split, removing the brain with a spoon.
3. Continue to split the backbone, down to the sacrum.
4. Remove the femur, fibula and tibia bones.
5. Remove the first five bones from each side of the rib cage.
6. Remove the scapula, humerus, radius and ulna bones.
7. Combine the marinade ingredients. Marinate the pig on the flesh side only, not the skin side. If possible, leave in the fridge overnight, otherwise continue to the next step.

Stretch, scald and hang the pig

8. Using the components of the suckling pig hanger, stretch the pig with a piece of wood from the head to the tail, one from shoulder to shoulder, and another to keep the trotters in place.
9. Starting from the bottom, pierce the suckling pig hanger through the legs without piercing the skin and go under the first two ribs and out and over. Continue to stake the pig through the shoulder bone, neck and cheek without piercing the skin.
10. Hang your suckling pig from a sturdy outdoor beam (for example a garage frame) and pour the boiling water over the skin to tighten and firm it up. Avoid getting any water on the flesh.
11. Once the skin has cooled, combine the maltose wash ingredients. Brush the skin with the maltose wash.
12. If possible, hang the pig in the fridge for up to 72 hours, brushing it again at least twice with the maltose wash during this time. Otherwise, hang somewhere cool and dry for 6 hours – it's best to cook it on the same day if you are not using a fridge. Use a fan to blow on the skin to help it to dry, and still brush twice with the maltose wash.

→

To serve

- Vietnamese lettuce or butter lettuce leaves
- rice paper sheets
- cucumber batons
- fresh pineapple, thinly sliced
- plantain, boiled until tender and thinly sliced
- Vietnamese mint, coriander (cilantro), perilla, fish mint, mint and/or sorrel leaves
- pickles (pages 62, 63, 64, 229)
- fermented soy bean sauce (page 34), hoisin or nước chấm (page 34), for dipping

Roast the pig

13 Remove the pig from the fridge and, while it is still firm, pitchfork it. To do so, remove the hanger and, using the pitchfork, repeat the same process as step 9. Let the pig come to room temperature before cooking.

14 Start your fire with wood. I like to use red gum or iron bark, as they impart a nice smoky smell and flavour.

15 While the fire is establishing, place the pig at an angle over the cool fire, skin side down, to begin to smoke for 30 minutes.

16 Flip to smoke the pig's flesh side for at least 1 hour over medium–low heat. After 1 hour, you will need to flip and rotate the pig to ensure even heat coverage. Sometimes, moving the fire around is easier than moving the pig.

17 At this stage, probe the pig in different areas to ensure all sections of the pig have reached 58°C (136°F). Also ensure your fire has an even layer of white charcoal, and the heating element is evenly hot, without flames or hot spots.

18 Continue to cook and rotate the pig from flesh to skin side over the fire, until the entire skin side is evenly cooked and coloured. Depending on your patience and heat of your fire, this should take around 45 minutes.

19 While the pig is cooking, use a skewer to pop the skin as it flares up or blisters. Popping the skin allows the skin to deflate and there will be no unsightly bubbles. Also regularly wipe the skin with paper towels to clean dripping fat as it will help prevent the pig from catching. You may need assistance with this part, especially if you are still holding on to the pig!

20 Leave to rest for at least 1 hour before portioning.

Portion the pig

21 Take the pig off the prongs, then remove the head, separate the legs, and cut along the ribs to remove.

22 Slice the meat into bite-sized chunks, and present on a large platter in a single layer.

Prepare the noodles

23 Up to 2 hours before serving, mix together the salted coconut cream ingredients.

24 Fold the fresh (or freshly cooked) bánh hỏi noodles in half, to make them easier to eat, and arrange on a plate. Brush the surface of the noodles with the salted coconut cream.

25 Keep the noodles covered with plastic wrap until ready to eat. Sprinkle spring onion oil and crushed peanuts over the top to serve.

To serve (the party)

26 Serve the suckling pig, noodles and various accompaniments together, and encourage guests to create their own wrappy guy (see page 210). Using a lettuce leaf or rice paper sheet as a vessel for the herbs and vegetables, a bit of suckling pig and some noodles, wrap it up, dip in sauce and eat.

Lẩu cơm mẻ

Fermented rice hot pot

Serves 4–6

2.5 litres (85 fl oz)	water
2	young lemongrass stems, cut into 4 cm (1½ inch) lengths
50 g (1¾ oz)	ginger, sliced (no need to peel)
1.5 kg (3 lb 5 oz)	beef shin, bone removed

Broth

1 litre (4 cups)	water
1	young lemongrass stem, cut into 4 cm (1½ inch) lengths
50 g (1¾ oz)	ginger, sliced (no need to peel)
2 teaspoons	salt
2 teaspoons	sugar
3	makrut lime leaves
1 cup (250 ml)	cơm mẻ (fermented rice, page 243)

Dipping sauce

100 g (3½ oz)	young lemongrass stems, roughly chopped
4	green scud chillies, roughly chopped
2 teaspoons	caster (superfine) sugar
1 teaspoon	salt
3 tablespoons	cơm mẻ (fermented rice, page 243)

To serve

1 bunch	chrysanthemum leaves (also known as tong ho or shungiku)
1 bunch	morning glory leaves and stalks
1 bunch	sweet potato leaves
1 bunch	mustard leaves
3	plantains, peeled, sliced and soaked (see note)

This lẩu uses the natural acidity and body of cơm mẻ to lift the broth and give it another dimension. Offal is a common protein for this dish though I have used beef shin in this instance. Some might regard the protein as the star, but it is the dipping sauce for this lẩu that keeps me enthralled. It shines bright on the palate alongside the brisk bursts of lemongrass.

Poach the beef shin

1. Place the water, lemongrass and ginger in a large saucepan and bring to the boil.
2. Cut the beef shin in half lengthways.
3. Add the beef shin to the poaching liquid and bring back to the boil, skimming off any impurities that rise to the surface.
4. Cook over medium heat for about 1 hour, until soft – you should be able to poke a chopstick through the meat.
5. Remove the shin, reserving the poaching liquid for the broth, and set aside to cool.

Make the broth

6. Strain the poaching liquid into a large clean saucepan. Add the water, lemongrass and ginger and bring to the boil.
7. Add the salt, sugar and lime leaves.
8. Mix the cup of cơm mẻ into 100 ml (3½ fl oz) of the broth, stirring to loosen the mixture.
9. Place a fine-meshed sieve over the saucepan and strain the cơm mẻ mixture into the broth, using the back of a ladle to press all the mash through.
10. Return to the boil, then leave to infuse over low heat for 20–30 minutes.

Make the dipping sauce

11. Using a mortar and pestle, pound the lemongrass and chilli with the sugar and salt until smooth.
12. Add the cơm mẻ and incorporate well.
13. The dipping sauce should be tangy and spicy on the front palate, with just a hint of sweetness, so adjust the flavours as needed.

Assemble the lẩu

14. Thinly slice the beef shin and fan onto a plate.
15. Wash the vegetables and arrange on serving plates.
16. Transfer the broth onto a gas cooker and place in the centre of the table with the meat, vegetables and dipping sauce. See page 87 for more on enjoying a hot pot.

Note

Plantains must be soaked to remove the sap. Mix 1 litre (4 cups) of water with 1 teaspoon of salt. Place the peeled and sliced plantains in a bowl and cover with salted water. Soak for 5 minutes, then drain and cover with fresh salted water to soak again for at least another 25 minutes.

Stir-fried livers with flowering garlic

Serves 3–4 as part of a larger meal

100 g (3½ oz)	chicken, duck or pork livers
1 teaspoon	cornflour (cornstarch)
2 teaspoons	egg white (from 1 egg)
3 tablespoons	vegetable oil
100 g (3½ oz)	bean sprouts
2	garlic cloves, minced
70 g (2½ oz)	garlic chive flowers, cut into thumb lengths
1	green scud chilli, sliced
1 teaspoon	fish sauce
1 teaspoon	shaoxing wine
2 teaspoons	sesame seeds
pinch of	sugar
pinch of	sea salt, to taste

A dish that bonds my eldest sister and me, with our shared love for delicious home-style flavours. It tastes like a hug. The slight gaminess from the livers keeps the dish exciting to eat, and the sprouts and chives add a wholesome element.

Marinating proteins or velveting in the traditions of Chinese cuisine is such an important part of the stir-fry process. Shaoxing wine, cornflour and sometimes bicarbonate of soda - alkali - is added to the marinade to help keep the proteins tender and prevent them from being overcooked (by starch forming a protective layer over the protein).

The rice wine helps keep the gaminess at bay. If you do not wish to use alcohol in your cooking, you can soak the chicken liver in cold water for 30 minutes to 1 hour before cooking, changing out the water a few times in between, to help release the blood from the liver and eliminate the gamey taste. I have used chicken livers in this recipe, but duck or pork liver works just as well.

1. Remove any connective tissue or membranes from the livers, and trim any discoloured parts.
2. Place the cornflour and egg white in a small bowl and whisk to combine. Coat the livers in the mixture.
3. Heat a wok over medium–high heat. Using 1 tablespoon of oil each time, half-cook the livers in two batches for 1–2 minutes. Remove from the wok and set aside.
4. Clean the wok out and place over high heat. Add the remaining oil.
5. Working fast, add the bean sprouts, garlic and garlic chive flowers and stir-fry for about 1 minute, until fragrant.
6. Return the livers to the wok and continue cooking for about 2–3 minutes, until they achieve your preferred level of doneness.
7. Add the remaining ingredients and stir-fry for 1 minute. Serve immediately.

Thịt heo ướp cám gạo

Pork marinated in rice bran

Serves 5–6

1 kg (2 lb 4 oz)	pork belly
30 g (1 oz)	salt (3% by weight ratio for pork; see note)
40 g (1½ oz)	rice bran (4% by weight)

To cook and serve

vegetable oil, for frying
vegetables (optional)
steamed rice

Note

This recipe can be scaled up or down according to the starting weight of the pork belly, based on the percentages listed in brackets after the other ingredients. For instance, if your pork belly starting weight is 500 grams, you would need 3% salt and 4% rice bran – which would be 15 g (½ oz) salt and 20 g (¾ oz) rice bran.

Pork was not a meat my mother had the luxury of consuming regularly while growing up. The family would only get access to pork if someone was killing a pig, and even then they would only get a portion. Pig's head congee is something Mum recalls fondly.

When they had access to pork belly, her father would salt it and roll it in rice bran, which they could source for free. *How long did he salt it?* I once asked, genuinely curious. *No idea*, Mum responded. *How much salt did he use?* She shrugged, completely unbothered that she knew nothing of this dish from her younger years apart from that it was deliciously salty, fried and eaten with hot rice.

I decided to redevelop the recipe because I thought it encapsulated the spirit of this book. A recipe with roots in frugality and one at risk of being lost because it should have been passed down the family but never was. However, I could never bring myself to tell Mum how much I paid to source organic rice bran in Australia.

The salting and drying takes up to 2 weeks. Extended hanging time will make the pork drier and allow time for the rice bran flavour to penetrate, before the salty pork is fried and served with hot rice.

Salt the pork overnight

1 Clean the slab of pork belly thoroughly by running it under cool running water. Leave to drain and pat dry.

2 Stab the pork using a needled meat tenderiser evenly on both sides of the belly, to allow the salt to penetrate evenly.

3 Place the pork in a glass or plastic container in which it can lie flat. Sprinkle half the salt all over the pork on both sides. Cover and leave to marinate in its own juices in the fridge overnight, turning it over twice during this time.

Hang the pork

4 The next day, toast the rice bran in a dry wok over medium heat for 2–3 minutes, until fragrant. Immediately remove from the heat and leave to cool.

5 Remove the pork from the container, discarding any juices; there's no need to pat the pork dry. Cut into 3.5 cm (1¼ inch) wide strips. Rub the pork with the remaining salt, then roll it in the rice bran to ensure it is well covered.

6 Hang the pork strips on meat hooks in a dark, cool, well-ventilated area. A pantry, underneath the stairs or in a charcuterie fridge (but not a standard fridge) would work. Leave to hang for at least 3 days before cooking. (After that, you can carve a bit off and cook to eat.) You can continue hanging the pork for up to 9 months. It will gradually dry and shrivel.

Cook and serve

7 Cut the pork into bite-sized pieces.

8 Stir-fry on its own, or with vegetables, and serve with rice.

Mì khô Nam Vang

Phnom Penh egg noodles

Serves 4

Pork bone broth

120 g (4¼ oz)	piece of pork meat (from the neck or shoulder)
600 g (1 lb 5 oz)	pork bones (use short ribs or pork knuckle)
100 g (3½ oz)	salted radish, from a packet
10 g (¼ oz)	dried prawns (page 54)
100 g (3½ oz)	old ginger, skin on, roughly chopped
½	brown onion, partially quartered keeping the root intact
4	dried longans, shelled
1 teaspoon	salt
2 tablespoons	fish sauce
1 teaspoon	cracked white pepper
100 g (3½ oz)	daikon (white radish), sliced into half-moons

Toppings

100 g (3½ oz)	pork liver
200 g (7 oz)	minced (ground) pork
2 teaspoons	minced garlic
pinch of	salt and cracked black pepper
120 g (4¼ oz)	squid, cleaned and scored
8	prawns (shrimp)

→

We used to make fresh egg noodles at the restaurant. While fresh egg noodles are substantially more tedious to make compared to fresh pasta, their distinct taste and aroma are without comparison.

The toppings in this dish are modelled after those found on hủ tiếu Nam Vang, rice noodles from Cambodia: pork mince, offal, quail eggs, calamari, onions, beans sprouts and greenery. Omitting the pork lard is possibly the healthy heart option, but consider the amount of flavour you are trading off.

Prepare the pork bone broth

1. Place the pork meat and bones in a large saucepan. Cover with water and bring to the boil. Drain, discarding all the liquid.
2. Run the bones and meat under cold running water to remove any scum. Leave to drain.
3. Scrub out the saucepan and return to the stovetop. Add the pork bones, meat, salted radish, dried prawns, ginger, onion and longans. Bring to the boil, then reduce the heat to a simmer.
4. Let the pork meat simmer for 45 minutes, or until the internal temperature reaches 80°C (176°F) or more. Remove from the broth and either dunk into an ice bath or run under cold running water to stop the cooking. Leave to drain, then pat dry.
5. Once the pork meat has cooled, wrap tightly in plastic wrap, into a log, then refrigerate until ready to serve (or even overnight, if desired).
6. Bring the broth back to the boil, then reduce the heat to medium, skimming off any scum. Leave the stock to infuse over low heat for at least 1 hour.
7. Taste the stock and season with the salt, fish sauce, white pepper and daikon. The daikon will soften in about 15 minutes.
8. Continue simmering over low heat until ready to use. Do not allow the broth to reduce.

Prepare the toppings

9. Rinse the pork liver thoroughly, then soak in cold water for 20 minutes. Drain and pat dry.
10. Place the liver in a saucepan, add enough water to cover and bring to the boil. Skim off any scum, reduce the heat and simmer for 5 minutes, until the liver is just cooked. Remove the liver and run it under cold water to stop the cooking. Drain and leave to cool, then thinly slice and set aside.
11. In a frying pan, sauté the minced pork with the garlic and a pinch of salt and pepper over medium heat for about 3–5 minutes, until cooked. Set aside.
12. Cook the squid and prawns in salted boiling water for 2 minutes, then drain, shell the prawns and set aside.
13. Remove the pork meat from the fridge, thinly slice and set aside.

→

Egg noodles (see notes)

500 g (1 lb 2 oz)	plain (all-purpose) flour
110 g (3¾ oz)	egg yolks (from 5–6 eggs)
100 g (3½ oz)	egg whites (from about 3 eggs)
2 teaspoons	grapeseed oil
1½ teaspoons	salt

Sauce

60 ml (¼ cup)	fish sauce
120 ml (4 fl oz)	oyster sauce
120 ml (4 fl oz)	soy sauce (Pearl River brand preferred)
1 tablespoon	dark soy sauce
1 tablespoon	sesame oil
60 g (2¼ oz)	caster (superfine) sugar

To serve

½ teaspoon	rendered pork lard per person (optional; see notes)
100 g (3½ oz)	Chinese celery
40 g (1½ oz)	garlic chives
200 g (7 oz)	bean sprouts
200 g (7 oz)	lettuce, finely shredded
8	quail eggs, soft-boiled and peeled (see notes)
	fried shallots (page 71)
	pickled garlic
	pickled green chilli
	lemon wedges
	chilli sauce

Make the noodles

14 Place the flour in a mound on a clean surface. Make a well and add the egg yolks and whites, oil and salt.

15 Use your fingertips to incorporate until a rough dough forms. It will be very difficult to knead given the amount of yolk – it may take 45–60 minutes. Do persevere. The results are worth it.

16 Allow the dough to rest for at least 30 minutes to let the gluten relax. Divide the dough into manageable portions, then flatten into a rough rectangle. Use a sharp knife or pasta machine to cut the dough –you may need to dust with flour. Aim for roughly 1.6–2 mm (1⁄20–1⁄16 inches) in diameter.

Cook the noodles

17 Bring a large saucepan of salted water to a rapid boil. Blanch the noodles for about 1 minute, or until cooked to your liking.

18 Drain and run under cold water to stop the noodles overcooking. You can leave them to sit for up to 15 minutes at this stage, although they may start to oxidise.

Assemble and serve

19 Mix all the sauce ingredients together until the sugar has dissolved.

20 Set out four noodle bowls and four broth bowls. Place about 1 tablespoon of the sauce in the bottom of each noodle bowl, with about ½ teaspoon of pork lard, if using. There will be some sauce left over; keep it in the fridge for your next quick meal.

21 Refresh the noodles in a large saucepan of fresh boiling water for 10 seconds, then drain and place in the bowls.

22 Repeat the same process with the Chinese celery, garlic chives and bean sprouts, blanching in the boiling water for about 10 seconds or until your preferred doneness. Place on the noodles.

23 Equally distribute the pork slices, liver slices, pork mince, squid, lettuce, quail eggs and prawns between the bowls.

24 Garnish with a pinch of fried shallots.

25 Ladle the hot pork bone broth into the four small side bowls (about 250 ml/1 cup of broth into each). Serve immediately, with your favourite accompaniments.

Notes

– You can also buy tins of boiled and peeled quail eggs at Asian grocers. Peeling your own boiled quail eggs is a pain, but they will be infinitely more delicious.

– If you prefer to buy your noodles, rather than make them yourself, use 650 g (1 lb 7 oz) thin fresh egg noodles and cook according to the packet instructions.

– To render pork lard, cut pork fat into 3–4 cm (1¼–1½ inch) chunks. Place in a saucepan and cover with cool water. Allow the water to come to a gentle boil over medium heat. Maintain the temperature and the water will eventually evaporate and the chunks of fat will liquefy. Keep a close eye on it and take care not to burn it. Strain and discard any gristly left-over bits, retaining the pork lard in a clean container. Refrigerate until required, up to 3 weeks.

Phở at home

J.Y.

One of the recurring conversations Thi and I have is the quality of produce in Australia and the way that quality translates in a dish. Phở in Vietnam is good because of the skill and the abundance of fresh produce, but phở done right in Australia is otherworldly, largely due to the quality of beef: pasture raised, more robust in flavour, with the promise of buttery fat leaching from the marrow.

When Thi and I were last visiting my parents back home in Brunei, Dad had it in his mind that he was going to learn to make this iconic Vietnamese dish. Dad is a keen camper and had been in a quiet cooking competition with his camping buddy; the pièce de résistance would be a pot of beef phở whipped up at the campsite.

Thi – never one to back down from a challenge and also the filial daughter-in-law – gamely agreed to the task of making beef phở if Dad was happy to take notes. Mum proceeded to pull a face and ask, *Why not chicken?* She pointed out to Thi that we were more likely to find water buffalo than beef in the local markets.

Thi remained characteristically undeterred and started making a list of beef cuts she would like to procure: brisket, tendon, marrow, tail, tripe, bones. I had not realised it at the time, but making a two-and-a-half-hour return journey to the wet market to procure these cuts turned out to be one of the easier parts of the process. For the record, Mum was also correct; very soon into the initial stages of cooking, Thi confirmed that we did indeed buy water buffalo parts, not beef.

As it were, making phở at home turned out to be quite the endeavour, and any returns that were promised diminished rapidly. It took us two days and a trip to the neighbouring town to find a bunch of sawtooth coriander. A bag of fresh rice noodles was procured via the back channels at a local coffee shop, and so too were Chinese doughnuts. All the while, we were also looking for black cardamom pods, which we never found.

Then Thi decided that beef phở required beef balls – of the springy variety that can easily be found in almost any Asian supermarket in Australia, even general inner-city supermarkets of a sufficient size. There were none to be found in Brunei. My parents were not in possession of a food processor, but still Thi persevered, mincing beef in a blender in small batches before we squeezed them into balls.

By this point, Mum showed substantially more aptitude and interest in what was happening in the kitchen than Dad, who was often caught snoozing in front of the television at key points of the process, otherwise snacking on the various cuts of beef in his travels in and out of the kitchen. I was ready to throw in the towel and daydreamed of just going down the road to buy a bowl of phở back home in Melbourne. Thi seemed only slightly perturbed.

When we did finally sit down to eat, my parents were sufficiently impressed. While slurping his noodles, Dad was considering just how he would present a bowl of phở on his next trip with his camping buddy. The only evidence of his note taking was a photo of the final product before he plunged his chopsticks into the bowl. *Well*, Dad pondered, *it is a lot of work, isn't it? I think I will just leave it to the professionals.*

Phở chiên phồng thịt bò xào

Fried phở chiên beef + vegetables

Serves 2 as a main meal

3 litres (100 fl oz)	vegetable oil, for deep-frying the noodles, plus extra for frying beef
250 g (9 oz)	rice noodle sheets (see bánh cuốn recipe, page 252), cut into 5 cm (2 inch) squares
130 g (4½ oz)	beef sirloin, thinly sliced, fat trimmed
2 teaspoons	cornflour (cornstarch)
15 g (½ oz)	egg white, from 1 egg
70 g (2½ oz)	red Asian shallots, peeled and cut into wedges lengthways
20 g (¾ oz)	ginger, julienned
2	garlic cloves, minced
160 g (5½ oz)	choy sum, chopped into 10 cm (4 inch) lengths
90 ml (3 fl oz)	water or stock

Marinade

1 tablespoon	light soy sauce (Pearl River brand preferred)
1 teaspoon	minced garlic
½ teaspoon	caster (superfine) sugar
½ teaspoon	cracked black pepper
¼ teaspoon	sesame oil

Slurry

2 tablespoons	cornflour (cornstarch)
1 tablespoon	cool water

Seasonings

100 ml (3½ fl oz)	shaoxing wine
2 tablespoons	light soy sauce (Pearl River brand preferred)
1 teaspoon	cracked black pepper

Phở chiên refers to both the noodle and the dish in this case: deep-fried squares typically topped with fried beef and vegetables and an accompanying sauce. A dish that is native to Hanoi and a great way to use what may have been left-over rice sheets from phở cuốn. The term 'pillow' is often bandied about in describing these squares, but do not expect a marshmallow-like situation or the mechanical properties of gnocco fritto. Do expect a light resistance or chew.

I have employed a velveting method for the beef, essentially allowing heat to be applied to the beef twice without seeing a deterioration in quality or mouthfeel. The cornflour mixture forms an outer layer over the beef pieces, which protects them during the extended cooking process and also offers a velvety mouthfeel. I have excluded bicarbonate of soda, which typically acts as a tenderiser; feel free to include a pinch if you are using a tougher cut of meat.

Double-fry the noodles

1. In a large saucepan or wok, heat the vegetable oil over medium heat.
2. Working in batches, add the rice noodle squares one by one, separated so they're not touching each other. Fry for 3 minutes, then drain and set aside at room temperature for up to 4 hours, until you are ready to serve. Do not discard the oil.
3. Just before serving, fry the squares again. (The first frying 'sets' the noodles; the second frying colours them.) Reheat the oil over medium heat and fry all the squares together for about 2–3 minutes, until golden brown.

Marinate the beef

4. In a bowl, mix together the marinade ingredients. Add the beef and toss to coat well with the mixture. Leave to sit on the bench for up to 20 minutes.

Cook the beef

5. Just before you start cooking the beef, whisk together the 2 teaspoons of cornflour and the egg white until well combined, then mix through the beef mixture. (The cornflour and egg white are part of the velveting process.)
6. In a wok, heat a little vegetable oil over medium–high heat. Add the beef and fry for 1–2 minutes, until the outside sets and it is almost cooked through. Remove from the wok and set aside.
7. Add the shallot, ginger and garlic and cook for about 50 seconds, or until the shallot has softened and the mixture is fragrant.
8. Add the choy sum and cook for about 2–3 minutes, until the stalk is tender, adding the water or stock if needed to help cook the choy sum.

→

9 Mix together the slurry ingredients until smooth, then add half the slurry to the wok. Add the seasonings and stir for about 1–2 minutes, until the sauce has thickened. You may need to stir in more slurry if you previously added a lot of water or stock.

10 Add the beef and toss well to combine. Taste and adjust the seasoning if needed, adding more soy sauce or black pepper.

To serve

11 Divide the rice noodle squares among two serving plates, allowing them to generally sit in a single layer. Top with your hot beef and vegetable stir-fry and serve immediately.

Nem chua gói lá chuối

Sour pork in banana leaf

Serves 12

1 kg (2 lb 4 oz)	lean pork loin or deboned leg
200 g (7 oz)	raw pork skin, or pre-shredded pork skin (available from Vietnamese butchers; 20% by weight ratio for pork; see notes)
50 ml (1¾ fl oz)	white rice vinegar
	banana leaves (see notes)

Cure

50 g (1¾ oz)	garlic cloves, minced (5% by weight)
30 g (1 oz)	green scud chillies, stems removed, thickly sliced, (3% by weight)
150 g (5½ oz)	white rice, cooked and cooled to 22–26°C (72–79°F) (15% by weight)
30 g (1 oz)	sea salt (3% by weight)
10 g (¼ oz)	white pepper, coarsely cracked (1% by weight)
30 g (1 oz)	caster (superfine) sugar (3% by weight)
2 g	salt cure #1 (pink salt; 0.002% by weight; optional)

To serve

scud chillies, thinly sliced
ginger, sliced and peeled and cut into 1 cm (½ inch cubes)

Nem or nem chua essentially refers to a sour fermented pork dish (though Mum likes making hers with beef). The Thais and Laotians have a dish of the same name, but the Vietnamese take is an exercise in patience and dedication.

The one thing I do not like about my mum's nem recipe is the use of nem seasoning powder – some sort of food preservative that helps sour the protein in the fermenting process; apart from its dubious chemical composition, I am also turned off by the resulting fluoro red colour it imparts. Past recipes I have experimented with remain just that, experiments – of varying success, varying levels of acid and chua (sourness), and varying confidence in consuming a fermented meat that is also typically served uncooked.

This recipe is adapted from Andy Ricker of Pok Pok fame. We had the joy of hosting Andy at the restaurant, and I was finally able to learn the art of nem without nem seasoning powder. In this recipe, the protein is cooked before serving.

You can skip the second stage if you are able to procure shredded pork skin from your local Vietnamese butcher. The recipe does call for the product to be fermented at a comfortable temperature of 28°C (82°F). You might have specialised equipment; my set-up may or may not include a wine fridge, a heater pad for beers, and a temperature control switch. Seek advice that suits your own circumstances.

Prepare the pork loin or leg

1. If using pork leg, debone it, ensuring there is no sinew or skin or fat. Dice up the pork into 5 cm (2 inch) pieces and chill in the freezer for 1 hour. You do not want it frozen but really cold, so that it can go through the mincer (grinder) easily.
2. Mince the pork to a very fine grade. Repeat if you need to, remembering to retain the chill by placing the mince in the freezer at intervals.
3. Place the pork in a large mixing bowl, cover with plastic wrap and set aside in the fridge for up to 3 hours.

Prepare the pork skin

4. Skip this stage if using pre-shredded pork skin. Otherwise, wash the pork skin under cold running water and scrape off any hairs with a sharp knife.
5. Place the pork skin in a saucepan of boiling water, ensuring the pork is immersed. Add the vinegar (it stops discolouration). Bring back to the boil, then reduce the heat to medium and poach for 20 minutes, removing any scum that rises to the surface. Do not overcook the pork skin; it is ready when you are able to just pierce the skin with a chopstick.
6. Remove from the heat. Working quickly while the skin is still hot, quickly scrape off any remaining fat using a spoon. Place the clean skin on a tray in one layer and chill in the fridge until cold.

→

7 Roll the cold skin tightly into a log, then use a sharp knife to slice it into very thin strips (the width of vermicelli noodles).

Cure and assemble

8 Finely blend the garlic and chilli using a food processor. Add the rice and continue to blend until smooth.

9 Transfer the mixture to a bowl. Add the salt, pepper, sugar and salt cure #1, if using, and mix until thoroughly combined.

10 Add the paste to the minced pork and shredded pork skin and mix well. The mixture should be bouncy and dense.

11 Place two pieces of banana leaf on top of each other on a flat work surface (the top leaf can be slightly smaller than the bottom leaf; two leaves together provide more structure).

12 Place 150 g (5½ oz) of pork mixture at the bottom of the leaf, in the centre, with some space either side.

13 Take the bottom edges of the banana leaf and roll tightly upwards to form a tight cylinder. Fold the edges of the cylinder under the section containing the mince. Pierce with toothpicks to hold, and place on a rack.

Ferment

14 Leave the parcels to ferment on the rack for 3–4 days at 28°C (82°F), ensuring they are out of the sun and in a well-ventilated area. Extra fermenting time will increase the sourness.

15 When ready, the pork should maintain a pink colour, and the smell should be sweet, like rice, with a smell of garlic and a tangy flavour. You don't want any alcohol smells or greying meat.

Cook and serve

16 To serve, throw on the barbecue (see page 104) on medium–low heat and cook for about 20 minutes, until the package becomes sticky and gelatinous (the gelatine from the skin leaches out).

17 Otherwise, preheat the oven to 180°C (350°F), and bake for 20 minutes. Unwrap the banana leaf and place under the grill (broiler) for the last few minutes to get some colour.

18 Serve with a cold beer, fresh scud chillies and cubes of ginger. Good drinking food.

Notes

- This recipe can be scaled up or down according to the starting weight of the pork, based on the percentages listed in brackets after the other ingredients.
- Asian grocers sell steamed banana leaves in vacuum-sealed bags, either frozen or at room temperature. Thaw if needed and dry the surface of each leaf using a tea (dish) towel or paper towel before use. You can also use fresh banana leaves. In this case, take care to clean the banana leaves with equal parts water and vinegar, then toast both surfaces of the leaf over an open flame to release the oils and soften the leaf before using.

Canh thịt heo khoai môn

Pork + taro soup

Serves 2–4 as part of a larger meal

280 g (10 oz)	fresh young taro
500 g (1 lb 2 oz)	minced (ground) pork
2 teaspoons	fish sauce
2–3 cloves	garlic, minced
¾ teaspoon	caster (superfine) sugar
1 teaspoon	coarsely ground white pepper
30 ml (1 fl oz)	vegetable oil
2 litres (8 cups)	chicken stock (page 43) or water
6	dried longans
30 ml (1 fl oz)	tapioca starch slurry (equal parts tapioca starch and cool water, mixed well)

To serve

spring onion (scallion) whites, cut into fine rounds

sawtooth coriander (culantro), rice paddy herb or garlic chives, roughly chopped

This dish nourishes the soul. The starchiness of the taro adds a body to the soup and the pork mince adds texture. You can choose to further halve the young taro, which does increase the soup's starchiness, but is also more manageable as a mouthful.

Soak the taro

1 Peel and wash the taro, then set aside to soak for 45 minutes in lightly salted water to prevent discolouration and leach any excess starch.

Marinate the pork

2 Place the pork in a mixing bowl, add the fish sauce, garlic, sugar and pepper and mix until well combined. Cover and set aside for an hour on the bench.

Simmer the soup

3 Add the oil to a heavy-based saucepan over high heat. Fry the pork mixture in batches for about 3–5 minutes per batch, until the meat has all been seared.

4 Add the taro and chicken stock and bring to the boil, skimming off any scum that rises to the surface.

5 Turn the heat down to a gentle simmer, then add the longans and simmer for 20–25 minutes. Check the seasoning – you may need to add a little more fish sauce to taste, but this soup should not be overly seasoned. Mix in the tapioca starch slurry.

Enjoy

6 Just before serving, bring the soup back to the boil.

7 Ladle into warmed serving bowls, add the garnishes, sprinkle with extra pepper if desired and serve immediately.

Lẩu bò nhúng dấm

Beef dipped in vinegar hot pot

Serves 2–4

200 g (7 oz)	beef sirloin, thinly sliced

Marinade

15 g (½ oz)	garlic, minced
3 teaspoons	oyster sauce
1½ teaspoons	sesame oil
1 teaspoon	cracked black pepper

Poaching liquid

2 litres (8 cups)	water
2	lemongrass stems
20 g (¾ oz)	ginger, sliced
3	garlic cloves, peeled
3	star anise
1	cinnamon stick
240 g (8½ oz)	brown onion, sliced
280 ml (10 fl oz)	rice vinegar
1	toasted dried chilli
15 g (½ oz)	rock sugar
1½ teaspoons	sea salt
1	young coconut, juice of, keeping flesh to serve as an accompaniment (or 250 ml/1 cup unsweetened coconut juice)
1½ teaspoons	whole black peppercorns

To serve (see notes)

200 g (7 oz)	cooked beef brisket, thinly sliced
100 g (3½ oz)	beef tongue, thinly sliced
100 g (3½ oz)	cooked beef tendon
5–6	pineapple slices, skin and core removed
130 ml (4½ fl oz)	pineapple mắm nêm per person (page 40)
	fresh vegetables and noodles (see note)

Garlic and lemongrass oil

50 ml (1¾ fl oz)	vegetable oil
20 g (¾ oz)	garlic cloves, minced
15 g (½ oz)	lemongrass stems, very finely chopped

Part of the joy of this lẩu is the delicate vinegar broth, which the dấm in its name refers to. Its counterpoint is its assertive sidekick, the mắm nêm dipping sauce.

Marinate the beef sirloin

1. Combine the marinade ingredients in a bowl. Add the sirloin and mix until well coated.
2. Cover and leave to marinate in the fridge for at least 3 hours.

Prepare the poaching liquid

3. Bring the water to a simmer in a large saucepan. Add the lemongrass, ginger, garlic, star anise and cinnamon stick. Leave to simmer for at least 15–20 minutes to infuse the flavours.
4. Add the onion, vinegar, chilli, sugar and salt. Add the coconut juice to your taste – the broth should be lightly seasoned (i.e. savoury), a little watery, and sour on the front palate.

Set up the table

5. Place a portable hot pot in the centre of the table (see page 87). Set the pot of poaching liquid on the hob and bring back up to a simmer.
6. Place the marinated sirloin, plus the brisket, tongue and tendon, the pineapple slices, the flesh of the coconut and any other accompaniments around the centre pot.
7. Set out plates and/or serving bowls for each diner. Everyone should also have their own small bowl of pineapple mắm nêm dipping sauce.

Make the garlic and lemongrass oil

8. Just before serving, heat the oil in a small saucepan, add the garlic and lemongrass and fry over medium heat for a minute or two, until fragrant.
9. Drizzle the hot sizzling garlic oil into the poaching broth just before starting.

To serve

10. Cook the beef and chosen accompaniments by dipping the slices into the hot broth, and pulling them out when done to your liking (see page 87 for more on enjoying a hot pot). You can also make rice paper rolls as you go, or create a bowl of meat and vegetables – there are no strict rules here.

Note

Other accompaniments you can prepare for your lẩu include sliced wombok, mushrooms, bok choy, plantain, cucumber, leaves and herbs such as shiso, Vietnamese lettuce, coriander (cilantro), spring onion (scallion) and watercress, tofu puffs, Chinese doughnuts, rice vermicelli noodles and rice paper sheets. You can also buy a variety of frozen meats from Asian grocers for the purposes of hot pot. These will not need to be cooked in advance.

Pork + chicken cartilage sausages

Makes approximately 35 sausages

300 g ($10\frac{1}{2}$ oz)	chicken cartilage
1 tablespoon	vinegar
pinch of	salt
3 kg (6 lb 12 oz)	pork leg, coarsely minced (ground)
6 metres (19 ft 8 inches)	fresh hog casing, approximately 32 mm ($1\frac{1}{4}$ inch) in diameter (see notes)
	fresh herbs, to serve

Filling

195 g (7 oz)	lemongrass stems, very finely chopped
150 g ($5\frac{1}{2}$ oz)	spring onion (scallions), cut into 3 mm ($\frac{1}{8}$ inch) rounds
120 g ($4\frac{1}{4}$ oz)	galangal, peeled and very finely chopped
120 ml (4 fl oz)	fish sauce
80 g ($2\frac{3}{4}$ oz)	makrut lime leaves
80 g ($2\frac{3}{4}$ oz)	caster (superfine) sugar
40 g ($1\frac{1}{2}$ oz)	coarsely cracked black pepper
40 g ($1\frac{1}{2}$ oz)	sea salt
40 g ($1\frac{1}{2}$ oz)	garlic cloves, chopped

We chanced upon a variation of this sausage in Hanoi, outside Đồng Xuân Market, just before dinnertime. There were a lot of sounds and light and movement, which bordered on overwhelming for someone of J.Y.'s neurodiverse tendencies. It was also raining, which is her kryptonite. Mercifully, we followed my nose to a cart selling – among other interesting things – pork sausages smoked and cooked over woodfire, and served wrapped in mulberry leaves. We did not find out till we got back to the rental apartment that these sausages also contained chicken cartilage, which was a very nice surprise when we bit into the sausages. You now have the advantage of such knowledge.

Follow your sausage stuffing machine's instructions when it comes to stuffing and linking. Some may require another person's help. YouTube videos may also be helpful. Leaving them to dry overnight helps prevent them bursting during cooking.

Prepare the chicken cartilage

1. Wash and rinse the chicken cartilage. Place it in a saucepan with enough water to cover it, then double the amount of water. Add the vinegar and salt.
2. Bring the mixture to the boil, removing any scum that rises to the surface. Reduce the heat and simmer the cartilage for 30 minutes.
3. Drain the cartilage and rinse under cold water.
4. Transfer to a food processor and pulverise the cartilage to resemble mince (ground meat).

Mix the filling and steep overnight

5. Place the cartilage in a large bowl with all the sausage filling ingredients, combining well to ensure everything is evenly mixed. Check the seasoning by frying off a little bit of the filling, and adjust to your liking; the mixture should be herbaceous and fragrant.
6. Cover and leave the mixture in the fridge overnight to marinate.

Stuff and link the sausages

7. If the sausage casings have been preserved in salt, soak them in a bowl of cold water for about 45 minutes to release the excess salt, then rinse thoroughly inside and out.
8. Following your sausage stuffing machine's instructions, fill your casing evenly with the chilled filling. Be careful not to overfill to prevent the casing from bursting.
9. Tie off or link the sausages at regular intervals – 16–17 cm ($6\frac{1}{4}$–$6\frac{1}{2}$ inch), or about 130 g ($4\frac{1}{2}$ oz) portions. Massage the length of each stuffed casing to even out the girth.
10. Hang the linked sausages up in the fridge to dry overnight.

→

Cook and enjoy

11 Bring the sausages to room temperature before cooking.

12 See page 104 for instructions on cooking over a grill, including smoking. I always prefer to smoke the sausage for about 20 minutes before cooking over direct heat. This avoids bursting, and the smoke adds a layer of flavour complexity.

13 The sausages can also be cooked in a pan over medium heat for about 10 minutes, with no extra oil required.

14 Serve with a plate of fresh herbs.

Notes

- Hog casings in Australia are sold in approximately 10 metre (33 feet) batches. You can store the unused casings covered in salt in an airtight container in the fridge. You can buy synthetic casings, but you will need more as they are smaller in diameter.
- When stuffing your sausages, air pockets can be massaged out of the casing if caught early – squeeze the air pocket back towards the stuffer to disperse. If there are holes in your casing, cut the casing where the holes are, remove the tail end of the mix, and tie off.

Thịt heo luộc ba rọi cuốn bánh tráng

White cut pork wrapped in rice paper

Serves 8–10

1 kg (2 lb 4 oz)	pork belly

Stock

200 ml (7 fl oz)	rice wine
100 g (3½ oz)	ginger, peeled and sliced
6	spring onions (scallions), white parts only
2 tablespoons	sea salt
1.5 litres (6 cups)	water

To serve

1 head	red butter lettuce, leaves separated
1 head	green butter lettuce, leaves separated
4	snake (yardlong) beans, cut into 4 cm (1½ inch) batons
1	Lebanese (short) cucumber, cored and cut into 5 cm (2 inch) batons
1	plantain, peeled and thinly sliced
5–10	green scud chillies (optional, to taste), sliced
1 bunch	Vietnamese mint
1 bunch	fish mint
2 bunches	shiso
1 bunch	mint
1 bunch	coriander (cilantro)
500 g (1 lb 2 oz)	fresh vermicelli noodles (or 250 g / 9 oz dried noodles, prepared according to the packet instructions)
1 × 340 g (12 oz)	packet rice paper sheets

Dipping sauce

Options include tamarind base (page 38), nước chấm ớt (page 34) and/or nước chấm tương hột (page 34)

This dish is designed to be served as an interactive main, as part of cuốn. This is one of my favourite ways to throw a dinner party, as the host is freed from the shackles of laborious meal prep. Guests help pick and clean the herbs while waiting for the pork belly to cook, and everyone builds their own lettuce cups or rice paper rolls when it comes time to eat.

I like cutting the pork lengthways and a little thicker, like the central Vietnamese style.

1. Place the pork in a saucepan and cover with water. Bring to the boil, skimming off any scum that rises to the surface.
2. Remove the pork from the pan, rinsing off all the impurities from the pork and the pan.
3. Place all the stock ingredients in the clean saucepan and bring to the boil. Add the pork and simmer for 30 minutes; do not allow the stock to reduce.
4. Remove the pork and place on a flat tray lined with baking paper. Place another piece of baking paper and then another flat tray on top and weigh down. Chill the pressing pork for 3 hours before slicing thinly, against the grain.
5. Set out your wrapping ingredients, sliced pork and individual bowls of dipping sauce and allow diners to build their own wrap and roll party.

Laotian sausage

J.Y.

Thi developed an aversion to Vietnamese cuisine as a child, preferring the flavours of televised suburban Australiana to a bowl of phở or the funk of fish sauce.

Her aversion was never framed by the 'lunchbox moment': the schoolyard experience of children of immigrants shamed by peers for the surprising contents of their lunchboxes. On the contrary, Thi found a lot of joy in swapping her school lunches for equivalent treasures. By then, the demographic composition of Doonside's residents allowed for a healthy mix of Turkish, Arabic and Filipino students. These schoolyard swaps would subsequently inform a lot of Thi's palate as a chef. Instead, her aversion to Vietnamese cuisine was informed by memories of ever-mounting tension at the family dining table.

Thi had even been convinced that she was allergic to fish sauce until her teens. Thi's mother was incredulous that her child could be allergic to fish sauce. *Well, I couldn't breathe*, Thi reasoned with me, *the same way I can't breathe when I start eating shellfish*. Allergies, however, are a very European concept.

In contrast, Thi has always been open with her love for Laotian cuisine and the happier memories she associated with it, going as far as opening a restaurant, Jeow, focusing on Laotian flavours.

It was her older sister who introduced Thi to the joys of sai oua, Laotian pork sausage. After a visit to the local Laotian takeaway, Thi's older sister would give her permission to consume not just one but sometimes two chunks of garlic-flecked sai oua in the car. Thi's mum had always drummed into her the Vietnamese term ăn xong, used to describe the poor etiquette of picking at food before everyone else is served, so this furtive snack felt like true freedom. There is a simple pleasure in unknotting the loops of a plastic bag while the warm and heady aromas of garlic, charred edges and spice-tinged herbaceousness curl into the olfactory senses, ahead of consuming a snack before the drive home.

The trips to the Laotian takeaway were also a guarantee of safety and camaraderie in a presence of a trusted adult. Thi's older sister had tried to help when the intervention of all other adults yielded no results beyond Thi being treated like an outcast.

We once chanced upon a Netflix show on Chinese Yunnanese cuisine in which they were making sapie or beef salad, also known as a laap in Laotian or northern Thai parlance. The beef salad was made with the use of bile, delivered either powdered or in its prized form: a neat parcel of a gallbladder or small intestine, tied off at either end, with the liquid swilling around within.

It reminded me of eating a raw beef laap in a suburban Laotian restaurant in Melbourne that we had very gamely agreed to have served with 'bitter.' We like bitter melon, was the reasoning at the time, bitter is good. Raw beef laap with bitter was, without over-playing its inherent qualities, foul, and I can offer no further elaboration beyond that. We accepted our fallacy and very quickly reordered another plate of raw beef laap without bitter. We did not know at the time what the aforementioned bitter referred to, knowing only that it was a powder. Years on, Netflix would enlighten us that it was in fact pure bile, in powdered form, which was less prized (read: less bitter) than its pure liquid counterpart.

I had always known that there was a crossover between Yunnanese and Laotian cuisine – borders and boundaries are socially constructed but the history and heritage of the ethnic tribes remained. In this instance, the crossover can be traced to the Dai ethnic group (not to be confused with Thai nationality or Tái ethnicity) living along the shared borders. To recognise the beef salad dish as wholly Yunnanese or Laotian would be to disregard the history of the ethnic tribes that live around the shared borders.

Acknowledging regional variations of dishes allows us to recognise the core elements of the dish. This notion is best exemplified in this book with the chéo references in a few recipes (chéo mắm tôm, page 37, chẩm chéo, page 37, and chéo xanh, page 168), attributable to the cuisine of Vietnam's northwest, bordering Laos. The similarly pronounced jeow is also dominant in Laotian food vocabulary, referring also to either a wet or dry mix of combined spices and ingredients.

Vegetables

Perhaps everything seems more extreme from the perspective of a child. I remember being forced to eat bitter melon, a vegetable that, as its name suggests, is bitter. I was not allowed to leave the dining table until every last piece of bitter melon on my plate was consumed.

It was unfathomable, as a six-year-old, that I had to force such a foul vegetable, with its textural oddity and its unnerving flavour, down my gullet. The bare skin of my arms would stick to the clear plastic that wrapped the dining table as I fidgeted, a lazy fly buzzing under fluorescent light in the thick Sydney evening air. I remember very dramatically wanting to throw up every time I bit down on a slice; the pungent flavour would flood my tongue, and then my olfactory senses, until every morsel of food that followed would taste horrid. In one of my more cinematic moments, I almost choked myself: a strategic decision to avoid chewing on, and instead attempt to swallow, a piece of bitter melon was thwarted by an accompanying strand of morning glory that ended up stuck down my throat. Oddly enough, while there are no recipes in this book that explicitly call for bitter melon, the vegetable has since become my poison of choice as an adult.

The collection of recipes in this vegetable section contains predominantly recipes that would find their roots, if not their ancestral home, across East Asia and Southeast Asia. I think it is a great reminder that 'authentic' cuisine is but a concept and that we ought to pay more attention to the influences of history and geography instead.

Bánh xèo

Sizzling crêpe

Possibly one of the more complex dishes to master in the Vietnamese cook's repertoire. Bánh xèo is iconic and wields mass appeal, but preferences are highly subjective – and someone's relative always has a better version.

I do not like referring to bánh xèo as a pancake, as many do. White-washing aside, it detracts from what I think is one of the dish's key elements, when done well: a thin, crisp, almost lacy shell. The origins of this dish remain ambiguous, although the general consensus is that central Vietnam plays a role. It may have evolved from bánh khoái – smaller, deep-fried and served with a peanut and liver sauce, from the imperial kitchens of Hue. It may have been influenced by the Chams, who were early adopters of wet-grinding rice into flours; a minority thinks it might have had French influence. I align closer to another school of thought, that bánh xèo may have been influenced by southern Indian cuisine. It is stylistically closer to a dosa in its physical attributes, ingredients and methods.

Apart from the thin and crispy factor, there is no right or wrong way to make bánh xèo. In Vietnam, the size of bánh xèo gets larger as one moves further south. The dipping sauces vary regionally from the aforementioned nut and liver sauce to nước mắm bases found in the south. The accompaniments also vary, from my personal favourite mustard leaves, through to rice paper and even star fruits and figs. Equally, there is versatility when it comes to the fillings. My go-to is fresh bamboo shoots, wood ear mushrooms and garlic flowers. I do also love eating bánh xèo in spring, with a bounty of spring vegetables. It is a nice way to shake it up from the pork, prawn, mung bean or bean sprout combo that is so widely available in many Australian Vietnamese restaurants. My hot tip is not to overfill the bánh xèo and to always eat it fresh.

I remember watching Mum make bánh xèo when I was a child. What I found fascinating then – and that fascination has not diminished over the years – is that Mum always had by the stove a hunk of pork fat, greasy and sticky, ready to be run over the surface of her wok. It left just the right amount of lubrication, in a way that a calculated spoonful of oil or a spray of fat-in-a-can could never do. A lesson for anyone attempting bánh xèo at home: Mum still doesn't believe that she has mastered the craft and instead spends a good part of every year thinking about the next tweak she can introduce to yield an even crispier and more delicate shell. This recipe has been provided by Emily Hua, a Sydney-based viet kieu, who also helped cook on the photoshoot for this book.

→

'Mum always had by the stove a hunk of pork fat, greasy and sticky, ready to be run over the surface of her wok.'

Makes 8–10

Batter

200 g (7 oz) rice flour
6 tablespoons cornflour (cornstarch)
8 g (¼ oz) ground turmeric
pinch of sea salt
400 ml (14 fl oz) filtered water
300 ml (10½ fl oz) coconut cream (Kara brand)
2 tablespoons coconut oil
40 g (1½ oz) garlic chives, chopped into 1 cm (½ inch) lengths
neutral-flavoured oil, for frying

Filling

150 g (5½ oz) dried split mung beans, soaked in cold water overnight
3 tablespoons vegetable oil
400 g (14 oz) brussels sprouts, quartered
250 g (9 oz) brown onions, thinly sliced
400 g (14 oz) winged beans, thinly sliced
1 garlic clove, crushed
pinch of sea salt
300 g (10½ oz) fresh palm hearts
250 g (9 oz) bean sprouts, rinsed

To serve

2 heads lettuce, such as butter, cos (romaine) or mustard lettuce, leaves separated
2 bunches mustard leaves
1 bunch each of sorrel, mint, Vietnamese mint, fish mint and shiso, leaves picked or whole
nước chấm (page 34)

Prepare the batter

1 Place the rice flour, cornflour, turmeric and salt in a large bowl and mix until well combined.

2 Add the water, coconut cream and coconut oil and mix well to ensure there are no powdery clumps. The batter should be homogenous and thin, with a yellow tinge from the turmeric; add a little more water to loosen the batter if required.

3 Stir in the garlic chives, then set aside to rest at room temperature for at least 1 hour.

Prepare the fillings and serving garnishes

4 Steam the mung beans for about 12 minutes, until soft, then set aside.

5 In a wok, heat the vegetable oil over medium–high heat. Stir-fry the brussels sprouts, onion, winged beans and garlic with a pinch of salt, for 3–4 minutes until just cooked. Remove from the heat and set aside, along with the palm hearts and bean sprouts.

6 Arrange your leafy wrappings and herbs on a platter, laid out ready for serving, and pour the nước chấm into individual dipping bowls.

Cook the batter

8 Arrange your frying oil, batter and fillings to be easily accessible from the stove – bánh xèo happens very quickly.

9 Using your best non-stick frying pan or wok on the largest flame or highest heat, add 1 tablespoon of oil and swirl to evenly coat the pan. Discard the excess oil (a little amount of oil is fine).

9 Swirl roughly 120 ml (4 fl oz) of batter into the pan to evenly coat it. Turn down the heat and cook for 3–4 minutes. While the bánh xèo cooks, add a drizzle of oil around the edges. This will help it become crispier and pull away from the pan.

10 In the centre of one side of the bánh xèo, add a small amount of stir-fried vegetable mix, roughly 75 g (2½ oz), and roughly 50 g (1¾ oz) of bean sprouts and palm hearts.

11 Using a flat spatula, fold the bánh xèo into a half moon. Let it cook for an additional minute.

12 Gently slide it out from the wok and serve immediately.

To eat

13 Best eaten with your hands. Break off some of the bánh xèo, making sure to get some filling. Add it to a lettuce leaf along with your choice of herbs, roll it up, then dip into your nước chấm. The idea is to master the art of wrapping because the bánh xèo will disappear fast!

Note

Resist the temptation to overfill your bánh xèo with vegetables; it will just make the bánh xèo sloppy. Work on the volume of batter that needs to go into your particular pan – practice makes perfect.

Nấm rừng nướng với mỡ hành

Grilled wild mushrooms + spring onion oil

Serves 3–4 as part of a larger meal

6	pine mushrooms (saffron milk caps)
15 g (½ oz)	unsalted butter
pinch of	sea salt
30 ml (1 fl oz)	spring onion oil (page 44)
25 g (1 oz)	roasted peanuts, lightly crushed

The perfect vessel for spring onion oil, as mushrooms soak up flavour. I have used pine mushrooms (saffron milk caps) in this recipe. Field mushrooms or lion's manes make fantastic substitutes.

1. Clean the mushrooms by brushing any debris off them, being careful not to damage the gills. Wipe off any persistent dirt with paper towel.
2. Melt the butter in a small pot and set aside.
3. Heat a chargrill pan over medium–high and place the mushrooms onto the grill. As they grill, lightly brush them with melted butter and season with a pinch of salt.
4. Cook for 2–3 minutes on each side, until the mushrooms slightly caramelise.
5. Transfer the mushrooms to a large serving plate and drizzle with the spring onion oil. Garnish with the nuts for texture and serve.

SPRING 'O

Ăn cuốn, the wrappy guy

Thi

Mum has always nurtured a garden: shiso, mint, Vietnamese mint and fish mint, rice paddy herb, assorted varieties of lettuce. She often frolics around the backyard in her dressing gown in the mid-afternoon sun, pruning and cutting herbs or other random bits she has grown, or giving them a quick spray from the garden hose. There is a familiar and immersive earthiness that hits the olfactory passage when Mum is in the garden – the air takes on a herbaceous quality, rounded by the sweet richness of turned dirt. What science calls petrichor, to describe the smell of rain, I associate with Mum in the garden.

I ate a lot of cuốn growing up; it's such a quintessential component of the Vietnamese diet, with leaves, herbs, the matriarch's choice of protein, potentially rice paper, and her mix of nước chấm. There is a Vietnamese term, râu thơm, which translates to 'fragrant herbs.' It is where this phrase, repeated across Asian-ish menus, hails from. Mum's cuốn is always composed of herbs and vegetables from her garden.

I spent three sweltering weeks in Singapore, Chiang Mai, Da Nang and Ho Chi Minh in mid 2023, both for work and leisure. As a chef – and hospitality workers around the world could possibly relate to this – my line of work often leaves me malnourished, either underfed or overfed. In this instance overseas, my hosts in Singapore ensured I was well fed, including visiting Singapore's famed hawker halls. Delicious as the hawker food was, I struggled with the carbohydrate- and protein-heavy nature of the dishes. I realised just how much I missed fresh vegetables and herbs. Not just as a garnish or an afterthought, but as a star of the dish.

It was not the first time that I had reflected on the dietary habits I had grown up with and how they contrasted with that of other nations and cultures, particularly the islands of Southeast Asia. Raw vegetables have never been a star there, perhaps because of water quality. Send a plate of raw herbs and lettuce to those customers as part of a cuốn plate and the green matter inevitably comes back to the kitchen untouched and goes straight into the organics bin. My best friend in my young adult years, Filipino in heritage and upbringing, often derided the 'rabbit food,' though he would later learn to appreciate their fresh companionship on a plate.

I found myself thinking about Mum and her garden increasingly on this trip. I would not have characterised the feeling as homesickness; it was probably more accurately a craving. I just wanted to bite into a cuốn, held together by a cool, fresh crispy outer, and bound internally by the cumin-citrus notes of perilla, the pungent leafiness of Vietnamese mint.

Some of my fondest food memories as an adult revolve around cuốn meals at Mum's dining table. I do not know how she does it so effortlessly, but all her herbs and vegetables seem to grow perfectly, without any blemishes or insect attacks. The result is a mound of fresh produce in plastic baskets on the dining table, ready to be transformed into a complete and uncomplicated meal. These are the moments that I treasure as a chef, and even more as a daughter.

+

For a long time, my relationship with my mother could be best described as tortured. It was a relationship formed in blood but moulded by anger. It has always been so hard for me to bring up the topic of our past, my childhood and what we endured as a family. I have so many questions, but it has never been clear how I could start asking them. Sometimes I wonder whether I have managed to work through my problems, other times I wonder whether I have just shut them out.

Regardless, all that burden is often put aside over a meal where Mum and I connect over the nuances of Vietnamese cuisine or the merits of growing a plant for its medicinal benefits. Deep down, I know she also hurts, and a shared meal is her way of showing her love and saying, *I am sorry*. It reminds me that I am in a good place, a safe place.

I love how we eat in my family – always fresh and flavourful, simple and with abundance. This memory guided my approach to cooking when we opened Anchovy. To that end, one of the hallmarks of the menu has always been a main served with leaves and herbs to wrap. *The wrappy guy* or *the leafy guy*, as we were prone to refer to it colloquially, or *the herb garden*. Frilly butter lettuce cups with their magenta-tinged edges, pickles in a riot of marigold-yellow flecked with mustard seeds, flamingo-pink and olive-green, and fresh herbs available through the market – garden mint, Vietnamese mint, perilla, coriander, the odd rice paddy herb, betel leaves or fish mint when the Melbourne weather deemed them affordable. A feast for the eyes and the soul.

×

Recipes featuring cuốn	
Cá mòi sống và gỏi dừa (sardines and coconut salad)	page 120
Bì cuốn bánh tráng (pork skin rice paper rolls)	page 167
Bánh hỏi và heo quay (pressed vermicelli with suckling pork)	page 174
Thịt heo luộc ba rọi cuốn bánh tráng (white cut pork wrapped in rice paper)	page 196
Nem rán (deep-fried spring rolls)	page 218
Bánh khọt (rice cakes with turmeric)	page 246

Grilled asparagus with fermented bean curd + Chinese black olives

Serves 3–4 as part of a larger meal

300 g ($10\frac{1}{2}$ oz)	medium-sized asparagus, trimmed
50 ml ($1\frac{3}{4}$ fl oz)	sweet ginger dressing (page 42)
1 tablespoon	roughly chopped dill
1 tablespoon	roughly chopped mint

Bean curd mayonnaise

2 tablespoons	mayonnaise
2 cubes	fermented bean curd (page 68), mashed
2 teaspoons	black olive and mustard green paste (Pengsheng brand preferred), finely chopped

This dish came about as spring was around the corner, and I was obsessed with the idea of using the fantastically delicious in-season zucchini as the star of a dish. I just was not sure how. I tried them steamed. Boiled. Raw. Oven baked. Grilled.

After one long day at the restaurant with no progress on new menu ideas, we went home, quite dejected, with two zucchini. Our fridge at home is the fridge of a busy household - often empty save for old faithful condiments that can always feed the hungry with little effort for maximum flavour. That night, we discovered that pan-fried zucchini was a great vessel for the creaminess of fermented bean curd and the earthy-rich oiliness of Chinese black olives. The dish was slightly heavy and unbalanced, but that was not a problem to be resolved at 2 am.

The next day in the kitchen, I added some ginger dressing, containing a natural sweetness and acid that lightened the combination. Finally, a little mint provided a fresh counterpoint to the salinity of the other ingredients.

I have subbed in asparagus as an equally delightful alternative here, but any spring vegetable would work.

The black olive and mustard green paste is a condiment used in Chinese cookery. The brand that is used here is Pengsheng from Hong Kong.

1. Heat a chargrill pan or barbecue (see page 104) to high heat. Meanwhile, mix together the ingredients for the bean curd mayonnaise.
2. Grill the asparagus until charred and tender, about 2–3 minutes, turning occasionally.
3. Transfer to a bowl and allow to cool briefly, then add the bean curd mayonnaise and the ginger dressing and toss until the asparagus is nicely coated.
4. Mix the herbs through and serve immediately.

Canh rau xanh

Leafy green soup

Serves 3–4 as part of a larger meal

½	garlic bulb, peeled
6–10	dried prawns (page 54)
1 litre (4 cups)	water
400 g (14 oz)	young mustard greens, washed well, cut into thirds (including the ribs)
1 teaspoon	cracked white pepper
2 tablespoons	fish sauce or soy sauce (optional, to taste)
2 pinches	fried shallots (page 71)

Leafy green soups were something my mother served on high rotation. They were also something my younger self associated with the gag reflex and incessant dining-table lecturing on the health benefits and curing properties of a bowl of liquid chlorophyll. I would have much preferred the all-Australian staple of a devon and tomato sauce sandwich.

I cannot remember the last time I ate a devon and tomato sauce sandwich and enjoyed it. I can, however, pinpoint the last time I consumed and thoroughly enjoyed a bowl of mustard green soup. It was simple and soulful, and it reminded me of Mum.

Any leafy green – tatsoi, bok choy, wombok – can be used as a substitute.

1. Lightly roast the garlic over an open flame for 6–8 minutes, or until tender. (If you do not have a gas flame, cook in a lightly oiled pan, cut side down, over medium heat for 5–8 minutes.) Leave until cool enough to handle.
2. Squeeze the roasted garlic from its skin into a large saucepan. Add the dried prawns and water and bring to the boil, skimming off any scum that rises to the surface.
3. Add the mustard greens and pepper, skimming again if needed. Simmer for 4–6 minutes, until the mustard greens are tender, but still vibrant green in colour. Season to taste with fish sauce or soy sauce, if needed.
4. Ladle into serving bowl, garnish with fried shallots and enjoy as part of a meal, or a nourishing soup for breakfast.

Dưa xào tỏi

Stir-fried choko with garlic

Serves 2–3 as part of a larger meal

300 g (10½ oz)	choko (chayote/ mirliton squash)
25 ml (¾ fl oz)	vegetable oil
2–3	garlic cloves, minced
pinch of	salt
pinch of	cracked white pepper
1½ teaspoons	fish sauce
2	spring onions (scallions), cut into 3 cm (1¼ inch) batons
	coriander (cilantro), to garnish

I have used choko in this recipe although any gourd or summer squash would be a suitable substitute. My favourite variation is young tromboncino when summer is breaking and the tromboncino vines in my garden have been very productive.

1. Peel the choko. Cut into 2 cm (¾ inch) rounds, then in half again, into half-moons. Set aside.
2. Heat the oil in a frying pan over medium heat. Sauté the garlic for a minute or two, until fragrant.
3. Add the choko and stir-fry for 4–5 minutes; you may need to add a splash of water to help it cook.
4. Season with the salt, pepper and fish sauce. Add the spring onion and stir-fry for a further 1 minute.
5. Transfer to a plate, garnish with coriander and serve.

Củ cải kho quẹt
Caramelised daikon

Serves 2–3 as part of a larger meal

300 g (10½ oz)	daikon (white radish)
15 ml (½ fl oz)	vegetable oil
1	red Asian shallot, minced
4	garlic cloves, chopped
1 tablespoon	raw sugar
225 ml (7½ fl oz)	young coconut juice (or unsweetened coconut juice)
1 tablespoon	fish sauce
1 teaspoon	Vietnamese caramel (nước màu; optional)
1 teaspoon	cracked black pepper

To serve

¼ teaspoon	cracked black pepper
2	spring onions (scallions), sliced
50 g (1¾ oz)	fresh young coconut meat, chopped
2–3	green scud chillies (optional), sliced

Stylistically, thịt kho tàu is distinct from thịt kho quẹt. The authenticity police appear to treat these inconsistencies (differences) as one and the same, with a cursory search online yielding a cacophony of recipes, degrees of caramelisation and variations in name. The one thing that everyone appears to have agreed on is the use of pork belly. Thịt kho tàu refers to the variation with a coconut-juice sauce and often includes boiled eggs, while thịt kho quẹt refers to the caramelised and often peppery version. I use daikon in place of pork belly for this version.

1. Peel the daikon, discarding the top. Cut the flesh into bite-sized chunks and set aside.
2. Heat a clay pot over medium heat. (A clay pot yields better flavour, but you can also use a heavy-based saucepan here.) Add the oil, shallot, garlic and sugar and cook for 6–8 minutes, until the sugar starts to caramelise.
3. Stir in the coconut juice to deglaze the pan.
4. Add the daikon and bring to the boil, skimming off any scum that rises to the surface.
5. Stir in the fish sauce, Vietnamese caramel and black pepper. Reduce the heat, then cover and gently simmer for 10–15 minutes, until the sauce absorbs into the daikon; I like my daikon quite soft.
6. Remove from the heat and serve in the clay pot, topped with black pepper, spring onion, coconut and chilli, if using. Best enjoyed with a bowl of rice.

An ode to nem rán

Thi

This deep-fried cylindrical item easily transcends borders, social classes, ethnicities and regions. It is acceptable at any time of the day: breakfast, lunch, dinner or a midday snack. It often starts your meal and yet would not be out of place as an addendum to the main course, and its versatility also finds it settled happily on dessert menus. If finger food had an Olympics, then this dish would win gold. It does not discriminate, it is gluten free, and it packs a punch.

Chinese trade and migration led to the spring roll's production across Southeast Asia, with varying fillings and dipping sauces and mostly with wheat-based wrappers – known as lumpia in Indonesia and the Philippines, its diminutive sumpia, and its namesake chun juen (literally: spring rolls) among the Southeast Asian diaspora. The latter's migration to Australia seeded the inspiration for the Chiko Roll, an icon of milk-bar Australiana.

In Vietnam, where rice is a staple, rice-based wrappers replace the wheat to create chả giò in the south and nem rán in the north, usually paired with a fish sauce–based dipping sauce. Nem rán then migrated to west Africa as a result of cross-cultural marriages between Vietnamese women and Senegalese riflemen drafted into the French-Indochina War. It is known as its northern Vietnamese diminutive nem in Senegal.

Each component and step in the nem rán production plays such an important role: the type and quality of wrapper employed, the rolling, the frying technique and even the quality of oil used. Do not let that scare you, however, because any deep-fried, crunchy item will generally find its way into the good books of most people.

I savoured very delicate versions of nem rán in Hanoi, accompanying bowls of bún chả procured from a street-side vendor and her roiling pot of hot fat: layers of deep-fried rice paper that shatter to release a curl of steam. It prompted me to consider the types of rice paper used.

Rice paper in the Australian market varies predominantly in composition – all rice, mainly rice with a little tapioca, and mainly tapioca. Aside from adding a springy and toothsome quality, tapioca starch brings the added benefit of stretch and resistance, which is always a welcome aid to the less-practised hand.

When making this recipe, look for rice paper designated for frying; the packaging will note as such. They are often substantially more delicate than their counterparts that require a pass through water. This delicate style reigns supreme because the deep-frying process is optimised where there are minimal liquids available to vaporise.

The astute reader would have noticed that I have not mentioned the filling, dipping sauce or any accompaniments in assessing the thrill of nem rán. The former is subjective and profoundly personal. The latter two are entirely optional in some cases: the sauce often has regional variations and is sometimes replaced altogether by a sweet chilli sauce, while the accompaniments of herbs and leaves are characteristic of southern Vietnamese cuisine. Optional as they are, the sensation yielded by a hot morsel of nem rán against the cool foil of crisp lettuce and chased by a savoury-sweet acid lick of nước mắm is an experience to relive time and time again.

Nem rán

Deep-fried spring rolls

Makes about 40

4 litres (135 fl oz)	vegetable oil, for deep frying
2 × 250 g (9 oz)	packets extra-thin rice paper sheets
	nước chấm, to serve; I like the Hanoi-style one on page 35 as it is less sweet, but you do you

Filling

30 g (1 oz)	dried shiitake mushrooms
100 g (3½ oz)	glass noodles
300 g (10½ oz)	taro, peeled and finely shredded
270 g (9½ oz)	carrots
270 g (9½ oz)	jicama
270 g (9½ oz)	daikon (white radish)
70 g (2½ oz)	spring onions (scallions), cut into thin rounds
80 g (2¾ oz)	fresh wood ear mushrooms, julienned, or 20 g (¾ oz) dried wood ear mushrooms
50 g (1¾ oz)	fried shallots (page 71)
10 g (¼ oz)	sea salt (plus extra for salting the grated vegetables)
30 g (1 oz)	black peppercorns, toasted (see page 268) and coarsely cracked
15 g (½ oz)	sugar
2	eggs, whisked

Maltose glaze (nước hàng)

10 g (¼ oz)	maltose syrup
100 ml (3½ fl oz)	hot water
100 ml (3½ fl oz)	cold water

I have struggled to find nem rán close to the ones I have had in Hanoi in any local Vietnamese restaurant here in Australia. I really want to replicate and master this dish, to make it my go-to for every family or social event.

I have included a recipe and steps for nước hàng. It translates directly as a caramel but it functions more closely to a maltose lacquer, which is used for glazing such things as the skin of a suckling pig to achieve superior crackles, and achieves the same result here.

Please note that air fryers are unsuitable for deep-frying nem rán from scratch. One could coat the rolls with neutral oil before following the instructions listed on the box, but that would detract from the masterclass in texture struck between a crisp exterior and a tender interior. I stand by the time-tested technique of deep-frying.

Prepare the filling

1. Place the dried shiitake mushrooms (and dried wood ear mushrooms, if using instead of fresh) in a bowl and cover with boiling water. Leave to rehydrate for 15 minutes, then drain and finely shred. Meanwhile, soak the glass noodles in cool water for about 20 minutes, until rehydrated, then cut into 5 cm (2 inch) lengths. Place them in a large mixing bowl with the rehydrated mushrooms and set aside.
2. Heat the oil in a deep-fryer or large saucepan to 180°C (350°F). Deep-fry the taro in batches for 3–5 minutes, until golden. Leave to drain and cool, reserving the oil for deep-frying the spring rolls.
3. Peel the carrots, jicama and daikon, then coarsely grate them. Place in a colander, sprinkle with a little salt and leave to drain for about 15 minutes. Using your hands, squeeze out as much water as possible.
4. Add the grated root vegetables and cooled taro to the bowl with the glass noodles. Add the remaining filling ingredients, including fresh wood ear mushrooms if using, and mix together. Check the seasoning and adjust to your taste. The mixture should not be overly seasoned – you should be able to taste the vegetables on your front palate and not the salt. Remember you will also have some dipping sauce on the side.

Make the maltose glaze

5. In a bowl, mix the maltose syrup and hot water together until diluted, then stir in the cold water and set aside.

Make the rolls

6. Place two sheets of rice paper together on a flat surface and lightly brush the top and underside with the maltose syrup.
7. Place about 2 teaspoons of the filling on the bottom half of the rice paper stack. Fold in the sides, then roll up tightly, forming a tight roll.

→

8 Repeat with the remaining filling, laying the rolls separately on a flat surface to dry for about 1 hour, until the maltose glaze has dried completely.

Deep-fry the rolls

9 Reheat the frying oil used for the taro to 165°C (330°F).

10 Deep-fry the rolls in batches for 6 minutes; you should not be expecting colour on your rolls at this stage. Set aside to drain on a wire rack until needed; you can leave them for up to 2–3 hours, or they can also be frozen at this point.

To serve

11 Just before serving, deep-fry the rolls again at 190°C (375°F) for 4–5 minutes, until golden brown. Drain briefly and serve hot, with nước chấm.

Đậu hũ sốt cà chua
Tofu + tomato

Serves 2–3 as part of a larger meal

400 g (14 oz)	tofu, cut into 3 × 5 cm (1¼ × 2 inch) chunks
1 litre (4 cups)	vegetable oil, for frying
2 tablespoons	olive oil
1	red Asian shallot, sliced
2	garlic cloves, minced
2 large	fresh red tomatoes, cut into wedges (do not use tinned ones)
50 ml (1¾ fl oz)	water or vegetable stock
1 tablespoon	soy sauce (Megachef brand preferred)
1 tablespoon	mushroom sauce (Megachef brand preferred)
½ teaspoon	raw sugar
½ teaspoon	cracked white pepper
40 g (1½ oz)	spring onions (scallions), cut into batons
3 tablespoons	chopped coriander (cilantro)

A simple dish that makes for a quick mid-week dinner or, in my case, a quick breakfast that can sustain me till we sit down for family meal in the restaurant at 4 pm. It is also a dish that transcends borders – I have seen it listed as part of a Chinese repertoire, and there are Southeast Asian variations with egg.

I like this dish on the saucier side so that I can spoon it over hot rice. I like using good-quality first-press olive oil to give the delicate flavours an added fruity zhush. I love making it when tomato season is in full swing, when the dish has potential to taste like sunshine and blue skies.

I have not used fish sauce in this instance. Fun fact: Mum considers fish sauce to be vegetarian because it does not contain any fish meat. I have used Megachef Soy Sauce and Megachef Premium Mushroom Sauce instead. Resist the urge to over-season this dish. The tomatoes should still be the life of this savoury party, not the soy.

1. Remove the moisture from the tofu by wrapping it in muslin (cheesecloth), placing it on a wire rack and gently weighing it down with a small plate for about 1 hour. (You can also use paper towels or tea/dish towels, whichever works for you.)
2. Cut the tofu into thick slices, measuring about 5 × 15 cm (⅝ × 2 inches).
3. Heat the vegetable oil in a large saucepan or wok to 180°C (350°F). Deep-fry the tofu in batches for 2–3 minutes, until golden brown, then set aside.
4. Heat the olive oil in a frying pan over medium heat. Sauté the shallot and garlic for 1–2 minutes, until translucent and fragrant.
5. Add the tomatoes and fried tofu and cook for 6–8 minutes, until the tomatoes have softened, adding the water to help cook down the tomatoes.
6. Add the soy sauce, mushroom sauce, sugar and white pepper. Stir well to combine, then simmer for 4–5 minutes, until the flavours meld together. Adjust the seasoning to your taste.
7. Toss the spring onion through just before serving.
8. Transfer to a plate and garnish with chopped coriander. Finish with good-quality olive oil and enjoy with hot rice, as part of a larger meal.

Note

If you can source fried tofu from your local Asian grocer, you won't need to deep-fry it. Also, instead of deep-frying the tofu, you can use an air fryer.

Đậu pháp xào với trứng vịt muối

Stir-fried green beans with salted duck egg

Serves 2–3 as part of a larger meal

300 g (10½ oz)	green beans
75 ml (2½ fl oz)	vegetable oil
1	red Asian shallot, sliced
2–3	garlic cloves, minced
1	salted duck egg, peeled and mashed
½ teaspoon	cracked white pepper

To serve

	fish sauce
	sliced fresh chilli

Salted duck egg snacks have been very on-trend over the past few years. This recipe is infinitely healthier. The duck eggs lend a richer, creamier and saline dimension to this dish that fish sauce and soy alone cannot achieve. If you do not have access to duck eggs from happy ducks, store-bought salted duck eggs are a nifty substitute – not to be confused with preserved duck eggs.

1. Top and tail the green beans and cut them in half on an angle. Rinse under cold running water and set aside to drain in a colander.
2. Heat the oil in a frying pan over medium heat. Sauté the shallot and garlic for about 2–3 minutes, until fragrant.
3. Add the green beans and stir-fry for 3–4 minutes, until just tender; you may need to add a splash of water to help them cook.
4. When the beans are done, add the salted duck egg and continue to cook for another 3–4 minutes, until hot.
5. Season with the pepper, transfer to a plate and serve with fish sauce and chilli.

white pot: pork + taro soup (page 191)
wok: stir-fried green beans with salted duck egg
green bowl: tofu + tomato (page 220)
white dish: stir-fried choko with garlic (page 214)

Canh khoai mỡ
Purple yam soup

Serves 2–4 as part of a larger meal

2 tablespoons	vegetable oil
130 g (4½ oz)	king brown (king oyster) mushrooms, cut into chunks
1	red Asian shallot, minced
1	garlic clove, minced
500 ml (2 cups)	vegetable stock or water
500 g (1 lb 2 oz)	purple yams, peeled and grated
1 tablespoon	vegetarian fish sauce
1 teaspoon	cracked white pepper
½ teaspoon	raw sugar (optional)

To serve

1 bunch	sawtooth coriander (culantro), leaves julienned
½ bunch	rice paddy herb, leaves picked

This soup is thick and luscious if prepared correctly, or adhesive and viscous if everything goes wrong. It is purple yam's inherent mucilaginous (read: slimy) quality that really makes this soup; other root vegetables, such as sweet potato, are poor substitutes. Vegetarian fish sauce has been used in this recipe, although the dish is historically paired with seafood, and any seafood-based flavour enhancers, such as dried prawns, would find themselves very much at home here. Frozen purple yam works well as a substitute.

1. Heat 1 tablespoon of the oil in a heavy-based saucepan. Add the mushrooms and fry over medium heat for about 5 minutes, until caramelised. Remove from the pan and set aside.
2. Add the remaining oil to the pan if needed and fry the shallot and garlic for 3–4 minutes, until fragrant. Stir in the vegetable stock to deglaze the pan.
3. Add the yam and bring to the boil, skimming off any scum that rises to the surface. Reduce the heat to a gentle simmer, then cover and cook for about 10 minutes, or until the yam is soft. If the mixture becomes too thick, stir in a little more stock or water.
4. Season with the fish sauce, pepper and sugar, adjusting the flavours to suit your taste.
5. Return the mushrooms to the pan and cook for a further 5 minutes, or until the mushrooms are hot again.
6. Ladle the soup into serving bowls, sprinkle with sawtooth coriander and rice paddy herb, and serve.

terracotta pot: leafy green soup (page 214)
blue bowl: purple yam soup
yellow plate: acacia omelette (page 228)
claypot: caramelised daikon (page 215)
pink and green plates: shrimp sauce (page 37) with some steamed veg

Gỏi bưởi va củ hư dừa

Pomelo + palm heart gỏi

Serves 2–3 as part of a larger meal

200 g (7 oz)	pomelo
60 g (2¼ oz)	fresh palm heart (see note)
1	red Asian shallot, thinly sliced
40 g (1½ oz)	mắm tép vinaigrette (page 32)
20 g (¾ oz)	mixed sawtooth coriander (culantro), mint and Vietnamese mint leaves

To serve

fried shallots (page 71)
roasted peanuts
dried prawns (optional, page 54)
prawn crackers (page 60)

Another gỏi that is no less alluring than the prawn and papaya version on page 114. To establish a great gỏi, look for textural variety and pops of flavour, steering clear of palate fatigue – of which the dressing is often a culprit.

1. Peel the pomelo and break it into bite-sized segments. Remove any seeds and separate the segments. Place in a large mixing bowl.
2. Peel off the outer layers of the palm heart, until you reach the tender centre. Cut the palm heart in half horizontally, then into thin half-moons.
3. Add the palm heart to the mixing bowl, along with the shallots and lightly dress with the mắm tép vinaigrette. The vegetables should be lightly coated. They shouldn't look limp and lifeless, or as if they are swimming in a pool.
4. Check the seasoning by adding more vinaigrette if required. Once you are happy with the flavour, add the herbs and lightly toss.
5. Transfer to a serving plate, garnish with fried shallots, roasted peanuts and dried prawns, if using. Serve immediately, with prawn crackers.

Note

If fresh palm hearts aren't available, you can use tinned ones. Pick a brand with a lower sodium content, and be sure to drain them thoroughly, then cut them into slightly larger chunks to help them retain their structural integrity, as tinned palm hearts are much softer in texture than fresh ones.

Rau thối với rau hấp

Acacia omelette + steamed vegetables

Serves 3–4 as part of a larger meal

200 g (7 oz)	okra, kept whole
1	hispi cabbage (savoy cabbage or wombok would also work), cut into wedges
1 bunch	broccolini (tenderstem broccoli), cut lengthways into largepieces
100 g (3½ oz)	young gai lan (Chinese broccoli), cut lengthways into large pieces
4	eggs
115 g (4 oz)	cha-om, stems discarded, fronds picked and roughly chopped
1¼ teaspoons	fish sauce
1¼ teaspoon	cracked white pepper
50 ml (1¾ fl oz)	vegetable oil
100 g (3½ oz)	chẻo mãm tôm (page 37)
	steamed rice, to serve (optional)

An easy joy of living in Australia, particularly in the major hubs, is the ready access to produce typically used in Southeast Asian cookery. However, that access can occasionally correlate with its own set of problems. The plant known as *Senegalia pennata* or cha-om, which is native to and widely used in the Indochinese regions, is an invasive bio-security risk in Australia, particularly in Queensland and New South Wales, where it competes with our native plants.

The Vietnamese charmingly refer to this acacia as rau thối, the smelly vegetable. It has historically been cultivated by the Khơ Mú and Tái ethnic groups, who move along the shared borders of northern Vietnam and Laos. It is also in this north-western region of Vietnam where chẩm chéo dip originates (see page 37). More accurately, chẩm chéo can be attributed to the Black Tái ethnic group whose geographical distribution spread includes parts of Yunnan (China), north-west Vietnam, Laos and Thailand. It should come as no surprise then that the Laotian jeow shares the same DNA.

The plant's use in this recipe, cooked with eggs, aligns more closely with a popular Thai or Burmese dish, cha-om omelette. Rau thối or cha-om can often be found frozen in Thai grocers, although I have chanced upon it fresh in Vietnamese grocers in Melbourne. The dish is simple but addictively pungent. The omelette can be consumed separately with rice, but I like channelling bagna càuda vibes and serving it together with a variety of steamed vegetables alongside chẻo mắm tôm (page 37) to dip.

Steam the vegetables

1 In a steamer over high heat, steam the okra, cabbage, broccolini and gai lan, in batches if necessary, for 5–6 minutes, or until tender, then remove from the steamer. (I like my vegetables just cooked, but my mother will cook the bejesus out of her vegetables until grey and declare them perfect.)

Make the omelette

2 Whisk the eggs in a large bowl. Add the cha-om and mix until the leaves are evenly distributed through the mixture. Season with fish sauce and pepper to taste.

3 Heat the oil in a non-stick frying pan over medium heat. Once the oil is hot, pour the egg mixture into the pan, spreading it out evenly to form a thin layer. Cook for 2–3 minutes, or until the bottom is golden brown and the edges start to set.

4 Using a spatula, carefully flip the omelette over and cook for a further 2–3 minutes on the other side, or until fully cooked through and golden brown.

To serve

5 Transfer the omelette to a serving plate. Cut into slices and serve hot with the steamed vegetables and chẻo mắm tôm, and with steamed rice for a larger meal.

Cà pháo
Pickled apple eggplant

Makes 2.1 kg (4 lb 10 oz)

50 g (1¾ fl oz)	shrimp paste; use a drier one such as belacan, rather than mắm tôm bắc, which is much wetter
2 kg (4 lb 8 oz)	Thai or apple eggplants (see note)

Salted lemon water

2 litres (8 cups)	cool water
1 tablespoon	sea salt
1	lemon, halved and juiced

Spice paste

300 g (10½ oz)	ginger, peeled and roughly chopped
300 g (10½ oz)	garlic cloves, peeled
20	red bird's eye chillies, stems removed
300 ml (10½ fl oz)	fish sauce
300 g (10½ oz)	sugar
60 g (2¼ oz)	salt
2 tablespoons	fermented chilli paste

You know you have hit the sweet spot with this pickle if all you can think about is fishing another cà pháo into your mouth to savour its intensity all over again. Like a sassy drag queen who is high on the adrenaline of dancing all night, it should be spicy, pungent and salty, with the slightest hint of sweetness if you search hard enough.

You can start using the pickle after a month, but the flavour starts to develop and go tangy after 3–4 months depending on the season. A great accompaniment to a meal – with rice and acacia omelette (opposite) or as part of a cuốn platter (see page 211).

1 Preheat the oven to 180°C (350°F). Wrap the shrimp paste loosely in foil, then bake for 15 minutes. Roasting the shrimp paste helps to dry the block and break it up, and also intensifies and concentrates the flavour by removing moisture from it. (You can also roast your shrimp paste in a pan, but do watch it closely.) Set aside.

2 Meanwhile, combine the salted lemon water ingredients (including the lemon shells) in a large bowl. Wash and trim the eggplants, then soak them for 1 hour in the salted lemon water to help remove the bitterness.

3 In a food processor, blend all the spice paste ingredients into a coarse paste.

4 Drain the eggplants and place in a large bowl. Add the spice paste and crumbled shrimp paste, mixing them through the eggplants.

5 Layer the mixture into a sterilised fermenting crockpot, ensuring that your eggplants are properly submerged in their own juices. (You can also use glass jars, but be sure to keep them in a dark place, otherwise light will discolour the eggplant. In a commercial setting, I use vacuum-sealed bags.)

6 Leave to pickle for 1 month. You can leave it longer, but the flavour starts to develop and turn tangy after 3–4 months, with warm weather hastening the fermentation process.

Note

Thai or apple eggplants are green in colour and are available at Asian grocers. They are very different to purple eggplant (aubergine).

Dậu phộng luộc
Boiled peanuts

Makes 2 takeaway containers

600 g (1 lb 5 oz)	raw peanuts, in their shells

Brine

80 g (2¾ oz)	lemongrass, cut into 5 cm (2 inch) lengths
4–5	star anise
1	cassia bark stick
2	fresh bay leaves
1	whole dried red chilli (optional)
30 g (1 oz)	rock sugar (optional)
25 g (1 oz)	sea salt
2.5 litres (85 fl oz)	water

A perfect accompaniment to a bottle of beer or a salted lime soda on a hot day. As a snack, boiled peanuts are as Vietnamese as they are African or Chinese or South American, which is to say they transcend borders and cultures. Boiled peanuts served in newspaper cones were a ubiquitous snack in Cabramatta while I was growing up, although they are impossible to find these days. Someone online suggested a Viet-Cajun peanut variation (see page 92 for more Viet-Cajun flavours). Perhaps that is one way to add a truly viet kieu dimension to this snack.

1. Rinse the raw peanuts under cold running water to remove any dirt or debris and place in a colander to drain.
2. Place all the brine ingredients in a large saucepan and bring to the boil. Add the peanuts and bring back to the boil. Reduce the heat and simmer gently with the lid on, skimming off any scum that rises to the surface.
3. Allow the peanuts to simmer for 2–3 hours, or until they reach your desired level of tenderness.
4. Once the peanuts are cooked, remove the pan from the heat and leave the peanuts to continue steeping in the brine overnight, for extra flavour.
5. The next day, remove the peanuts from the brine and store in an airtight container in the fridge, where they'll keep for up to a week. (To store the brine, bring it back to the boil for at least 5 minutes, then leave to cool in a clean container. It will keep in the fridge for up to 3 weeks and can be used to cook up another batch of peanuts.)
6. Serve the boiled peanuts warm or at room temperature, shelling them just before eating. You can warm the peanuts by re-boiling them in their own brine, or steaming them. For me, there is nothing like warm peanuts.

Accidental restaurateurs

J.Y.

I remember walking into what would become Anchovy's dining room after we first picked up the keys for the leasehold, and Thi asking me what I thought the dining room should look like. I drew a blank. I had never really considered what the restaurant we had planned to open would *look* like – perhaps with some tables and chairs? Having spent the preceding decade buried in academic papers, I would have been better equipped if she had asked me whether we ought to express our future sales figures in the form of a line chart or a bar chart. Thankfully, Thi started to draw her arms around some imaginary axis of the room, describing where she thought the bar and the waiter's station ought to be, saving me from offering a semi-coherent response that might pass as restaurateur speak.

Looking back, we were not prepared to embark on the whirlwind journey of Anchovy. The restaurant started as a manifesto with simple goals: to showcase Vietnamese cuisine and its foundations within an Australian context – produce, service, hospitality. It was an idea that had not yet fully developed when we signed the lease to take over a non-descript shopfront on Bridge Road in inner Melbourne's Richmond back in 2015. The intent was formed only in broad strokes – Thi felt like she could do better, *she had to do better*, than the glut of poorly executed Vietnamese or Southeast Asian–leaning restaurants that were popping up in Melbourne. Vietnamese cuisine was bedded in a culture that went back across dynasties, yet the average consumer in Australia was familiar with the largely French colonial street eats and locally brewed beer of backpacker trips to Ho Chi Minh, or the ambitiously large menus of (admittedly delicious) suburban Australian eateries.

In our early years as a couple, we spent the very little time we had together dining out. Throughout, Thi continued to lament the quality and reputation of Southeast Asian restaurants opening in Melbourne. It was not that they were not good, more so that they lacked what Thi considered the soul that made Southeast Asian cookery. It was as if Thi felt a responsibility to control the rhetoric of modern Vietnamese cuisine.

After some discussion of the restaurant idea, we spent a few months attending commercial property viewings and assessing them like one would assess a residential rental property – *That cupboard is missing a door*; *This is a big kitchen; Oh, there's car parking*. The shopfront on Bridge Road was our first real attempt at negotiating a lease. Thi was still considering other locations after we'd signed a five-year lease. We had, dare I say, accidentally started down path of restaurant ownership.

'Thi had been determined to attach a Vietnamese name to the business. The words ăn chơi or "to eat for fun" were ingrained in her mind. A playful side-step took us to Anchovy.'

The name Anchovy came a few weeks later. Thi had been determined to attach a Vietnamese name to the business. The words ăn chơi or 'to eat for fun' were ingrained in her mind. A playful side-step took us to Anchovy. Besides, anchovies are the main ingredient in fish sauce, and fish sauce is the key ingredient in Southeast Asian cuisine.

We consciously distanced ourselves from the 'Asian fusion' tag for fear of its inherent stigmas, choosing instead to label the restaurant: *Modern Asian. Modern Australian. A little bit in between.* Anchovy's early menu incarnations were very much a reflection of who Thi was as an Asian Australian, as a viet kieu. They were driven by our Southeast Asian roots and influenced by the contemporary dining landscape as well as memories of growing up in the western suburbs of Sydney, but the dishes were always grounded in Vietnamese cuisine. Soy-cured trout rice paper rolls existed alongside cauliflower fried rice and Turkish sucuk alongside periwinkles with mustard green velouté. Over time, the DNA of Thi's cooking and of Anchovy evolved, from her language to her visual language to, most importantly, her palate.

We continued to jump into new challenges. Turning the space upstairs at the restaurant into a private dining room ourselves when we had zero construction experience to speak of and while the business was flailing in debt. Taking out a commercial lease for the space next door to expand on a business opportunity while the world was battling a respiratory virus. Acquiring a car loan for a commercial van to turn into a campervan so that we had a carriage to take us away over the weekends when we needed distance from the restaurant.

The campervan subsequently gave us the freedom to see a lot of Victoria and with that freedom came a vision to acquire a thatched-roof country house, perched on a hill with rolling greenery around it. We came across a 36-hectare property in Irishtown, 150 kilometres west of Melbourne. It was, in Thi's mind, perfect. Where I saw a slog – barren undulating land, Sifton bush spurting out of unfertile dirt, and overgrown brambles by the seasonal creek at the bottom of the property – Thi envisioned a landscape I have come to associate with Mường, Thai and Hmong tribes in Vietnam: long, neat green terraces laddered up the geography of the land, punctuated by fruit-bearing trees and edible shrubs. In her mind, swales would criss-cross the land, transferring whatever limited water was available through the 750-millimetre annual rainfall to the roots of crops. The terraced rice field has always been associated with rice agriculture in Asia, but Thi saw crops of mustards and witlof, of tomatoes, eggplants and zucchini when the season was right, and of radishes, nasturtiums and tatsois when the mercury starts to fall.

While we haven't yet bought our own farm, we have always focused on local produce. This approach occasionally draws outrage at the cost of dining at a Vietnamese restaurant, a function of the cost of produce. I have always been at pains to stress a few things relating to pricing: that our overheads and expenses are factored as Australian dollars rather than a currency of more favourable rates; that our culture and heritage are worth more than a single digit; that our offerings as a business are the antecedents for Vietnamese, and Asian cuisine in general, to be priced equally to their occidental equivalents in Australia.

Rice

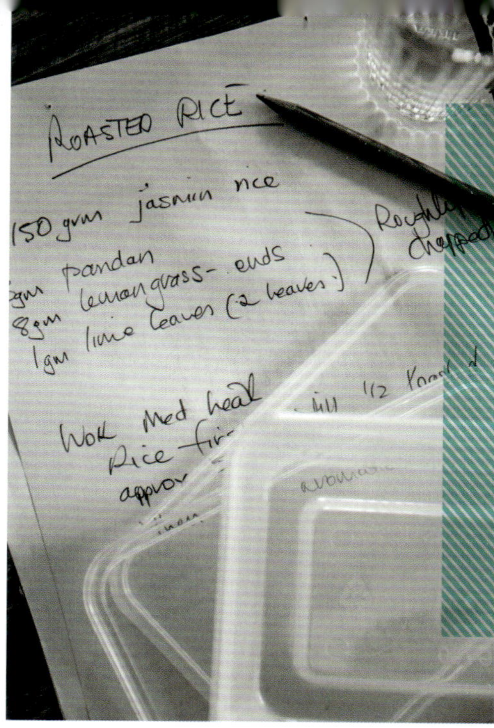

Until recently, buying rice in Australia has felt a bit like an afterthought, particularly outside the ethnic enclaves of rice-eating cultures. Buy it in kilo bags of varying quantities – one, two, five, ten or the occasional twenty. Buy it ready-cooked in single-serve pouches. Buy it in short, medium or long grains, in colours of white, brown or, more recently, red. Jasmine, basmati or glutinous. Wander into the Italian delis or the pasta aisle of the major supermarkets and find appropriately labelled arborio or carnaroli. Missing are the vendors who make their living plying rice varieties to consumers, and who might be able to hold an educated conversation around the nuances of japonica and indica rice, or the amylose and amylopectin content of the varieties.

The same fate befalls the various rice starches. We usually distinguish them by brand, Erawan being preferred. The difference comes down to dry-milling versus the preferred wet-milling, where the rice is soaked first and thus yields a finer and silkier end-product compared to dry-milled.

Unfortunately, I once spent quite a lot of money on a mill, to then find that it was only suited for dry-milling. A bag of organic Australian-grown white koshihikari rice, when dry-milled, yielded a rather coarse and disappointing batter that was not suited for the task of bánh cuốn (page 252). Looking at a picture of a granite wet mill, J.Y. realised that her parents were in fact in possession of that very mill some five and a half thousand kilometres away – on the corner of their fishpond as part of a garden water feature.

As a viet kieu and a chef, I feel the occasional frustration when I am trying to relearn and document all the knowledge that was once an integral part of Vietnamese everyday life. It is frustrating that industrialisation, globalisation and technology mean that we no longer choose to make time or devote attention to a dish or ingredient – that forgoing the taste and aromas of freshly ground rice is an acceptable trade-off for the convenience of buying rice flour off the shelf.

I look forward to the day that rice and rice flour are treated with the same reverence in Asian kitchens as artisanal grains and flours are given in bakeries; spoken of in the same way that coffee processors or winemakers speak of their raw materials and the impact on the resulting product.

Bánh bèo

Steamed rice cakes with pork fat relish

Makes 35

Batter

1.5 litres (6 cups)	water
450 g (1 lb)	rice flour
15 g (½ oz)	sea salt
15 ml (½ fl oz)	vegetable oil
50 g (1¾ oz)	tapioca starch

Pork fat relish

35 g (1¼ oz)	dried prawns
35 ml (1¼ fl oz)	room-temperature water, for soaking the prawns
200 g (7 oz)	pork back fat, diced into 1 cm (½ inch) cubes
5 tablespoons	cornflour (cornstarch), for coating
60 ml (¼ cup)	vegetable oil
200 g (7 oz)	red Asian shallots
35 g (1¼ oz)	lemongrass stalk, roughly chopped
3	Thai red bird's eye chillies, stems removed
35 g (1¼ oz)	garlic cloves, peeled
50 g (1¾ oz)	palm sugar (jaggery), shaved and pounded
35 g (1¼ oz)	salted soy beans, drained and crushed
35 ml (1¼ fl oz)	fish sauce

To serve

nước chấm ớt (page 34)
spring onion oil (page 44)

This dish was originally an attempt to use all the animal fat (pork, beef, lamb and even Murray cod) accumulating at the restaurant as a result of whole-animal butchery. Animal fat cooked out with aromatics, sugar, soy beans and dried prawns yielded the perfect flavour bomb to go alongside a mouthful of steamed rice cake, texturally velvety but otherwise void of flavour.

Bánh bèo is a street snack that can be traced back to the imperial kitchens of Hue in central Vietnam. The soft and pliable nature of the rice cakes is delightful. They are topped with regional variations, from mung beans through prawn floss, and accompanied by spring onion oil and a fish-sauce based dipping sauce of some description.

The relish is versatile – it could also be used on grilled fish wings, and I have dug spoonfuls of it to amp up a bowl of pasta. It is best to make the batter for the bánh bèo the night before as it gives the batter a chance to rest and bloom properly.

Prepare the batter

1 In a large bowl, whisk together all the batter ingredients, ensuring there are no lumps. Cover and leave to rest overnight in a cool spot (on the bench or in the fridge). The batter will split overnight, but that is normal. Stir again just before using.

Prepare the pork fat relish

2 Soak the dried prawns in the water until soft; this might take a few hours. Once soft, scoop out the rehydrated prawns, reserving the soaking water as it is full of prawn flavour. Pulse the prawns in a mini food processor until flossy, then remove and set aside.

3 Quickly blanch the pork fat in a small saucepan of boiling water for 1 minute, to remove any impurities. Remove from the water and pat dry.

4 Lightly coat the pork fat in the cornflour and fry in a small saucepan with enough oil to cover for about 5 minutes, until crispy. Drain off any oil and reserve for frying the aromatics in step 6. Finely dice the pork fat and set aside.

5 Finely dice the shallots. Place the lemongrass, chillies and garlic in the mini food processor and pulse until they are roughly the same size as the shallots.

6 Heat the reserved oil in a wok or frying pan and slowly fry off the shallot and spice mixture for 3–5 minutes, until golden and aromatic. Add the prawn floss and cook out for 5 minutes.

7 Add the pork fat, palm sugar and reserved prawn-soaking water and cook for a further 5–8 minutes, until the sugar has dissolved and is caramelised. Stir in the soy beans and fish sauce.

8 Once cooled, your pork fat relish will keep in a clean plastic container in the fridge for up to 1 month.

→

Steam the rice cakes

9 Set up a steamer. Half-fill a wok or large saucepan with water and place over high heat. Place a steaming basket inside the wok, or on top of the saucepan, and put the lid on.

10 Give the batter a good stir to re-emulsify the mixture.

11 Working in batches, pour the batter into small ramekins, to about 5 mm (¼ inch) from the rims. (I use ceramic soy sauce dipping ramekins, about 45 ml/1½ fl oz in capacity.)

12 When the water starts boiling vigorously, place the ramekins in the steamer basket. Cover and steam over high heat for 12–13 minutes, taking care to top up the water level when it gets low. Once cooked, the batter should not be gluey.

To serve

13 Remove the ramekins from the steamer and serve straight away. Eat the rice cakes out of the ramekins, topping each with a teaspoon of warmed pork fat relish, a teaspoon of nước chấm ớt and some spring onion from the spring onion oil.

Cơm mẻ
Fermented rice

200 g (7 oz)	jasmine rice
1 litre (4 cups)	water

Brewing cơm mẻ is reminiscent of maintaining a Tamagotchi, with the added superstition of an old wives' tale. Cơm mẻ is a fermented condiment made with rice and native yeasts; its end state is a milky, creamy paste that is used as a souring agent. Like a Tamagotchi, it does need to be entertained and fed regularly (stirred and topped with more rice) lest it sees a miserable end. The eye-rollingly unfortunate old wives' tale is that women who are menstruating should not open the (typically opaque) jar of cơm mẻ as their eye contact would somehow kill the microbes in the ferment.

In warm weather, this process will take 6–7 days, in winter expect 12–14.

1. Place the rice in a large bowl filled with water and gently stir the rice around with your fingertips to remove any debris and dust. Rinse the rice, discarding the water. Repeat this process another three times.
2. Place the rice in a clean saucepan and add the litre of water. Bring to the boil, then reduce the heat and simmer for about 15 minutes, until the rice is cooked and translucent. It is fine (and in fact preferable) to overcook the rice slightly, as it will break down faster during the next stages.
3. Drain off all the excess water into a bowl or jug to cool, reserving it for later.
4. Cook the rice in the pan with a lid on until all the water evaporates. Transfer the rice to a bowl and let it cool. (You can let the rice cool down in the pan, but it will take longer.)
5. Have a large sterilised glass jar ready – at least 3 litres (100 fl oz) in size, depending on your feeding schedule.
6. Transfer the cooled rice and reserved rice water to the jar, in a ratio of 1 part rice to 2 parts rice water. Cover with muslin (cheesecloth) and leave in a cool dark place.
7. Stir the mixture twice a day for 1 week, until the rice becomes creamy, with a sour aroma. In warm weather, this process will take 6–7 days, but in winter expect the ferment to take 12–14 days.
8. Once this state has been achieved, feed the ferment every 3–4 days with 50 g (1¾ oz) of cooled cooked rice, stirring it in thoroughly each time.
9. If the mixture starts to get too thick, add more rice water. The aim is to settle on a loose mixture of about 1 part rice to 2 parts rice water.
10. You can start using your cơm mẻ at this stage, storing it in a sterilised jar in a cool dark place. Like a sourdough starter or ginger bug, it will keep for years, if you do not let it die. As the cơm mẻ ages over the years, you will notice that it will become whiter, thicker and creamier.

Bánh căn
Rice cakes

Makes 14–16

120 g (4¼ oz)	cooked jasmine rice
565 ml (19½ fl oz)	water
175 g (6 oz)	rice flour
pinch of	salt
	cooking oil spray
14–16	quail eggs (optional)

To serve

picked leaves and herbs
nước chấm ớt (page 34)
spring onion oil (page 44)

The thing that makes bánh căn so good is the earthenware they are cooked in – a clay plate with round moulds and accompanying hats, which allows for a crisp and smoky exterior, and a moist and chewy interior. To prepare this dish without the clay pan is akin to organising a barbecue with a microwave. Sure, it will cook, but will it taste the same? Will it feel the same without the ritual of charcoal and smoke?

I recognise that there are logistical challenges in sourcing this earthenware plate, but I have decided to include this recipe for posterity. For the creative cooks out there looking to hack a cooking vessel, the earthenware plate allows for a combination of dry baking and steaming. If you are one of the lucky ones to procure a clay bánh căn plate, remember to soak the plate, which prevents cracking, and to season it with oil in between uses.

Like most bánhs, bánh căn serves as a versatile vessel for ingredients and sauces: protein from pork through prawns, toppings like pork rind or quail eggs, accompaniments of raw herbs and vegetables or sour mangoes, peanut-flecked sauces or a simple, balanced nước chấm.

Ferment the rice

1. In a clean container with a lid, mix the cooked rice and 165 ml (5½ fl oz) water together and stir until smooth and clump free.
2. Pop the lid on and leave to ferment for 2–3 days at room temperature. This step lightens the batter and yields a less-heavy result, and also accentuates the flavour of the rice.

Cook the batter

3. Soak a clay bánh căn plate in cool water for at least 1½ hours before using. (Its little 'hats' do not need to be soaked.)
4. Heat the clay plate on the stove over medium heat until hot, then lightly oil the clay plate with cooking oil spray.
5. Meanwhile, blend the fermented rice mixture until very smooth.
6. Place the 400 ml (14 fl oz) water, rice flour and salt in a bowl and mix until incorporated. Add the fermented rice mixture and mix well.
7. Fill each indent in the clay plate with batter, until just under the rim, and pop the hats on.
8. Cook over medium heat for 3 minutes with the hats on. The edges of the cakes should start to lift from the plate. (You can use a palette knife to lift the cakes off the plate to check the bottom, remembering to replace the hats each time.)
9. If using quail eggs, crack them onto the top of the rice cakes when they are three-quarters cooked. Place the hats on top and take them off every other minute, so the quail eggs cook but remain runny.
10. With or without quail eggs, the rice cakes should take about 5–6 minutes to cook. Serve warm with picked leaves and herbs, nước chấm ớt and spring onion oil.

Bánh khọt

Rice cakes with turmeric

Makes 66

150 g (5½ oz)	cooked jasmine rice
180 ml (6 fl oz)	coconut milk
875 ml (30 fl oz)	water
400 g (14 oz)	rice flour
25 g (1 oz)	cornflour (cornstarch)
1½ teaspoons	ground turmeric
1 teaspoon	sea salt
	vegetable oil, for cooking

Toppings (optional)

dried split peas or mung beans, soaked
quail eggs
dried prawns (page 54), rehydrated

To serve

picked leaves and herbs
nước chấm ớt (page 34)
spring onion oil (page 44)

I have tried variations of bánh khọt in Vietnamese eateries across Melbourne and Sydney, and in the various regions of Vietnam. I then made my own using freshly ground rice when the pandemic rolled around. The restaurant was in takeaway mode and one of our offerings was a wrap and roll party pack. I wanted something fun and textural to go into the pack and settled on bánh khọt. I had time to put towards research, and I had also recently come across a biodynamic rice producer in Victoria whose product I was keen to try. It was this dish that cemented my understanding of 'simplicity in produce'.

This recipe uses a metal bánh khọt pan. I have also found success using poffertjes pans.

Make the batter

1 In a food processor, blend the cooked rice and coconut milk until smooth.

2 Add the remaining ingredients, apart from the oil, and blend again to a smooth crêpe batter consistency. You can prepare this batter a day in advance and store it in an airtight container in the fridge; ensure you bring the batter back to room temperature before cooking.

Cook

3 Heat a metal bánh khọt pan on the stove until it smokes. Half-fill each divot with vegetable oil.

4 Stir the batter again, then fill each divot with about 25 ml (¾ fl oz) of batter.

5 Cook over medium heat for about 2–3 minutes, until the batter half sets.

6 At this point, add your soaked split peas or mung beans, if using, and cook for a further 1 minute. Add any additional toppings, then remove from the heat.

7 Repeat the process until the mixture is finished or save the batter for another day. It will keep in an airtight container in the fridge for up to 5 days.

To serve

8 Serve warm, with picked leaves and herbs, nước chấm ớt and spring onion oil.

Dreaming of bánh cuốn

Thi

My earliest memory of dining out finds the family on a warm Sunday afternoon. We would have driven 30 minutes from our local church to Cabramatta, a hub for the Vietnamese community in Sydney. The Sunday crush is a familiar place for any ethnic diaspora. As in many neighbourhoods around the world, the little arcades and lanes that connect the carpark to the main strip of John Street would be packed full of bodies of different heights, girths and odours. You were jammed in, shoulder-to-shoulder, trying to fight through the waves of crowds while not losing the family train as everyone made their way to their preferred food joints. Mum would hold my hand and drag me along so I would not get lost.

While the entire family's go-to meal out was phở, I dreamt of bánh cuốn. I would happily devour the dish in its entirety, savouring every mouthful of cuốn, inhaling the cinnamon-flecked chả and crunching through the semi-burnt mound of crispy shallots that sat atop as a garnish.

Bánh cuốn is a rice batter that is steamed on linen-lined steamers into translucent sheets. It is often rolled with savoury ingredients and eaten with a dip, or paired with charcuterie and other morsels. Bánh cuốn has always been the epitome of Vietnamese food. I liken it to the Scout's badge of honour; you are not a real Vietnamese cook if you have not been able master this dish and its related techniques: to ladle a layer of milky rice batter of perfect viscosity, for that layer of batter to eventually yield an even, translucent sheet, to flick that rice sheet off the steamer sheet with a bamboo stick.

I am still very fond of bánh cuốn and its close cousin, bánh ướt (page 164). At home, it was always mesmerising to watch my mother confidently cut batons of cucumber to mound over my bánh ướt: Kiwi-branded knife in one hand, and a piece of cucumber held aloft in the other. It was fun to watch; I wanted more than anything to be just as good as her.

My family never made bánh cuốn from scratch at home. We would always order it from one of the aunties – bored at home, in need of a side hustle, and most importantly, skilled.

A few years ago, I watched one auntie, one of Mum's friends, in her bánh cuốn process. It was at this point that I learned to distinguish the step from knowledge to skill, and from skill to craft. There was something inherently different about her bánh cuốn – the texture and clean, floral aroma were transcendent. I then discovered that she soaked and milled her own rice. It was a revelation to me as a second-generation Vietnamese.

I asked her to show me how she steamed her bánh cuốn. Her response both amused me and left an unyielding impression on me. *Anyone can steam it,* she exclaimed. *It's the bamboo stick you need to have a destiny with.* Destiny, or định mệnh. Who the heck thinks about their affinity with a bamboo stick before steaming bánh cuốn? Well, apparently Auntie does.

She proceeded to take me on a tour of her garden to show me the bamboo plant from which she harvests her bamboo sticks to dry in order to make her bánh cuốn. *Not all the bamboo pieces work. You need to pick the right stick to dry, and one that matches your skill set,* she advised.

Then she showed me the dried coconut husk ladle she carved herself, which allows for the right amount of rice batter to be ladled onto the steamer so that her very specific bamboo stick can then pick it up. It was wild.

I remembered the first time I made bánh cuốn, years earlier. It was the first – and only – time I managed to lift a sheet of translucent bánh cuốn off my steamer with an unwieldy bamboo stick I had procured for the purpose. *It's not that hard*, I had thought to myself, admiring the glossy, translucent sheet that hung in the air, my free hand hovering over my digital timer. Then I repeated a second, third, and subsequent attempts – I never was able to get that perfectly viscous swirl in the batter again, nor was I able to rid my steamed sheets of their pock marks betraying my ladling skill, or lack of. It appeared that my destined fate with my bamboo stick was not meant to be.

'Bánh cuốn has always been the epitome of Vietnamese food. I liken it to the Scout's badge of honour.'

Bánh cuốn

Steamed rice rolls

Serves 3–4

Batter

150 g (5½ oz)	rice starch
150 g (5½ oz)	tapioca starch
¼ teaspoon	salt
900 ml (31 fl oz)	cold water

Filling (see note)

1 tablespoon	vegetable oil
120 g (4¼ oz)	red Asian shallots, finely chopped
6	garlic cloves, minced
250 g (9 oz)	pork, coarsely minced (ground)
80 g (2¾ oz)	fresh wood ear mushrooms, julienned
3 teaspoons	fish sauce
2 teaspoons	black peppercorns, toasted (see page 268) and cracked
1 teaspoon	caster (superfine) sugar

To serve

sliced chả quế (cinnamon pork loaf, available from Vietnamese butchers)
fried shallots (page 71)
coriander (cilantro) sprigs
mint leaves
nước chấm (page 34)
red bird's eye chilli
cracked black pepper

The skill of making bánh cuốn lies firstly in its fragile yet tensile but translucent nature, secondly in the tenderness of the rolled sheets, and finally in the balance of the accompanying dressing. As a chef who values craftsmanship, it is a bit heartbreaking to know that the skill and history of steaming bánh cuốn is being lost, to some variation of a Teflon-coated pan or a Pyrex dish in a microwave. The recipe uses linen cloth and a metal bánh cuốn steamer mould.

Make the batter

1. In a bowl, combine the rice starch, tapioca starch and salt. Add the water and mix well to ensure there are no lumps.
2. Let the batter rest for at least 1 hour, to ensure the batter is well hydrated, for a smoother result.
3. When you are ready to steam the rice rolls, give the batter a good mix before using.

Make the filling

4. Heat the oil in a frying pan, then stir-fry the shallot and garlic until fragrant.
5. Add the pork and wood ear mushrooms and stir-fry for a further 3–4 minutes.
6. Add the fish sauce, pepper and sugar. Cook for an additional 2 minutes, then check the seasoning and transfer to a bowl.

Steam the rice sheets

7. Line the bánh cuốn steamer mould with unbleached linen cloth. Ensure it is tight.
8. Half-fill a wok or large saucepan with water and place over high heat. Place the mould inside the wok, or on top of the saucepan, and put the lid on. Turn the heat down to medium.
9. Using a small ladle, spoon the batter into the centre of the mould and immediately swirl in one direction to ensure an even, thin spread. Put the lid back on, to keep the moisture in, and steam the sheet for 2–3 minutes, until it lifts off the cloth.
10. Transfer the cooked sheet to a large greased tray or work surface, and spread about 2 tablespoons of the filling on the edge closest to you. Roll the sheet away from you to form a log, and set aside.
11. Repeat with the remaining batter and filling.

To serve

12. Transfer two or three rolls to each serving plate. Serve with the accompaniments, including a good heap of pepper.

Note

As an alternative to the pork and mushroom mix, you can crack an egg onto the bánh cuốn while it is steaming. If you are using an egg, fold the rice noodle sheet onto it like an enclosed envelope, instead of rolling.

Rượu nếp
Glutinous rice wine

Makes 1.5 litres (6 cups)

1 kg (2 lb 4 oz)	sweet glutinous (sticky) rice
4 litres (135 fl oz)	natural spring water, filtered water or distilled water
½ teaspoon	Chinese yeast (see note)
	sugar, if needed

It appears that brewing rice wine runs in the family – both my maternal grandmother and eldest sister used to do so, the latter in the refugee camp to help with an extra source of income for Mum. I was inspired by their proficiencies at brewing rice wine, though my early attempts were hindered by the lack of documentation. It has taken several years of experiments, various conversations with Mum and my sister, and much interrogation of the literature around Chinese rice wine to have finally yielded results I am quite happy with.

Soak the rice

1. Wash the rice with filtered tap water until the water runs clear; there should not be any starch left in the rice.
2. Soak the rice overnight in 2 litres (8 cups) of the spring water. Drain before steaming.

Steam the rice

3. Line a steamer basket with muslin (cheesecloth). Add the rice, spreading it in an even layer, and put the lid on.
4. Half-fill a wok or large saucepan with water and place over high heat. Place the steaming basket inside the wok, or on top of the saucepan. Steam the rice for about 30 minutes, until it is transparent and sticky, taking care to top up the water level when it gets low. Do not cook the rice to mush. The rice should be firm and hold its shape, and you should be able to see individual grains.
5. Spread the rice on a sterilised tray (if you have a pot large enough, stick the whole thing in boiling water) and cool to 26°C (79°F). I use a stainless-steel tray measuring roughly 53 x 32.5 cm (21 x 13 inches).

Ferment the rice

6. Crush the yeast ball into a powder. Dust the yeast over the rice and mix well to evenly inoculate the rice grains.
7. Transfer the rice to a clean 3 litre (100 fl oz) container with a fermentation airlock; I use a large glass jar. Add the remaining 1 litre (4 cups) of spring water and stir until incorporated. Seal the lid on, with the airlock in place.
8. The rice mash should sit out of direct sunlight and at 26–27°C (79–81°F) – no higher, or you will kill the yeast. A lower temperature – say, 22–23°C (72–73°F) – is also fine, but your rice will take longer to ferment. (In cooler months you can use a brewer's heating pad and keep the jar in the cupboard to keep the temperature consistent.)
9. Stir the mixture twice a day for 5 days, once in the morning and once in the evening. You may initially think there is insufficient water, but the rice will break down, and more liquid will soon be expelled from the rice. There should be a lot of activity in the first few days.

→

When to stop the first fermentation

10 You might start to smell some yeasty fragrances and a little alcohol coming on. You might want to use it at this stage, as it will be a little sweeter – quite tropical, fruity and fizzy.

11 After 2 weeks, the activity should have stopped, and the rice mash will separate into layers.

12 Strain and press the mixture through muslin (cheesecloth) into a clean bowl, squeezing out as much liquid as possible, then transfer the liquid into a clean, sterilised air-locked bottle. You can keep the mash: in Chinese cuisine it is used for a range of dishes, including being stirred into breakfast congee, in savoury marinades and in desserts, including a variation of the sticky rice dumplings on page 292. Keep the mash refrigerated in a clean airtight container and use within 2 weeks.

Second fermentation (optional)

13 At this stage, if the rice wine tastes a little bitter, add some sugar to sweeten it; it will also create fizz. You can add 1 teaspoon to a 500 ml (2 cup) bottle and replace the lid so it is airtight. Leave out at room temperature for 2 days to let the second fermentation begin.

Store the rice wine

14 The rice wine (at either stage of fermentation) can be funnelled into clean bottles and kept refrigerated or in a very cool, dark place. Consume within 4–7 weeks, depending on your personal taste. The rice wine is a 'living' product, as we haven't hit the mixture with any sulphur – so micro-fermentation will continue, given the presence of starches, and the flavour will change over time.

15 The fermentation will peak, and the quality of the rice wine will start to degrade – again, the optimal point of peaking and degradation is a matter of personal taste. Making a few batches over time will help you identify your preferred style.

Notes

- You will find balls of Chinese yeast in Asian grocers in the dried goods section. It is used as a starter for fermentation, in the same way winemakers and brewers use either indigenous yeasts or commercial yeasts.
- This wine will be moderately alcoholic – if you want to test the ABV level, you can use a hydrometer before and after fermentation. They are available from brewing shops.

Bánh giầy
Steamed glutinous rice cakes

Makes 8 portions (16 discs)

370 g (13 oz)	glutinous (sticky) rice starch
25 g (1 oz)	pork lard
½ teaspoon	sea salt
280 ml (10 fl oz)	boiling water
	banana leaves, for lining the steamer (use thawed frozen leaves, if you can't get fresh ones)
	oil, for brushing
	terrine or pork loaf, to serve

Garlic oil

1	garlic bulb
185 ml (¾ cup)	vegetable oil

Note

Bánh giầy stands out for being one of the few savoury rice-based bánh dishes in this book made with glutinous (sticky) rice. Legend has it that the dish is from the first Vietnamese state of Văn Lang, which geographically encompassed northern and north-central Vietnam, as well as parts of current-day China. Indigenous sticky rice varieties have always been cultivated in the mountainous areas in the country's north by the Mường, one of the largest ethnic groups in Vietnam. Most of the other rice-based bánh dishes in this book have their roots in the Mekong Delta towards the south, where jasmine rice is the dominant variety.

Bánh giầy is a lovely snack: simple, textural, fragranced with banana leaves and slicked with a touch of pork fat. A thick slab of chả lụa or pork loaf is commonly sandwiched between two white, chewy bánh giầy discs and served for breakfast. I prefer a slab of terrine sandwiched between my bánh giầy, perhaps a pork, duck liver and macadamia terrine, or even a generous slab of giò thủ – a pig's head terrine flecked with the cartilage of pig's ears, the chewiness of its skin and the satisfying meatiness from the tongue and cheeks.

Make the garlic oil

1. Peel the garlic, separating the cloves. Place in a small saucepan with the oil over low heat. Leave to infuse for at least 30 minutes, or up to 1½ hours. Leave to cool, then store in a clean dry container until needed; it should last for a few months.

Make the dough

2. Place the rice starch, pork lard and salt in a bowl. Add the boiling water in three batches, quickly incorporating into a dough with a wooden spoon, and ensuring the dough is not too wet or sticky.
3. When cool to the touch, knead the dough until smooth. Shape into a ball, cover with plastic wrap and leave to rest for 30 minutes.
4. Portion the dough into 40 g (1½ oz) balls.

Steam the dough

5. Half-fill a wok or large saucepan with water and place over high heat. Place a steaming basket inside the wok, or on top of the saucepan, with the lid on. Bring the water to the boil.
6. Cut your banana leaves into 9 cm (3½ inch) squares. Place on a flat surface and brush the surface with the garlic oil.
7. Place the dough on one piece of banana leaf, then place another piece of banana leaf on top, pressing down lightly. The dough should be roughly 1.5 cm (⅝ inch) thick, sandwiched in between the banana leaves.
8. Repeat with the remaining portions.
9. Place as many pieces as you can fit in your steamer. Cover and steam over a rolling boil for 7–8 minutes. When cooked, the discs should have an even colour and not look gritty. They will have a light and chewy texture.
10. Cook the remaining rice cakes in the same way, taking care to top up the water underneath the steamer when it gets low.

To serve

11. Sandwich a generous slab of terrine or pork loaf in between two discs that have come straight off the steamer. Remove the banana leaves before consuming.

Cơm nị cà púa

Turmeric rice clay pot + Cham braised beef

Serves 6–10

Cà púa

2 tablespoons	annatto oil (page 45)
25 g (1 oz)	mild curry powder
2 teaspoons	salt
1 tablespoon	cracked black pepper
½ teaspoon	raw sugar
1.5 kg (3 lb 5 oz)	beef shanks, cut into 3 × 5 cm (1¼ × 2 inches) chunks
100 g (3½ oz)	ginger, peeled and minced
50 g (1¾ oz)	garlic cloves, peeled and minced
50 g (1¾ oz)	lemongrass stalks, roughly chopped
4	red bird's eye chillies, finely chopped
80 ml (⅓ cup)	coconut oil (see note)
200 g (7 oz)	red Asian shallots, thinly sliced
6	star anise
1	cassia bark stick, about 6 cm (2½ inches) long
2	curry leaf sprigs
1 tablespoon	coriander seeds, ground
1 tablespoon	whole cloves, ground
250 ml (1 cup)	coconut water (no added sugar, if using a commercially packaged version)
50 g (1¾ oz)	côm mé (page 243)
165 ml (5½fl oz)	coconut milk

→

While cơm nị and cà púa are two separate dishes, they are often eaten together. This is a dish from the An Giang province in southern Vietnam, attributable to the Cham ethnic group. Those more familiar with the cuisine of the Southeast Asian islands, where the Chams were historically active commercially and by sea, will readily identify cơm nị and cà púa as rice clay pot and braised beef respectively.

Prepare the cà púa

1 Combine the annatto oil, curry powder, salt, pepper and sugar in a large bowl. Add the beef shanks and coat them all over, then set aside to marinate overnight or for at least 8 hours.

2 In a food processor, blend the ginger, garlic, lemongrass and chilli to a fine paste and set aside.

3 Warm the coconut oil in a heavy-based saucepan over medium heat. Add the shallot, star anise, cassia stick and curry leaves and fry for about 3–4 minutes, until fragrant. Stir in the blended spice paste and fry over low heat for 5 minutes.

4 Add the beef and stir to coat. Add the coriander seeds, cloves, coconut water and cơm mẻ and bring to the boil. Reduce the heat, then cover and simmer for 30 minutes. Continue to cook on low for an additional 60 minutes. At this point, the gravy should have reduced by half.

5 Stir in the coconut milk and check the seasoning. Leaving the lid slightly ajar, simmer for another 30 minutes.

Prepare the cơm nị

6 While the beef is simmering, heat a clay pot or heavy-based saucepan over medium heat. Add the oil and fry the shallot for 3–4 minutes, until crispy and caramelised.

7 Add the cassia stick, star anise, cardamom pods, curry leaves, bay leaves, ginger, garlic and turmeric and stir for 2–3 minutes, until fragrant.

8 Stir in the rice and toast for 3–5 minutes, until fragrant.

9 Turn the heat down to medium–low, stir in the water and raisins and bring to the boil. Reduce the heat to low, then cover and simmer the rice for 25 minutes, until the liquid has evaporated.

10 Once the rice is cooked, stir in the coconut milk and butter (do not be tempted to add it any earlier). Using a fork or chopstick, fluff the rice to loosen the individual grains. Put the lid back on to keep the rice warm.

→

Cơm nị

30 ml (1 fl oz)	vegetable oil
200 g (7 oz)	red Asian shallots, thinly sliced
1	cassia bark stick, about 6 cm (2½ inches) long
6	star anise
6	green cardamom pods, crushed
20–30	curry leaves
3	fresh bay leaves
1 teaspoon	minced ginger
1 teaspoon	minced garlic
½ teaspoon	ground turmeric
500 g (1 lb 2 oz)	jasmine rice, washed thoroughly and drained
500 ml (2 cups)	cold water
100 g (3½ oz)	raisins
150 ml (5 fl oz)	coconut milk
60 g (2¼ oz)	butter or ghee

To serve

	whole roasted peanuts
	salt, pepper and citrus (page 40)

To serve

11 Sprinkle the beef braise with a small handful of peanuts and serve with the rice, salt, pepper and citrus.

Note

To make your own coconut oil, warm 1 litre (4 cups) coconut cream in a saucepan over high heat until it splits, stirring continuously – do not walk away from the pan. After 5 minutes, turn the heat down to low and keep stirring. The mixture will separate, and you can strain off the oil to use in recipes. The cream curdles, so discard.

The authenticity police

J.Y.

A customer and I once had a short but robust discussion about món cuốn at the restaurant. The guest and her party had just finished the savoury component of their meal, which had ended with a cuốn (see page 210), alongside a cut of pork steak for the table and a vegan alternative for herself. She made a point of standing up and coming over to me – often a good sign if accompanied by a smile, sometimes terrifying where there is a frown.

The bò lá lốt, she started, *it was really good.* I accepted the compliment, but the dish the table had just consumed was not bò lá lốt. Yes, the cuốn happened to contain betel leaves, but that was where the similarity ended.

I proceeded to describe some attributes of món cuốn. *So it is not quite bò lá lốt, although stylistically consuming bò lá lốt falls into the category that is món cuốn, with all the leaves and herbs* – that was what I had wanted to end with, but never did quite get the chance.

I travelled around Vietnam for seven weeks, the customer stated quite firmly while I was mid-sentence, with very assertive eye contact, *and what we had just now was bò lá lốt.*

I moved to clear the table. The discussion left me quietly outraged. Here I was, presented with a logic that lived experience yields credibility and power: in this instance, the guest had decided that she knew Vietnam and was able to represent her subset of knowledge. There is nothing wrong with that; we all do it, and it is exemplified no more clearly than in Thi, a viet kieu, opening a restaurant to serve the food that represents part of who she is. However, in this case, the guest's logic was incorrect. It was also frustrating that this information was presented from an occidental's viewpoint.

I do recognise that leading this discussion from purely an orientalist perspective is also unfair. To do so overlooks the human tendency to treat the various Southeast Asian cuisines as discrete sets, and sometimes a single homogenous entity. I have similarly been told that our restaurant's rendition of bánh bèo (page 240) is incorrect and been offered advice on how we can fix the dish. At Anchovy, we topped our bánh bèo with some form of suet relish and other accompaniments, very much to the delight of guests, particularly those of Vietnamese heritage. It was with best intentions that this guest offered their insight on how we had messed up the dish but that it could easily be remedied by removing all the toppings in favour of preserved radishes and a good hit of chilli sauce. *That*, he said with a flourish, *is how you should serve chwee kueh properly.*

For the uninitiated, chwee kueh is a Singaporean cousin of the bánh bèo – it shares the same bloodlines (mix rice flour and water, then steam the batter) but differs in toppings.

Both incidents suggest several things – that the concepts of authenticity and what is 'correct' in the context of food are murky at best, and should in fact yield to our understanding of the range of cultural, geographical, historical and socio-economic factors that can influence a recipe; and that while globalisation has not fundamentally changed cuisines, it has hastened the impact of migration and trade on their evolution.

These ideas can also be twisted in another direction. As lived experience yields credibility and power, it is often asked if a cook wielding her tools has had some – preferably formal – experience preparing the proposed cuisine. There have been so many times where a disappointed, *Oh,* punctuates the answer, *No,* when the question is asked of Thi's cheffing experience: *Had you cooked Vietnamese food in a restaurant before opening Anchovy?*

I do think that our knowledge of food and application of ingredients will continue to change as we move away from the ancestral home of cuisines. I would like to think that this book and its spirit exists because it is ever more so important to record what is there before it is lost, and to make careful study of the key elements – the history, the sociology and the environment – that make up a dish.

Sweets

The joy of sweets in Vietnamese cuisine is that they can be, and are, consumed at any time of the day. Perhaps the 'true' dessert, being the course that most often concludes a meal, is fruit (see page 272). Most commonly oranges or watermelon, but any combination of ripe, in-season fruit makes for a great way to finish a meal and the best gift to bring to a dinner party.

I have chosen to name this section sweets rather than desserts to stay true to the Vietnamese spirit of all-day sugar hits.

Bánh lọt with soy panna cotta + gula melaka syrup

Serves 6

Bánh lọt

30 g (1 oz)	pandan leaves
270 ml (9½ fl oz)	water, plus an extra 950 ml (33 fl oz) water
196 g (6¾ oz)	water chestnut flour
34 g (1¼ oz)	mung bean starch
22 g (¾ oz)	caster (superfine) sugar
½ teaspoon	pandan essence
pinch of	salt
	ice bath

Soy panna cotta

7 g (1/6 oz)	gelatine leaves (gold strength)
30 ml (1 fl oz)	cool water
480 ml (16½ fl oz)	unsweetened soy milk (page 69)

Gula melaka syrup

600 g (1 lb 5 oz)	gula melaka (dark palm sugar)
300 ml (10½ fl oz)	water

Gula melaka coconut sauce

900 ml (31 fl oz)	coconut milk
300 g (10½ oz)	gula melaka (dark palm sugar)

To serve

900 g (2 lb)	shaved or crushed ice

This is not one of those sweets that can be whipped up on a whim. You can scratch the itch if there is a chè shop nearby. Alternatively, have some of these components on hand to halve the effort when you do decide to embark on this undertaking.

The beauty is that the various components can also be reassembled with other sweets in this book to form different desserts that are just as good. Perhaps swap out the panna cottas with the coconut flan (page 288), or add a small scoop of durian and white chocolate parfait (page 270). You will need a noodle press or potato ricer.

Make the bánh lọt

1. Roughly chop the pandan leaves, then place in a blender with the 270 ml (9½ fl oz) of water. Blitz on high speed for about 3–5 minutes, until the water becomes a little warm.
2. Place the water chestnut flour, mung bean starch, caster sugar, pandan essence, salt and extra 950 ml (33 fl oz) water – mixing well. Stir in the pandan water and leave to infuse for 1 hour.
3. Prepare the ice bath and have a noodle press or potato ricer handy.
4. Strain the mixture twice into a saucepan. Place over medium heat and keep stirring until the mixture starts to gel and the colour starts to change. After about 10 minutes, the mixture should start to become translucent.
5. Working over the ice bath, fill your noodle press two-thirds full with the pandan mixture and gently press down to extrude the noodles. Adjust your pressing rate and pressure applied depending on the length of noodles you are after – the length of your pinky finger is normally a good guide. Extrude the noodles straight into the ice bath, as the chill will help to set them. Run your fingers through the noodles in the ice bath to ensure they haven't stuck to each other on their way out of the press.
6. Repeat with the remaining pandan mixture, working quickly before the mixture sets. Discard any noodles that are stuck together.
7. Strain the bánh lọt and transfer to a clean container, then cover with fresh cool water.
8. The bánh lọt will keep in the fridge for up to 2 days until ready to use, but the pandan flavour will dissipate the longer the bánh lọt is soaked.

Make the soy panna cotta

9. Place the gelatine leaves in a small bowl, cover with the water and leave to bloom for 10–15 minutes; it should form a gel-like mass.
10. In a saucepan, warm about half the soy milk to 60°C (140°F).
11. Add the bloomed gelatine and stir until dissolved, then stir in the remaining cold soy milk.

→

12 Strain, then dispense into six serving glasses, pouring about 80 ml (⅓ cup) into each.

13 Refrigerate until ready to use, for up to 2–3 days.

Make the gula melaka syrup

14 Gently heat the gula melaka and water in a saucepan and stir until the sugar has dissolved.

15 The syrup will keep indefinitely in a clean sealed container in the fridge.

Make the gula melaka coconut sauce

16 Place the coconut milk and gula melaka in a saucepan and stir over medium heat until the sugar has dissolved.

17 Set aside until needed, for up to 2 days.

To assemble

18 Using a slotted spoon, scoop 2–3 tablespoons of bánh lọt onto each panna cotta.

19 Dress each with 2 tablespoons of the coconut sauce.

20 Divide shaved or crushed ice between six glasses. Dress with a drizzle of the gula melaka syrup and serve.

Kem tiêu và dâu tây

Pepper ice-cream + strawberries

Makes 1 litre (4 cups)

15 g (½ oz)	red peppercorns, to taste
660 ml (23 fl oz)	full-cream (whole) milk
110 ml (3¾ fl oz)	thickened (whipping) cream
65 g (2¼ oz)	egg yolks
155 g (5½ oz)	caster (superfine) sugar
	ice bath

Macerated strawberries

500 g (1 lb 2 oz)	strawberries, hulled and thinly sliced
80 ml (⅓ cup)	Grand Marnier (or Cointreau; see note)
1 teaspoon	caster (superfine) sugar

I love really retro desserts, particularly those that involve ice-creams, custards and jelly. This dessert is a throwback to ones I used to regularly enjoy at an all-Australian family's house, involving tinned fruits, custards and a healthy splash of Cointreau.

This dessert is all at once cold and warming, with its creaminess offset by the macerated strawberries. Best attempted when strawberries are in season. Do use good-quality pepper as it will make a difference. I have used red pepper from Phú Quốc, famed for its riper and fruiter notes.

Make the ice-cream

1 Toast the peppercorns in a dry frying pan over medium-high heat for about 1 minute, until fragrant. Remove from the pan and leave to cool for 5 minutes, then finely grind using a spice grinder or mortar and pestle.

2 Place the ground peppercorns in a saucepan, add the milk and cream and bring to a simmer.

3 Meanwhile, whisk the egg yolks and sugar in a bowl for about 1 minute, until pale. Whisking continuously, gradually add the warm milk mixture.

4 Return the mixture to the pan and stir continuously over low heat until the mixture reaches 82°C (180°F) on a sugar thermometer and just coats the spoon; this can take 10–15 minutes.

5 Pour into bowl placed over the ice bath – you can strain the mixture through a fine-meshed sieve if you would prefer no peppercorns to remain – and stir occasionally until chilled, 1–1½ hours.

6 Churn in an ice-cream machine, following the manufacturer's instructions, and freeze until required. (This ice-cream is best served on the day it's made.)

7 Serve the strawberries with a scoop of the pepper ice-cream.

Macerate the strawberries

8 Combine the strawberries, liqueur and sugar in a bowl, then leave to stand for 15–20 minutes for the strawberries to macerate and release their juices.

Note

If you are using Cointreau rather than Grand Marnier, reduce the amount of sugar slightly, as Cointreau is substantially sweeter than Grand Marnier.

Kem bơ
Avocado ice-cream

Serves 1–2

300 g (10½ oz)	ripe avocado flesh (about 2 large avocados)
75 ml (2½ fl oz)	condensed milk (or evaporated milk, for a lighter and less sweet option)
6	jackfruit chips, crushed into fragments
generous scoop	durian and white chocolate parfait (page 270) or vanilla ice-cream

Avocado was introduced to Vietnam via the French in 1940; avocado wood is still used in central Vietnam to fire bread. Kem bơ, which translates literally to avocado ice-cream, is a bit of a misnomer, as the entity is closer to an avocado thick shake with toppings. Regardless, this tasty treat is referred to as a kem (ice-cream) on the streets of Da Nang.

1. In a blender, blitz the avocado and condensed milk until smooth.
2. Chill the mixture in the fridge for about 1 hour, or until cold.
3. To serve, spoon 2 tablespoons of the avocado mixture into a glass. Layer with some of the crushed jackfruit chips.
4. Spoon more avocado mixture into the glass, then top with a generous scoop of parfait or ice-cream and a few more jackfruit chips. Serve immediately. The mixture will last 1 day in a clean airtight container in the fridge, but you will eat it before then.

Kem sầu riêng

Durian + white chocolate parfait

Serves 8–10

450 ml (16 fl oz)	thickened (whipping) cream
100 g ($3\frac{1}{2}$ oz)	egg yolks
170 g ($\frac{3}{4}$ cup)	caster (superfine) sugar
45 ml ($1\frac{1}{2}$ fl oz)	water
large pinch of	sea salt
60 g ($2\frac{1}{4}$ oz)	white chocolate, melted
10 ml ($\frac{1}{4}$ fl oz)	vodka

Durian cream

150 g ($5\frac{1}{2}$ oz)	durian flesh
100 ml ($3\frac{1}{2}$ fl oz)	thickened (whipping) cream

I felt compelled to introduce a durian dessert to the menu at Anchovy because I love durian. The original iteration of this dessert took 3 months to crack. The assembly included a scoop of lemon sorbet, raspberry powder, a dribble of olive oil and a pinch of salt. It was an incredible dessert. I have only included the durian and white chocolate component here, in the interest of simplicity and also because it stands its own ground as an excellent scoop of ice-cream.

The vodka is used to stop the parfait from freezing into a rock-solid block and to maintain some level of scoopability, since vodka does not freeze. Grainshaker produce a delicious Australian corn vodka that is gluten-free.

1. Place the durian cream ingredients in a blender or food processor and blend until smooth. Refrigerate until needed.
2. Using an electric mixer, whisk the cream to medium peaks; do not overwhip. Set aside in the fridge until required.
3. Using clean beaters, whisk the egg yolks on high speed until creamed and pale.
4. Start heating the sugar and water in a saucepan, to 121°C (250°F). The temperature is quite critical here – it ensures the sugar is fully dissolved, for the perfect texture, density and mouthfeel, adding to the perception of creaminess and preventing ice crystals forming in the parfait.
5. With the mixer on medium speed, pour the syrup down the side of the mixing bowl until incorporated into the creamed egg yolks. If the syrup is flicking around the bowl, simply whisk the syrup in by hand.
6. Add the salt and continue whisking until the mixture cools to body temperature – about 7–8 minutes.
7. Once the mixture has cooled, fold the melted chocolate and vodka through. Fold the chilled durian cream through, then finally the chilled whipped cream. The texture should be smooth and velvety.
8. Churn in an ice-cream machine following the manufacturer's instructions, and serve immediately.
9. To store, pack into airtight containers and keep in the freezer for up to 3–4 days.

Fruit platter

The ideal way to organise a fruit platter is to buy fruits in season and splurge on tropical fruits, even if it might cost you a little more. There are three ways to buy fruits from a Vietnamese grocer: trái cây để ăn bây giờ, trái cây ăn sau, trái cây cho cúng – to eat now, to eat later and for the altar. The first two are somewhat obvious, with the insinuation that ripe fruits ready-to-eat are for now, and those that require a few more days of ripening for later. Fruits 'for the altar' come rock solid – so that they can ripen slowly and not rot as they play their roles as objects of offerings to the ancestors.

Vignettes on death

Thi

The handful of Vietnamese funerals I have attended in Australia over the past few decades have always been similar. The template is etched in my memory – the rituals and symbols, the mourners, and the bánh mì, handed out by the family in a gesture that says, *Thank you for coming and celebrating a life with us today.* As refugees re-establishing ourselves away from the ancestral home, all we had by way of identity were the customs and behaviours that reminded us of our roots.

+

The death of my brother-in-law struck a particular chord with my eight-year-old self. He had gained my gratitude for confronting the stepfather about the abuse he had inflicted on me. Unlike the other adults in my orbit who stood on the sidelines and were reluctant to interfere with a 'family matter', my brother-in-law made me and my protection his responsibility. He had cast aside any deference for tradition and the family hierarchy to allow me a safer passage into adolescence. I had always recognised and been indebted to his actions. Yet cancer took over, and a crushing anxiety grew in me as his tumour did in him. I grieved by myself, and for myself, on the day of his passing, not trusting that there would be other adults who would attempt to look out for me as he had.

I met my maternal grandmother for the first time when she was on her deathbed and I was a belligerent 16-year-old, on that first trip on Cà Mau. I remember saying to her the only thing I had the language faculties to express – *Hello Grandmother, I am* Bich Phuong – although I was unsure if she had the mental faculties to recognise me.

By that point, my mother had not seen her own family in 18 years and so much had changed. The family had lost the farm during the war, her brother had gambled away the family home, her father had passed away, and her mother was paralysed after a fall down the stairs.

My grandmother and I spent many hours in each other's company on that trip, staring at each other with nary a conversation between us – separated by the deep chasm of a language barrier, and with her paralysis limiting even non-verbal communication. I spent the time reflecting on the many what ifs. *Would I have been more protected if my grandparents had been around me growing up? Would Mum have walked around battered and with black eyes?* I reflected on my mother's losses and at that moment decided I did not want to suffer similar losses – not the cultural ties, not the connection to my mother's homeland or my maternal family's history.

Perhaps it was the intoxication or perhaps we were just caught up in the moment of a fun night, but the thought of setting off my friend's car alarm made me breathlessly giddy. It was parked in a laneway and we thought she might have been upstairs with a sexual equal. But the alarm never went off, because the car was unlocked. I remember opening the back door and being greeted with a distinct stench of early-stage decomposition. The events leading up to her death – by overdose – maddened me because they could have been avoided had she been surrounded by people who cared for her. It was a turning point in my own relationship with drugs, which I had relied on to relieve myself of my deafening inner-voice and the intrusive thoughts intent on presenting themselves.

My mother informed me of my abuser's health condition early one morning as I was leaving for work. Stage 4 terminal cancer. Those four words ruined my day. His impending death would liberate him from any compunction I had hoped would have lived with him rent-free. Months later, my mother reported that he passed away peacefully surrounded by family. I remain trapped in my infernal cell, unable to free myself from the consequences of his violations.

My auntie and I are bound together by birth and the afterlife. Thirty-eight years to the day and even to the hour that I was born, my auntie was laid to rest in a burial plot in Cà Mau. That precise coincidence left me with a sense of unease, though my mind was already busy hoarding existential questions on that trip.

It had been almost ten years since I had last returned to Cà Mau, and the maturity I had brought back with me allowed a renewed level of vigour and insight. I reflected upon the loss of my aunt in the same way I was considering the loss of culinary skill and food traditions around me. I felt the loss of opportunity in both cases to gain further knowledge.

My aunt's funeral in Vietnam was a substantially different affair from what I had experienced in Australia. Apart from the fact that I was family and was privy to the behind-the-scenes workings of it all, what struck me was the food – not just a meal but an endless rotation of fresh dishes that appeared at mealtimes, three times a day, three days in a row, and with snacks in between. It would have been nothing short of incredible had the mood not been as sombre.

Kẹo chuối
Banana candy

Makes 3 logs

170 g (6 oz)	pineapple flesh
425 g (15 oz)	caster (superfine) sugar
130 g (4½ oz)	skinless peanuts
45 g (1½ oz)	sesame seeds
85 g (3 oz)	old ginger
3 teaspoons	lime juice
850 g (1 lb 14 oz)	ripe sugar bananas (unpeeled weight)
6	large coconut rice paper sheets

I fell for this snacky dessert in Bến Tre, and found myself accidentally scoffing four or five in a moment of weakness. Perhaps I was taken by the subtle heat of the ginger, or the fragrance of the bananas.

I tested this dessert for a set menu the day it was due. There was a bit of discussion on just exactly which type of rice paper was required – neither the varieties for rice paper rolls nor nem rán felt appropriate. We thought of communion wafers, as they shared similar properties. Coconut rice paper was the final choice – quite thin, almost communion wafer-like, and dissolvable on the tongue. I had dashed out an hour before dinner service started in an effort to source this rice paper. J.Y. did not even bother printing the dessert on the menu, so sure was she that my experiment would be unsuccessful. Let the record show that it was a hit.

1. Finely chop the pineapple flesh. Place in a bowl, add the sugar, mix well and leave to macerate for 30 minutes.
2. Meanwhile, preheat the oven to 170°C (350°F). Spread the peanuts and sesame seeds on two separate baking trays and roast for 13–15 minutes, until golden brown. Check them at the 8-minute mark, then keep a close eye on them to make sure they do not burn. Remove from the oven and leave to cool, then lightly crush the peanuts and set aside.
3. Peel and julienne the ginger. Place in a bowl with the lime juice and set aside to marinate until required.
4. Warm the macerated pineapple mixture in a heavy-based saucepan over low heat, ensuring all the sugar melts. Turn the heat up to medium and allow to cook out for 15 minutes.
5. Peel the bananas, crush them using a fork, then stir them through the pineapple mixture. Cook for about 1 hour, or until caramelised, stirring regularly so the mixture does not burn on the bottom of the pan. The mixture should reduce substantially, by about 40 per cent of its original volume.
6. Stir in the ginger and lime mixture and cook for a further 15–20 minutes, until you have a thick, dark caramel. The mixture will be hard to stir, but do persevere. Do also note that the acid in the lime juice will prevent the sugar solidifying – so if you add your ginger and lime mixture into the banana mixture too early (before it caramelises properly, or has reduced properly), the mixture may not set.
7. Remove from the heat, stir the crushed peanuts and sesame seeds through and set aside.
8. Lay out a double sheet of plastic wrap, to make a rectangle measuring about 60 × 30 cm (24 × 12 inches).
9. In a large frying pan, and working one at a time, lightly toast two coconut rice paper sheets on one side – just to warm them, not to heat them. Double-stack the two rice paper sheets on the plastic wrap.

→

10 Evenly smear one-third of the fruit mixture over the rice paper, about 1.5 cm (5⁄8 inch) thick. Roll into a tight log using the plastic wrap, then tie a knot at both ends. Leave to cool.
11 Repeat with the remaining rice paper sheets and fruit mixture, using two rice paper sheets per log.
12 Once cooled, the fruit mixture should be firm enough to cut into 1 cm (½ inch) slices. Stored in an airtight container in the pantry, these treats will last for months.

Note

Rather than wrapping the fruit logs in the rice paper sheets, you can skip steps 8–11 and simply set the fruit mixture in a container before cutting into 1 cm (½ inch) slices.

Bánh bò nướng
Caramelised honeycomb cake

Serves 6–8

310 g (11 oz)	granulated white sugar
310 ml (11 fl oz)	hot water
30 g (1 oz)	heavy dark syrup, such as agave or rice syrup
112 g (4 oz)	tapioca starch
112 g (4 oz)	rice flour
4 g (⅛ oz)	bicarbonate of soda (baking soda)
3 g (1⁄10 oz)	baking powder
5	eggs
pinch of	salt
112 g (4 oz)	unsalted butter

Pandan coconut cream

250 ml (1 cup)	coconut cream (Kara brand)
3	fresh pandan leaves, knotted
25 g (1 oz)	granulated white sugar
pinch of	sea salt

Bánh bò nướng shares its roots with the Indonesian bika ambon and the Malaysian kek sarang. It is a cake that yields a honeycomb crumb structure and an intensely caramelised aroma. The tapioca starch gives the cake resistance and spring; it should not be chewy or firm. It is baked and not steamed – the nướng in its name alludes to the baked nature. There is also the steamed variety, known simply as bánh bò.

This recipe leans on caramelised sugars for the colour and flavour as opposed to some varieties that rely on the pandan and thus are green in colour.

Bake the cake

1. Preheat the oven to 180°C (350°F). Place a 36 × 16.5 × 8 cm (14¼ × 6½ × 3¼ inch) non-stick baking tray in the oven to heat up.
2. Make a dry caramel with the sugar by heating the sugar in a saucepan over low heat. Take it very dark – over 220°C (425°F) – then deglaze the pan with the hot water, being very careful as the mixture will bubble up. Simmer gently for 3–5 minutes, until the hardened caramel is dissolved. You should end up with about 540 g (1 lb 3 oz) of syrup.
3. Weigh out 510 g (1 lb 2 oz) of the caramel syrup – you should have a small amount left over (try it drizzled on ice-cream). Add the agave or rice syrup and stir to dissolve, then leave to cool to body temperature.
4. Sieve the tapioca starch, rice flour, bicarbonate of soda and baking powder into a bowl. Stir to dissolve any lumps, then set aside.
5. Whisk the eggs with the salt, then pass through a sieve, into a clean bowl, to remove any lumpy bits.
6. Melt the butter until warm.
7. Just before mixing the batter ingredients together, lightly grease the hot tray with oil and return to the oven.
8. You will need to work quickly at this point, otherwise your cake won't rise properly in the oven. Add the whisked eggs to the flour mixture and whisk until smooth. Add the caramel syrup and whisk again. Add the butter and whisk until incorporated.
9. Remove the tray from the oven and quickly tip the batter into the tray. Loosely cover the tray with foil and place on the bottom rack of the oven.
10. Bake for 22 minutes, then rotate the tray and bake for another 22 minutes; the cake should be fully set at this stage.
11. Remove the foil and bake for another 10 minutes.
12. Remove from the oven and invert the tray to transfer the cake to a wire rack to cool and help retain the honeycomb webbing.
13. Once cooled, remove the cake from the tray and slice into 2.5 cm (1 inch) portions.

→

Make the pandan coconut cream

14 Place the coconut cream in a saucepan over medium-low heat, scooping or shaking out any coagulated bits stuck inside the tin. Tie each pandan leaf into a knot and add to the pan with the sugar and salt.

15 Leave to infuse for 30–45 minutes, being careful not to let the coconut cream reduce in volume.

16 Either use immediately, or pour into a clean container with a lid and leave to cool, then keep in the fridge for 3–5 days.

To serve

17 Serve the cake warm with the pandan coconut cream on the side. Store the cake in an airtight container at room temperature on the first day, then refrigerate for up to an additional 2 days, gently reheating in the microwave for serving.

Rau câu
Three-layer jellies

Makes one 28 × 18 cm (11 × 7 inch) glass Perspex dish

Black coffee jelly

800 ml (28 fl oz)	water
20 g (¾ oz)	instant coffee granules
100 g (3½ oz)	caster (superfine) sugar
8 g (¼ oz)	agar agar powder

Coconut jelly

420 ml (14½ fl oz)	coconut milk (Aroy-D brand preferred, which is lighter than Kara)
280 ml (10 fl oz)	water
70 g (2½ oz)	caster (superfine) sugar
pinch of	sea salt, to taste
77 g (2¾ oz)	agar agar powder

Pandan jelly

350 ml (12 fl oz)	water
25 g (1 oz)	pandan leaves, bruised
50 g (1¾ oz)	caster (superfine) sugar
1 drop	pandan essence
4 g (⅛ oz)	agar agar powder

Layers of agar jelly with coffee, coconut and pandan: the clean snap, inherently refreshing, and not actually that bad for you as far as sweets go. These can be made in a glass Perspex dish or in individual moulds. You can build up as many or as few layers as you like, and in whatever order you like. Just remember, if you are using a mould, that whatever colour you use first will end up on the top when you unmould.

Make the black coffee jelly

1. Bring the water to the boil in a saucepan, add the coffee and sugar and stir until dissolved.
2. Bring the water temperature to 70°C (158°F).
3. Whisk in the agar agar, bring back to the boil, then remove from the heat.
4. Strain through a fine-meshed sieve and dispense into the dish or moulds, about 3–5 mm (⅛–¼ inch) per layer, depending on how thick you want your jelly layer to be. Allow to set at room temperature for 10–15 minutes. As this is setting, prepare the coconut jelly.

Make the coconut jelly

5. In a saucepan, combine the coconut milk, water, sugar and sea salt. Stir over medium heat until the sugar and salt have dissolved.
6. Bring the water temperature to 70°C (158°F).
7. Whisk in the agar agar, bring back to the boil, then remove from the heat.
8. Strain through a fine-meshed sieve and allow to set at room temperature for 10–15 minutes, until the temperature is 50–60°C (122–140°F), then pour a layer over the coffee jelly. Any hotter and the mixture will melt the existing jelly layer; any cooler and it may not be properly pourable.

Make the pandan jelly

9. In a saucepan, bring the water and pandan leaves to the boil. Remove from the heat and leave to infuse for 30 minutes.
10. Strain through a fine-meshed sieve, then top up with more water to make up 350 ml (12 fl oz) in total.
11. Return to the pan, add the sugar and pandan essence, and bring the temperature to 70°C (158°F).
12. Whisk in the agar agar, bring back to the boil, then remove from the heat.
13. Strain through a fine-meshed sieve and allow to set at room temperature for 10–15 minutes, until the temperature is 50–60°C (122–140°F), then pour a layer over the coconut jelly.

To serve

14. Carefully unmould the jellies, if using moulds. Cover tightly with plastic wrap; the jelly will keep in the fridge for up to 1 week.

Bánh ít
Sticky rice dumplings

Makes 14–16

Filling

50 g (1¾ oz)	shelled macadamia nuts
125 g (4½ oz)	gula melaka (dark palm sugar) or coconut sugar
50 ml (1¾ fl oz)	water
190 g (6¾ oz)	fresh mature coconut flesh, shredded (or thawed frozen shredded coconut)
pinch of	sea salt
30 g (1 oz)	white sesame seeds
1	orange, zested

Dough

180 g (6 oz)	glutinous (sticky) rice flour
10 g (¼ oz)	tapioca starch
50 g (1¾ oz)	sugar
pinch of	sea salt
130 ml (4½ fl oz)	unsweetened coconut water
110 g (3¾ oz)	starchy potato, peeled

To serve

	freshly grated coconut

Like chè xôi nước (page 292), bánh ít is very unimaginatively referred to as a sticky rice dumpling or a glutinous rice ball among the English-literate. Like chè xôi nước, it is often also filled with mung beans. Where it differs is in its versatility, in that the filling can be both savoury (such as pork) or sweet.

This recipe is adapted from the version we serve at the restaurant. I have used potato in the dough recipe to help with its pliability, a trick I picked up from Mum.

Prepare the filling

1. Spread the macadamias on a baking tray and roast in a preheated 160°C (325°F) oven for 10–15 minutes, until dark golden. Start checking after 8 minutes, stirring to ensure even roasting. The nuts will continue to cook and colour from the residual heat after you remove them from the oven, so do not over-roast. Remove from the oven and leave to cool, then roughly chop and set aside in a bowl.
2. In a saucepan over medium heat, dissolve the gula melaka in the water. Add the coconut and salt and cook for about 4–8 minutes, until the water has evaporated and the mixture is sticky, stirring to ensure the mixture does not catch on the base of the pan. Set aside to cool.
3. Meanwhile, evenly toast the sesame seeds in a dry frying pan until a dark golden colour, taking care they do not burn. Add them to the chopped macadamias.
4. Once the coconut mixture has cooled, add the macadamias, sesame seeds and orange zest, mixing well. The flavour should be fresh and zesty.
5. Shape the mixture into tight 15 g (½ oz) balls (about the size of a cherry tomato).
6. Place the balls on a baking tray lined with baking paper and freeze for 2–3 hours, or until solid.

Make the dough

7. Begin by mixing the glutinous rice flour, tapioca starch, sugar and salt in a bowl with the coconut water. The dough should be a crumbly mixture. Cover the bowl with plastic wrap and rest for 40 minutes.
8. Meanwhile, steam the potato until a fork passes through without resistance. (Do not boil the potato, as this will introduce too much moisture into the dough.)
9. While still hot, mash the potato into the dough, mixing until the potato is evenly distributed and the dough is smooth.
10. Cover with plastic wrap and leave to rest at room temperature for 20 minutes.

Form the balls

11. Roll the dough into a tube of 15 cm (⅝ inch) diameter.
12. Portion into 25 g (1 oz) balls (about the size of a golf ball).

→

13 Flatten each dough ball into a disc 50 per cent larger than the diameter of the coconut balls. Be sure to leave the centre of each disc thicker than the edges.
14 Place a coconut ball in the centre of a dough disc, then bring the edges in over the filling. Once completely covered, roll the ball so it is smooth. Repeat with the remaining dough and filling.
15 Freeze in an airtight container, or on a tray wrapped well with plastic wrap, for up to 2 weeks.

Steam the balls from frozen

16 Place the balls in a steamer lined with baking paper. Steam over high heat for 10–12 minutes, until opaque. Test with a cake tester; the inside should be warm.
17 Immediately after steaming, roll the balls in freshly grated coconut to cover them evenly. The freshly steamed balls might feel tricky to work with, especially if the dough wrapper is too thin, but they will firm up slightly as they cool. The coconut will stick to the balls more easily when fresh out of the steamer.
18 Best served at room temperature – rest for 20 minutes.

Mứt
Candied sweets

These candied fruits, vegetables and seeds were once the centrepiece of Tết, the Lunar New Year festival, but are now falling by the wayside given the easy accessibility of sugar and confectionery in general. Mứt appeals to the chef in me, as it is a great way to use skins and peels of fruits that would otherwise end up in the bin. I have included three variations here – for ginger, passionfruit pith, and lotus root – though there are many others.

Candied ginger

Makes 500 g (1 lb 2 oz)

1.5 litres (6 cups)	cool water, plus extra to blanch
1	lime, quartered
1 kg (2 lb 4 oz)	fresh ginger
300 g (10½ oz)	raw sugar, approximately
1 teaspoon	sea salt

Make the acid water

1 Pour the water into a clean bowl. Juice the lime straight into the water, without any concern for pips. Throw the lime shells in as well, then set aside.

Prepare the ginger

2 Peel the ginger skin (easiest done with a spoon). Rinse the ginger and pat dry with paper towel.

3 Using a sharp knife or mandoline, slice the ginger about 4 mm (3⁄16 inch) thick, or to your preferred thickness.

4 Soak the ginger slices in the acid water for at least 2 hours. This step helps to retain the colour and texture of the ginger during the cooking process.

Blanch the ginger

5 Transfer the ginger and acid water to a saucepan and bring to the boil. Immediately remove from the heat and drain the ginger, discarding the lime shells and acid water.

6 Place the ginger back in the saucepan, cover with fresh cool water and bring back to the boil, then drain again. If you are using old ginger, repeat this blanching step one more time, to reduce its spicy heat.

Macerate the ginger

7 Weigh the ginger, then transfer to a clean bowl.

8 Add one-third of the ginger's blanched weight in sugar – so, if your ginger now weighs 900 g (2 lb), you will need 300 g (10½ oz) raw sugar. Add the sea salt and mix well.

9 Cover and leave to macerate at room temperature for about 1 hour, until the sugar has dissolved.

→

Cook the ginger

10 Transfer the macerated ginger and sugar mixture to a non-stick saucepan.

11 Bring to a gentle simmer over medium heat, then cook, stirring occasionally, for 45–60 minutes, until the sugars thicken and the ginger is candied. Do not allow the contents to burn or colour. Keep a close eye on your pan, as the sugars will eventually turn into a syrup.

12 If you prefer your candy to be chewier, cook it out for less time. Conversely, if you prefer it crispier and harder, cook it out longer.

Cool and dry

13 Transfer the ginger pieces to a flat tray lined with baking paper, spreading them out in a single layer. Leave to cool and dry at room temperature overnight – do not store in the fridge. You can also dry the ginger slices in a dehydrator at 80°C (46°F) for 3 hours.

14 Once cooled, your candied ginger is ready to eat. Pack into clean airtight containers and store in a cool place out of direct sunlight. It will keep for up to 4 months.

Candied passionfruit pith

Makes 2 takeaway containers

500 g (1 lb 2 oz)	passionfruit shells, pulp removed
2 litres (8 cups)	water
2 teaspoons	sea salt
50 ml (1¾ fl oz)	lime juice
50 g (1¾ oz)	raw sugar

Peel the passionfruit shells

1 Wash the passionfruit shells. Peel the skin using a vegetable peeler or paring knife, discarding the skin, but retaining the white pith.

2 Cut the pith into thumb-sized chunks.

Soak the passionfruit pith

3 Pour 1 litre (4 cups) of the water into a clean bowl, add 1 teaspoon of the sea salt and mix to dissolve.

4 Add the passionfruit pith and leave to soak for 15 minutes. The salted water helps draw out moisture, improving the texture of the end product.

5 Drain the pith, discarding the water.

Blanch the pith

6 In a saucepan, bring the remaining 1 litre (4 cups) of water to a gentle boil. Add the remaining 1 teaspoon of salt and allow to dissolve.

7 Add the passionfruit pith and blanch for 1 minute. Drain, rinse under cold water and pat dry.

Macerate the pith

8 Weigh the passionfruit pith, then transfer to a clean bowl. You should be left with about 200 g (7 oz) pith at this point.

9 Add the lime juice and sugar, mixing well.

10 Cover and leave to macerate at room temperature for 30 minutes, until the sugar has dissolved.

→

Cook the pith

11 Transfer the macerated passionfruit pith and sugar mixture to a non-stick saucepan.

12 Bring to a gentle simmer over medium heat, then cook, stirring occasionally, for 45–60 minutes, until the sugars thicken and the pith is candied. Do not allow the contents to burn or colour. Keep a close eye on your pan, as the sugars will eventually turn into a syrup.

Cool and dry

13 Transfer the passionfruit pith to a tray lined with baking paper, spreading it out in a single layer. Leave to cool and dry at room temperature overnight – do not store in the fridge. (I prefer my pith dried naturally, and not in a dehydrator.)

14 Once cooled, your candied passionfruit pith is ready to eat. Pack into clean airtight containers and store in a cool place out of direct sunlight. It will keep for up to 4 months.

Note

This recipe is a fantastic way to use up lots of passionfruit shells.

Candied lotus root

Makes 2 takeaway containers

2.5 litres (85 fl oz)	cool water
1	lemon, quartered
450 g (1 lb)	fresh lotus root, cleaned
1¼ teaspoons	sea salt
120 g (4¼ oz)	raw sugar, approximately
1	vanilla pod

Make the acid water

1 Pour 1 litre (4 cups) of the water into a clean bowl. Juice the lemon straight into the water, without concern for the pips. Throw the lemon shells in as well and set aside.

Soak the lotus root

2 Peel your lotus, then cut into 3 mm (⅛ inch) slices on the circular face.

3 Add the lotus root pieces to the acid water and leave to soak for 3 hours. Drain and set aside.

Blanch the lotus root

4 Pour the remaining 1.5 litres (6 cups) of water into a large saucepan. Add 1 teaspoon of the salt and bring to the boil.

5 Add the lotus root, in batches if needed, and blanch for 1 minute. Rinse under cold water and pat dry.

Macerate the lotus root

6 Weigh the lotus root pieces, then transfer to a clean bowl. Add 30% of their blanched weight in sugar – so, if you now have 400 g (14 oz) of lotus root, add 120 g (4¼ oz) of raw sugar.

7 Add the remaining ¼ teaspoon of salt and mix thoroughly.

8 Cover and leave to macerate at room temperature for up to 4 hours, until the sugar has dissolved.

Cook the lotus root

9 Transfer the lotus root and sugar mixture to a non-stick saucepan. (Do not crowd the pan; you may need to work in batches.)

→

10 Bring to the boil over medium heat. Reduce the heat to low and cook for 5 minutes, stirring occasionally.
11 Split the vanilla pod and scrape the seeds into the pan. Simmer for another 5–10 minutes, until there is no more liquid in the pan.

Cool and dry

12 Transfer the lotus root pieces to a tray lined with baking paper, spreading them out in a single layer. Leave to cool and dry at room temperature overnight – do not store in the fridge. You can also dry the lotus root in a dehydrator at 80°C (46°F) for 3 hours.
13 Once cooled, your candied lotus root is ready to eat. Pack into clean airtight containers and store in a cool place out of direct sunlight. It will keep for up to 4 months.

Bánh flan dừa

Coconut flan

Serves 6–8

Caramel

300 g (10½ oz)	caster (superfine) sugar
2 teaspoons	orange juice

Custard

3	eggs
6	egg yolks
70 g (2½ oz)	light brown sugar
500 ml (2 cups)	coconut milk (Aroy-D brand, which is lighter than Kara)

A classic Vietnamese dessert, if one were to start Vietnam's culinary history at the arrival of French colonists in the nineteenth century. Similar to its European brethren, a custard base is prepared and cooked. Ovens are not common in the typical household in Vietnam so the mixture is often steamed rather than baked in a bain-marie. Eat it by itself or tip it out into a bowl with crushed ice, bánh lọt (page 266), chewy jellies and coconut milk. Add the flesh of the best durian you can source for a power move.

Prepare a bain-marie

1 Have a 21 cm (8¼ inch) square glass baking dish handy, to bake your flan in. Find a larger vessel that your flan dish will comfortably sit inside, then half-fill the larger vessel with boiling water as your bain-marie.

2 Carefully transfer the larger vessel to the oven and preheat the oven to 160°C (320°F).

Make a dry caramel

3 Place the sugar in a wide-based saucepan over medium heat, slowly allowing the sugar to dissolve evenly without stirring, swirling the pan instead.

4 Once the sugar has liquified (which may take about 5–8 minutes), continue cooking over low heat until the colour turns dark amber.

5 Add the orange juice and continue swirling the saucepan to deglaze the pan. The acid in the orange juice will help prevent the caramel setting rock-solid.

6 When the bubbling stops, pour the caramel directly into your glass baking dish, swirling the hot caramel around the edges of the dish, coating one-third of the way up each side.

7 Leave to cool until set.

Make the custard

8 Place the eggs, egg yolks and sugar in a large bowl. Using an electric mixer, whisk until the sugar has dissolved. Add about one-third of the coconut milk and whisk to loosen the mixture.

9 Using a spatula (to avoid introducing too much more air), mix in the remaining coconut milk.

10 Strain the custard into your caramel-lined baking dish. Remove any bubbles by either tapping the dish on a solid surface, or lightly blow-torching the surface with a kitchen blow torch.

11 Tightly cover your flan dish with foil; I fold a large sheet of foil in half, to double its tensile strength.

Bake the flan

12 Gently place the baking dish in the centre of the bain-marie. The water level should sit just above the level of the custard, so remove or add more boiling water as required.

→

13 Bake at 160°C (320°F) for 55 minutes, then gently shake the dish and check if the flan jiggles. It should have a slight wobble without any visible liquid seeping out.
14 Carefully remove the bain-marie from the oven and allow the flan to cool in the bain-marie.
15 Serve at room temperature – either straight from the baking dish (as J.Y. has been known to do), or flipped on a serving tray or plate. The flan will keep, covered tightly with plastic wrap, for up to 3 days in the fridge.

To flip the flan out

16 Find a serving tray or plate larger than your baking dish. Place the serving tray or plate on your baking dish, holding them together firmly, then flip them both over in a single quick motion.

Bánh bông lan lá dứa

Pandan chiffon cake

Serves 12

8	egg yolks
200 g (7 oz)	caster (superfine) sugar
100 ml (3½ fl oz)	pandan juice (see notes)
50 ml (1¾ fl oz)	coconut cream
60 ml (¼ cup)	vegetable oil
¾ teaspoon	pandan essence
¾ teaspoon	natural vanilla extract
150 g (5½ oz)	plain (all-purpose) flour, sifted
2 teaspoons	baking powder
pinch of	salt
10	egg whites
1 teaspoon	cream of tartar

Coconut whipped cream

3 g (1/10 oz)	gelatine leaves (gold strength)
2½ teaspoons	cool water
130 g (4½ oz)	white chocolate callets
325 ml (11 fl oz)	thickened (whipping) cream
175 ml (2/3 cup)	coconut cream, at room temperature

Salted coconut

200 g (7 oz)	freshly grated mature coconut
pinch of	sea salt

Notes

You can make the pandan juice by blitzing 500 g (1 lb 2 oz) pandan leaves with 100 ml (3½ fl oz) water. Strain the mixture before using.

Pandan essence is necessary for both its aroma and aesthetics. Find it with the food colouring at the supermarket.

The cake tin is the same one used for angel food cake, 25 cm (10 inches) in diameter.

A pandan chiffon cake represents a childhood memory for many of us. Some of us scoff it balled up into a single dense morsel; others eat it slowly, mesmerised by its fragrance and lightness. Pandan is an interesting food item to describe. The aroma is vanilla-like, cut with a bit of greenness. I find dog owners understand the smell innately – it is the smell of a dog's paw pads, a sweet grassy note. I owe the development and refinement of this recipe to Kim Chin, a fellow kieu, who is as passionate about nostalgic desserts as I am.

Make the cake

1. Preheat the oven to 170°C (350°F).
2. Place the egg yolks and 120 g (4¼ oz) of the caster sugar in a mixing bowl. Using an electric mixer, whisk until light and aerated.
3. Whisk in the pandan juice, coconut cream, oil, pandan essence and vanilla. Stir the sifted flour, baking powder and salt through.
4. In a separate bowl, using clean beaters, whisk the egg whites until frothy. Gradually add the remaining 80 g (2¾ oz) of caster sugar and the cream of tartar, whisking until firm peaks form.
5. Gently fold one-third of the egg white meringue at a time through the yolk mixture.
6. Pour the batter into a large ungreased 25 cm (10 inch) angel food cake tin. Smooth the surface. Run a skewer through the batter, then drop the tin once from a height to pop any large air bubbles.
7. Bake for 40–42 minutes, then check for doneness. Use your finger to gently press on the centre of the cake. If the cake springs back, then it is done. If your finger indent remains, cook a little longer.
8. Remove from the oven and leave to cool upside down in the tin.
9. Once fully cooled, remove the cake from the tin by running a sharp paring knife around the inside of the tin.
10. Without the icing, the cake will keep for up to 3 days in the fridge if properly covered with plastic wrap.

Make the coconut whipped cream

11. Place the gelatine leaves in a small bowl, cover with the water and leave to bloom for 10–15 minutes; it should form a gel-like mass.
12. Place the chocolate in a heatproof bowl.
13. Heat the cream in a saucepan over medium heat, being careful not to let it boil. Pour it over the chocolate and stir until melted.
14. Add the gelatine and stir until dissolved, then stir in the coconut cream.
15. Strain the mixture through a fine-meshed sieve and chill to set for at least 1 hour.
16. Whip the coconut cream to stiff peaks. Set aside.

Ice the cake

17. Place the cake on a rotating cake stand. Using a palette knife and the help of the cake stand, spread the coconut whipped cream all over and around the cake.
18. Mix the salted coconut ingredients together and sprinkle over the cake. Once iced, the cake will keep for 2 days in the fridge, but it's best eaten on the same day.

Chè xôi nước

Glutinous mung bean balls

Makes 10–12

Filling

180 g (6 oz)	yellow split peas, soaked overnight in cool water
1 teaspoon	caster (superfine) sugar
pinch of	sea salt
2 teaspoons	vegetable oil
1 tablespoon	spring onion (scallion) rounds

Dough

115 g (4 oz)	purple sweet potato (see note)
250 g (9 oz)	glutinous (sticky) rice flour
200 g (7 oz)	cool water

Pandan syrup

1 litre (4 cups)	water
200 g (7 oz)	rock sugar
25 g (1 oz)	ginger, peeled and sliced
20 g (¾ oz)	fresh pandan leaves
pinch of	sea salt

Coconut milk

300 ml (10½ fl oz)	coconut milk
pinch of	sea salt
40 g (1½ oz)	caster (superfine) sugar

To serve

toasted sesame seeds

One of Mum's favourite desserts. Variations of these glutinous rice balls are found across East and Southeast Asia. Do not be put off by the addition of spring onion rounds. The heat accentuates the allium's natural sweetness. In the absence of mung beans, any legume can be used – I used split peas in this instance. You can adjust the steaming time accordingly.

Make the filling

1. Drain the soaked split peas, then steam for 30–45 minutes, until very soft. (You can also steam the sweet potato for the dough at the same time, but in a different vessel.)
2. Place the steamed split peas in a mixing bowl, sprinkle with the sugar and salt, then mash and set aside.
3. Heat the oil in a small saucepan over medium heat. When the oil starts to smoke, add the spring onion rounds and immediately take off the heat. Stir well to colour the spring onion.
4. Add the spring onion mixture to the split peas and incorporate well. Set aside.

Make the dough

5. Peel the sweet potato and steam for 25 minutes, or until very soft.
6. Place in a bowl and mash until smooth, using a potato ricer or fork.
7. Incorporate the glutinous rice flour, mixing well.
8. Add the water and knead in the bowl until a smooth ball forms.
9. Allow to rest in a sealed zip-lock bag at room temperature for at least 1 hour.

Shape the balls

10. Weigh the filling into 16 g (½ oz) portions and roll into tight balls.
11. Roll the dough into a log, then cut into 30 g (1 oz) portions. Roll each one into a smooth ball, then flatten each into a disc on your palm.
12. Place a ball of filling in the centre of a dough disc, then fold the dough around the filling to enclose. Roll again to seal the seams, ensuring that the filling isn't spilling out of the seams.
13. Repeat with the remaining dough and filling. If you have any left-over dough, you can roll it into balls without any filling and poach them – they will taste just as good.

Prepare the pandan syrup

14. Bring all the syrup ingredients to the boil in a saucepan.
15. Turn the heat down to a gentle simmer and stir to ensure the sugar has dissolved. Set aside.

Prepare the coconut milk

16. Place the ingredients in a saucepan and warm to dissolve the salt and sugar. Set aside.

→

Poach the balls

17 Bring a large saucepan of water to the boil.

18 Individually drop the balls into the water, stirring to ensure they do not stick together, and taking care not to overcrowd the pan.

19 Once the balls float to the surface, about 4–5 minutes, allow another minute of cooking, then transfer to a serving bowl.

To serve

20 While still hot, place one or two filled balls in each serving bowl, plus a few small unfilled balls.

21 Ladle 60 ml (¼ cup) of the pandan syrup and a tablespoon of the coconut milk into each serving bowl.

22 Top with a pinch of sesame seeds and serve hot.

Note

Purple sweet potato should not be confused with purple yam; starchy potato makes a suitable substitute. Starches from the root vegetable add to the pliability of the dough.

Epilogue
Thi

In May 2022, five months after signing a book deal and just after celebrating seven years of Anchovy, J.Y. and I decided to press pause on our restaurant. We had spent the months prior agonising over the decision. Mental fatigue had been brewing and eventually bubbled over. We announced the hibernation of Anchovy and went camping that same afternoon. It immediately felt like the shackles had been removed.

We continued to operate the other arms of the business while I tried to take a step back from being the face and the driving force of the restaurant. It gave me the indulgence of time that I had not expected to need to undertake this book.

It seemed improbable to interrogate my cooking and career without delving into my past, and with that interrogation came a tumble of suppressed memories. The emotional turmoil caught me off-guard. Members of my family were also up in arms over how much of our family history I would reveal, and whose story that was to tell.

The perseverance required pushed me to the edge on many occasions. At times, I resented giving up a part of myself when no one helped me at my most vulnerable. I had previously considered quitting cheffing to be more purposeful on the social justice front. I hope that this book might empower even just one person to find themselves and pursue their dream, regardless of the deck life has dealt them.

We reopened Anchovy in June 2024, though the pain and chaos in my personal life continued to tighten its grip. By then, we had submitted the first substantial draft of the book and finished the photoshoot. It was the creative outlet of cooking that once again liberated me from the turmoil. I found freedom in the easy distraction, the rigour and routine, and could once again forge my own way.

I had also experienced the luxury of spending an inordinate amount of the past two years thinking about the mechanics of Vietnamese cuisine. It had given me a deeper understanding of what my cooking stood for – that my food is neither native nor adopted, but simply reflects a Vietnamese identity naturalised in Australia. This book tells that story of adaptation and preservation – as a refugee's daughter, as a chef-owner, as a survivor, as a viet kieu.

Index

Index of essays

Acknowledgements

Thi

To Millie and the Kellys: thank you for being my turning point and allowing me to realise my passion early in my career. It is something that I will forever cherish.

Anthony Redondi, Christine Manfield, Andrew McConnell and David Verheul – I can't even express my gratitude for what each of you has taught me during my time in your kitchens. Your guidance and creativity have had a profound impact on me not only as a chef, but as a person.

It may seem unusual to thank a restaurant, but Anchovy has played a crucial role in anchoring my career, rebuilding my relationship with my mother through cooking, and unravelling what it means to be Vietnamese in Australia today. To our patrons, it's been such a pleasure, discovering these flavours with you.

Jane Willson, it is not every day that anyone gets the opportunity to write a book like this. Thank you for your patience and for rallying the best team to support my journey in bringing this book to life, including Justin Wolfers, Sarah Odgers, Emily Hart, Katri Hilden and Ariana Klepac.

Mark Chew for photography, Klarissa Pfisterer for the design and Kirsten Jenkins for styling. You have opened your creative world and allowed me to open mine. It has been such a beautiful process, and I cannot wait to work with you all again.

I would also like to thank the entire Anchovy crew, past and present. This restaurant would be nothing without you. Special thanks to Hannah Cox, Emily Hua and Zoe Nguyen for holding down the fort while we were writing this book, and to Kim Chin for your contributions in helping to develop the nostalgic desserts.

Sarah Porz – your mentorship, listening ear, welcoming home and unwavering support have become pillars of our journey.

Chen and Sok Sim – if angels walked the earth, it would be you both.

Lengers and Wazzah (my in-laws), thank you for embracing me in your family and for raising the most loving, smart, articulate, supportive, humorous partner someone could ask for.

To my elder sisters, thank you for everything you have sacrificed for us and the family. To my youngest, Linda – you have pushed me to not be afraid to have a voice.

My beautiful mother – I will always remember our photo on the steps of Parliament House. Two fearless young women conquering this world together. Because of you, I want to share our story and celebrate the resilient woman you are.

And to J.Y. You have made this world a better place. You have taken my thoughts and made them safe. Your unconditional love and support are unparalleled. From one penguin to another, you have shown me what true love means. Because of you, I now believe that dreams can come true.

×

Published in 2025 by Murdoch Books,
an imprint of Allen & Unwin

Murdoch Books Australia
Cammeraygal Country
83 Alexander Street
Crows Nest NSW 2065
Phone: +61 (0)2 8425 0100
murdochbooks.com.au
info@murdochbooks.com.au

Murdoch Books UK
Ormond House
26–27 Boswell Street
London WC1N 3JZ
Phone: +44 (0) 20 8785 5995
murdochbooks.co.uk
info@murdochbooks.co.uk

For corporate orders and custom publishing, contact our business development team at salesenquiries@murdochbooks.com.au

Publisher: Jane Willson
Editorial manager: Justin Wolfers
Design manager: Sarah Odgers
Design: Pfisterer + Freeman
Editors: Emily Hart and Katri Hilden
Photographer: Mark Chew
Stylist: Kirsten Jenkins
Photoshoot chefs: Sarah Porz and Emily Hua
Production manager: Natalie Crouch

Murdoch Books acknowledges the Traditional Owners of the Country on which we live and work. We pay our respects to all Aboriginal and Torres Strait Islander Elders, past and present.

ISBN 9 781 92261 640 1

NATIONAL LIBRARY OF AUSTRALIA
A catalogue record for this book is available from the National Library of Australia

A catalogue record for this book is available from the British Library

Colour reproduction by Splitting Image Colour Studio Pty Ltd, Wantirna, Victoria

Printed in China by C&C Offset Printing Co., Ltd.

FSC www.fsc.org MIX Paper | Supporting responsible forestry FSC® C008047

10 9 8 7 6 5 4 3 2 1

OVEN GUIDE:
You may find cooking times vary depending on the oven and oven setting you are using. Unless otherwise noted, recipes in this book were tested using a fan-forced (convection) oven. As a general rule, for conventional ovens, set the oven temperature to 20°C (25–50°F) higher than indicated in the recipe.

TABLESPOON MEASURES:
We have used 20 ml (4 teaspoon) tablespoon measures. If you are using a 15 ml (3 teaspoon) tablespoon add an extra teaspoon of the ingredient for each tablespoon specified.

IMPORTANT:
Those who might be at risk from the effects of salmonella poisoning (the elderly, pregnant women, young children and those suffering from immune deficiency diseases) should consult their doctor with any concerns about eating raw eggs. Please ensure that all seafood, beef, or other meat products to be eaten raw or lightly cooked are very fresh and of the highest quality.